The WHAT and HOW of
Reading Instruction

SECOND EDITION

J. David Cooper

Edna W. Warncke

Dorothy A. Shipman

Ball State University

Merrill Publishing Company

A Bell & Howell Information Company

Columbus • Toronto • London • Melbourne

Cover photo: © Merrill, Andy Brunk

Published by Merrill Publishing Company
A Bell & Howell Information Company
Columbus, Ohio 43216

This book was set in Times Roman.

Administrative Editor: Jeff Johnston
Production Coordinator: Linda Hillis Bayma
Art Coordinator: Mark D. Garrett
Cover Designer: Cathy Watterson

Library of Congress Catalog Card Number: 87-63312
International Standard Book Number: 0-675-20504-2
Printed in the United States of America
2   3   4   5   6   7   8   9—92   91   90   89

Contents

Preface

The basic purpose of *The What and How of Reading Instruction* is to teach preservice teachers how to teach reading by helping them develop a basic foundation. In revising this text, we wanted to:

1. Account for the most recent research and practice in teaching reading.
2. Provide students a textbook written with their study needs in mind.
3. Make changes suggested by users and at the same time retain features that have been considered helpful to instructors and students.

This text has thirteen chapters designed to help preservice teachers develop a basic knowledge about how to teach reading. Each chapter contains two features designed to help students read and understand the text more effectively: marginal questions and a practice exercise. These features are explained in the section entitled "How to Use This Textbook" that follows the preface.

The basic organization of the text is built around the concepts of what to teach in reading and how to teach reading. The *what* of reading instruction is developed in the following chapters:

1. Reading and Factors That Influence It
2. Prereading

3. Comprehension
4. Word Recognition Skills
5. Study Skills

These chapters develop the concept that reading is a process of constructing meaning and that skills should not be stressed in isolation.

The *how* of reading instruction is developed in the following chapters:

6. The Directed Reading Lesson—An Overview
7. Strategies for Prereading and Skill Teaching
8. Background and Vocabulary Development
9. Reading and Discussing the Selection
10. Enrichment
11. Effective Approaches to Teaching Reading
12. Informal Classroom Assessment
13. Classroom Organization and Management

The focus of these chapters is on combining direct instruction with the directed reading lesson concept to teach reading. Step-by-step instructions for basic strategies of how to teach reading are presented.

This edition of *The What and How of Reading Instruction* would be useful in any undergraduate or graduate-level course focusing on the basics of teaching reading in the elementary school. It would also be a useful text in an inservice program where teachers needed to refresh or update their basic teaching strategies.

Acknowledgments

We want to thank all of the instructors and students who have used the first edition of this text and provided input for its revision. We would like to acknowledge the assistance of our reviewers; namely, Jerry Garrett, University of Arkansas at Monticello; Calvin Greatsinger, Central Washington University; Tom Potter, California State University—Northridge; and Pauline Travis, Southwestern Oklahoma State University. Special thanks go to our colleague and friend, Dr. Peggy A. Ramstad, for her input and support as a co-author of the first edition. Brenda Stone Anderson, our typist, worked long hours from a pasted manuscript to see this revision to fruition. Finally, to Jeff Johnston, editor at Merrill Publishing, thanks for seeing the need for this revision.

J. David Cooper
Edna W. Warncke
Dorothy A. Shipman

How to Use This Text

This edition of *The What and How of Reading Instruction* was written to help you learn as much as possible from your textbook. Each chapter has two important features that you should learn to use: marginal questions and a practice exercise.

The marginal questions in each chapter will help bring out the important information in the chapter. The practice exercise will help you review the information from the chapter and prepare for your instructor's tests. We suggest that you use the marginal questions and practice exercises in the following pattern to improve your own reading of this textbook:

1. Before you begin to read
   a. Skim each chapter to get a general idea of what it is about. Read the title, subheadings, and captions on illustrations, diagrams, or figures.
   b. Try to think of other information that you have read that relates to the chapter topic.
2. During your reading
   a. Read each marginal question and then read the text that follows.
   b. Underline the text or take notes that answer the marginal questions. (If you take notes, you may find it helpful to make a written outline for the chapter.)

     c. If you are unable to answer the question, reread the section pertaining to it immediately to clarify what you have missed. If you are still having difficulty locating an answer, check with another student in your class or your instructor.

3. After reading

     a. Look back over the chapter to review the answers to your questions.

     b. Reread any parts that caused you difficulty or were unclear.

     c. Think about how the information you gained will help you in teaching reading.

     d. Complete the practice exercise.

CHAPTER 1

Reading and Factors That Influence It

As you read each chapter, we recommend that you record the answers to the questions presented in the margin. These questions are provided to direct your attention to the important points in the text. After completing each chapter, we suggest that you complete the practice exercise to help develop your understanding of the material presented.

What will be learned about reading in this chapter?

~my paper~

In this chapter, discussion will evolve around (1) a basic definition for reading, (2) how background and oral language influence reading, (3) the components of the reading process, (4) why reading is a strategic process, (5) factors that influence reading, and (6) the reading needs of special students.

READING DEFINED

What should be learned about the definition of reading?

Linguists, educators, psychologists, and a variety of scholars from other fields continue to debate and discuss the question, "What is reading?" (Samuels & Kamil, 1984). There are many different theories and definitions available that attempt to explain and define the complex act of reading. What a teacher believes about the definition of reading directly influences how reading will be taught (Mitchell, 1980). Therefore, at early points in the professional development of teachers, it is important to focus on developing a basic understanding of how reading is defined. It is not necessary to know all the different definitions and theories of reading; as experience is gained in teaching, and professional knowledge is broadened through further study, teachers continuously change and expand their understanding of reading in light of new research and information.

To assist in the process of defining reading, read the following paragraph:

Sara and Mark were having a wonderful Easter. They couldn't stop laughing when their father came hopping across the yard in his white costume with a fuzzy tail. They were enjoying hunting for beautifully colored eggs and placing them carefully in their baskets. Both of them were really surprised when he gave them a beautiful krashanky which they placed in their baskets with the other eggs.

As this paragraph was read, there probably was no difficulty in recognizing most of the words. The mind recalled things known about Easter and hunting for eggs, including any of the reader's experiences with Easter and Easter egg hunts. These experiences and the background knowledge of the reader relative to Easter made it possible to figure out that father was dressed as a rabbit. The text didn't provide this information. The text only gave clues such as it was Easter and father came hopping across the yard in a white costume with a fuzzy tail. These clues plus background experience were used to determine that father was dressed as an Easter bunny. In this way, interaction with the text took place. Clues were taken from the text and related to prior knowledge or background experience to read or construct.

The last sentence may have contained one word whose pronunciation was unknown, *krashanky*. The reader may not have seen or heard this word before. Possible pronunciations might have been krā shank ē, krə shawnk ē, krăsh ank ē, and so forth. Even if the word krashanky was unknown, the reader's background experience with Easter and the others words in the text probably helped determine that a krashanky is some type of Easter egg. Actually, a krashanky is a beautifully hand painted or elaborately colored Ukrainian Easter egg. Again, interacting with the text to construct meaning or understanding took place.

Even when the reader did not recognize all the words in the paragraph, enough were recognized to draw clues from experience to construct or develop meaning; most readers have some understanding that Sara and Mark were hunting Easter eggs and their father who was dressed as a rabbit gave them an egg that was different. Each reader's exact understanding of this paragraph will vary somewhat because each reader's background experiences vary. This is always true in reading. Readers often construct different variations of meaning for the same text because their backgrounds vary.

The process of reading can be illustrated even more clearly with the following text:

Mingleup was plocking her tomp. She plocked it for her varump.

As these sentences were read, more difficulty in determining the words existed. Most readers aren't sure how to pronounce them, having never seen them before, and they are not in the reader's oral language. Readers have had no experience with *Mingleup, plocking, tomp,* or *varump*. It is not possible to recognize these words or formulate any meaning for them or the ideas which they represent in this paragraph. Therefore, this paragraph could not be read. The reader may have been able to recognize a few of the words or attempt to sound out some of the others, but could not construct meaning for the paragraph.

FIGURE 1-1
Interaction Between Reader's Prior Knowledge and Clues from Text

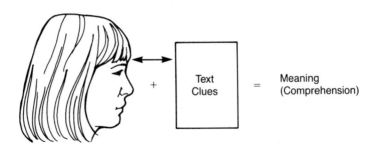

What is reading?   Both of these examples illustrate how the reading process depends upon the reader's background experiences and oral language (Adams & Bertram, 1980; Menyuk, 1984). In order to perform this process, students must be taught to recognize words quickly (Anderson, Hiebert, Scott, & Wilkinson, 1985) and to use the processes needed to construct their meanings by using information from the text and relating it to their prior experiences. That is what was done as a reader attempted to read these two examples. More success was possible with the first one because of the reader's background and oral language that made it possible to construct meaning.

Therefore, based on these two examples, what is reading? Reading is a process of constructing or developing meaning for printed text. To do this, the reader brings prior knowledge or experiences to the text. The clues in the text trigger the reader's experiences relative to the topic. The reader uses clues from the text in combination with prior knowledge to form meaning; the use of these two elements together is the interaction between the reader and the text; Figure 1-1 illustrates this concept.

ORAL LANGUAGE, BACKGROUND EXPERIENCE, AND READING

Why should the language arts be related in teaching?   Reading is one of the four language arts—listening, speaking, writing, and reading. Figure 1-2 shows how these four areas are closely related. Speaking and writing are the expressive areas of the language arts; the user of these processes is expressing or communicating information to someone else. Listening and reading are the receptive areas of the language arts; when these processes are being used, the individual is receiving information. Research has clearly demonstrated that there is a close relationship among listening, speaking, reading, and writing (Loban, 1963). As will be learned throughout this text, teachers should relate these four areas in the instructional program in language arts and reading as much as possible because they are closely related to each other.

FIGURE 1-2
The Language Arts

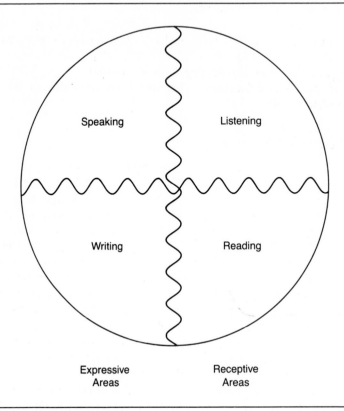

Speaking

Listening

Writing

Reading

Expressive
Areas

Receptive
Areas

Oral Language

Why is oral language important to reading?

Language consists of the oral and written symbols that represent thoughts and ideas. Oral language uses the oral symbols and involves speaking and listening. It is from this oral language base that students develop the ability to use the written symbols in reading and writing.

Oral language is clearly the foundation on which all reading is built (Menyuk, 1984). Think back to the two examples read earlier. In the one about Easter, there was little difficulty in constructing meaning because the words and sentences were in the reader's oral language experience. The only word which was probably not in the reader's oral language was krashanky. However, what was known about oral language helped the reader use the other words around krashanky, or the context, to get some idea of what it meant even if an exact meaning was not determined.

The second example, about Mingleup, was more difficult; in fact, no real reading took place. Most of the words were not in our oral language experience and had not been heard or spoken in the language. The oral language base necessary for successful reading was missing. In order to teach someone to read the paragraph about Mingleup, someone would first have to help develop the oral language relative to the language used in the example.

When students come to school with limited oral language or come from language backgrounds other than English, their instructional program in reading must begin by developing oral language. However, throughout reading instruction, oral language must be continuously developed for all students, not just those who are ''language different.'' Oral language is the foundation on which all growth in reading and writing is built.

Background Experience

Why is background experience important to reading?

Closely related to the reader's oral language is background experience. Background experience consists of all those things known about as a result of talking to others, seeing things, reading, going places, and so forth. Language is the representation of these experiences. Everything that one does in life builds background experiences.

Background experience is an important element in the reading process (Adams & Bertram, 1980; Johnston, 1981; Johnston & Pearson, 1982). Think back again to the two examples used to illustrate that process. Readers probably had background experience with Easter and most of the ideas presented in that paragraph. Therefore, they were able to use their prior experiences plus the clues in the text to construct understanding for the passage. Only the word krashanky caused any difficulty because it probably was not a part of the reader's background experience. In the example about Mingleup, there was no prior knowledge or background experience from which to draw. Even if words were sounded out, readers were unable to construct meaning for the passage because of their lack of background.

What is schema, and why is it important in reading?

Background experience helps develop a framework of ideas in the mind. For example, when reading the paragraph about Easter, immediate thoughts are related to this topic. They may be about such things as Easter eggs, egg hunts, rabbits, baskets, flowers, getting new clothes, going out to dinner, spring, and so forth. Whatever the reader's thoughts are about Easter, along with all the other things known about Easter, is the *schema* for Easter. Schema (singular) or schemata (plural) are the structures representing the information stored in memory (Rumelhart, 1980). These structures can be thought of as little storage units where information or ideas that have been experienced are filed. As one reads, one is constantly drawing on schemata to help construct meaning. There was no schema for Mingleup; therefore, nothing was in the mind to draw from to enable the construction of meaning for that passage. During the reading process, the reader is continuously using the clues and information provided by the text to draw from schemata to construct meaning for what is read. Understanding this aspect of the reading process is very important to knowing how to teach reading, as will be seen when studying the Directed Reading Lesson later in this text.

COMPONENTS OF THE READING PROCESS

What is decoding, and how does it fit into the reading process?

Think of the reading process as involving two components: *decoding* and *comprehension*. There are several definitions for decoding (Samuels & Kamil, 1984). From one point of view, decoding is defined as the process of associating meaning with letters or sounds. From another, decoding is defined as associating sounds with letters in words.

In this text, we take the position that decoding is being able to associate the sounds with the symbols for words; this results in orally pronouncing the words or silently thinking the words. Since the reader is using the process of comprehension simultaneously with decoding, meaning usually will be immediately associated with the word. Therefore, decoding, as we present it, is being able to know the sounds that go with the letters to form words.

Decoding is an important part of the reading process. Effective readers are able to do this quickly and accurately (Lesgold, Resnick, & Hammond, 1985). If the reader is unable to decode, attention is focused on analyzing each individual word rather than on interpreting the text and constructing meaning. The skill of decoding must be developed to the point where the reader performs it quickly and automatically with little attention being paid to the process (Anderson, Hiebert, Scott, & Wilkinson, 1985). When reading the passage about Easter, very little attention was paid to figuring out the words until the word krashanky was encountered. In the paragraph about Mingleup, more attention was paid to the words because they were unfamiliar. In the first example, decoding was almost completely automatic and quick; in the second example it was not. Therefore, the reader encountered more difficulty in reading the second passage.

It is not necessary for the reader to be able to decode every word on the page with 100 percent accuracy in order to be able to read. A reader may not know how to decode krashanky but still be able to form or construct meaning for the passage. The reader must develop sufficient skill with decoding so that attention can be focused on formulating meaning for the text rather than analyzing each individual word.

What is comprehension, and how does the reader use it in the reading process?

Comprehension is the process of constructing meaning. Readers perform the tasks of decoding and comprehending together as they read. In fact, readers use many different skills and processes simultaneously as they read. While reading the paragraphs about Easter and Mingleup, the decoding and comprehension processes were used together. When decoding became a problem, comprehension slowed down or stopped.

As has been seen in the examples presented in this chapter, decoding and comprehension are both influenced by the reader's oral language and background experience. The diagram in Figure 1-3 shows that as the reader becomes more mature, his or her conscious concern shifts from thinking about decoding words to interpreting the text. Existing evidence supports that this is what most good readers actually do (Perfetti & Lesgold, 1977). While examining the figure, note that the beginning reader is more concerned about decoding, but even at this stage, comprehension is involved. As the reader matures and decoding becomes automatic, comprehension becomes the conscious concern of the reader, but some element of decoding is still present in the process of reading.

FIGURE 1-3
Components of the Reading Process

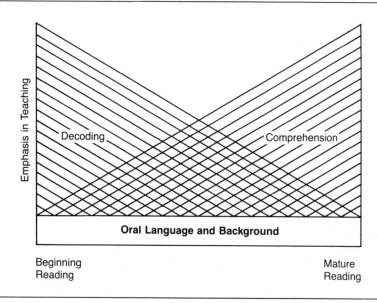

Teaching students to decode words involves what is called *word recognition*. The *only reason* for teaching students to recognize and decode words is to help them construct meaning. The teaching of word recognition does not automatically lead to reading. It is just one of the steps in developing the overall process of reading. Chapter 3 will focus on what should be included in comprehension, Chapter 4 will present what should be taught as a part of word recognition, and Chapter 5 will focus on study skills. Chapters 6, 7, 8, and 9 will help you learn how to integrate and weave together the teaching of word recognition and comprehension so that each element *will not be used in isolation*. Having a basic understanding of how the reading process works will help teachers better understand the procedures used in the teaching of reading.

READING IS STRATEGIC

Why is reading strategic, and how does one monitor reading?

A strategy is a plan for doing something; different tasks require different strategies. Reading is a process that requires strategy; therefore, reading is strategic (Anderson, Hiebert, Scott, & Wilkinson, 1985). This means that the reader must be flexible and adjust the way he or she reads to the type of text being read and the purpose for reading. For example, when reading a chapter to study for a multiple-choice test, one reads more carefully, focusing on specific details, than when one reads a murder mystery for fun. Good readers are able to change and adjust their reading to their purpose (Anderson, Hiebert, Scott, & Wilkinson, 1985).

Good readers monitor their reading (Brown, 1980). Monitoring means keeping track of how something is doing. An important part of a good reader's strategy for reading is being able to monitor reading during the process and be aware of whether or not what is being read is making sense (Baker & Brown, 1984b; Brown, 1980). This is called *comprehension monitoring* or *cognitive monitoring*. Good readers know when their reading is not making sense, and they know how to use different strategies to correct this problem (Baker & Brown, 1984a). This is an important part of the reading process that must be taught to students.

FACTORS THAT INFLUENCE READING

What factors influence reading?

As has already been noted, reading is a complex process. The explanation of this process provided thus far is a basic one, intended to develop an understanding of reading that will lead the teacher to see why certain strategies and procedures are used in teaching. The complexity of the reading process is further compounded by the many factors influencing it, including the reader's motivation for reading, purpose for reading, social-emotional status, and physical status. All of these factors interact with each other and the other elements of the reading process that have been described.

Motivation for Reading

Good readers are motivated to read and are interested in it. A student who has the desire to read and is interested in reading is more likely to be easier to teach and therefore likely to learn more readily than one who is not.

Many students come to school with this motivation and interest well developed. Others do not. Therefore, the way in which each student will learn to read and use the reading process will be directly influenced by his or her motivation and interest. A student's motivation and interest can be used when developing teaching strategies and selecting materials for instruction. A student who lacks the motivation and interest for reading must be approached differently from one who does not.

Purpose for Reading

A student's reading is influenced by the purpose for reading. Students may not have an overall purpose for reading and may not see its importance. Such students may be the same ones who are unmotivated to read. An important part of helping students learn to read is to help them see how reading can be used in their lives and the lives of those who are important around them.

Students must learn that different types of reading require a different purpose and different strategies. Reading the newspaper cartoons for fun is not the same as reading a recipe to make a cake. Each type of reading has a different purpose and requires the reader to use different skills and strategies. Students must be taught this directly; they must be taught to know their purpose for reading.

Social-Emotional Status

Reading is also influenced by the student's social and emotional status. A student who gets along well with peers and has a positive self-concept and attitude is likely to learn to read much more readily than one who does not (Strang, 1968).

Problems at home, school, or in other areas may cause a student to become emotionally upset. Such circumstances will have a direct influence on reading. A student's emotional status can change from day to day, and the student's performance in reading can be affected by this emotional state.

Physical Status

Reading is also influenced by the student's physical status. This includes such factors as overall health, vision, and hearing. In general, it can be concluded that a student who is healthy and has good vision and good hearing is more likely to learn to read effectively than one who does not (Spache, 1976).

A student who comes to school hungry, sleepy, or who is sick frequently is not going to be in good physical condition to learn. Frequent illnesses take away a student's energy for learning and often remove him or her from the opportunity to learn.

Being able to see and hear is important to learning to read. Therefore, students should have their vision and hearing checked regularly to ensure that they have no problems in these areas.

All of these factors can influence reading and must constantly be considered by the classroom teacher. Each factor is involved in the process of reading and adds to its complexity.

FACTORS THAT INFLUENCE SPECIAL NEEDS STUDENTS

Who are special needs students, and how can each group be helped to learn to read?

In every school there may be students who are somewhat different from the majority of those in the school. These students may be bilingual; have cultural, dialectical, or language differences; be handicapped learners; or be gifted readers.

All children come to school bringing many language skills. The teacher must help them develop these skills further and teach them to read the language they already understand, just as with regular students. Teachers must remember the importance of the oral language and experiences of the students in the process of teaching them to read. Therefore, when teaching children with special needs, the teacher must always develop their oral language and experience backgrounds before attempting to get students to read. By making specific adjustments to the methods presented in this text, they will be appropriate for use with students who have special needs.

Bilingual Learners

Bilingual students are those who have limited proficiency with English and who speak another language fluently (Vacca, Vacca, & Gove, 1987). The major difference between bilingual students and English-speaking students is their competency with English. Because of this difference, non-English speakers may be frustrated when learning to read. First, the teacher must develop in the students the ability to speak a language that may be quite different in its linguistic components from the students' native language. For example, in some languages, adjectives normally follow nouns and/or negatives may be at the beginning of the sentence rather than close to the verb as in English. In general, bilingual students find it easier to learn nouns and verbs than they do to learn the placement of words in sentences and the use of auxiliary words in standard English (Sinatra, 1981).

In teaching bilingual children to read, it is important to expose them to many natural oral language situations where they hear the language being spoken. Teachers should read to them, allowing them to see the print and pictures. Opportunities for conversations and informal sharing should also be abundant. Dramatic play is often helpful to bilingual students in helping them relate English words to meaningful situations.

Perhaps the most effective method of teaching bilingual students to read English is through the use of the Language Experience Approach (see Chapter 11) where students talk about their own experiences and culture, and it is written for them to read. After a time bilingual students may also be instructed using basal readers if the teacher provides instruction on linguistic structures and forms. Aukerman and Aukerman (1981) recommend that teachers should speak in standard English using natural grammatical sequences as a model for students to follow.

Cultural, Dialectical, or Language Different Learners

When teaching reading, consideration needs to be given to groups of students who have cultural, dialectical, or language differences from the majority of students in the classroom. These groups might include such students as those with a black dialect, Appalachian dialect, Mexican-Americans, students who actively belong to an Indian tribe, refugees, and/or foreign-born speakers of English. Many times such groups of students have vastly different experience backgrounds. These differences will likely produce language differences that may affect progress in learning to read standard English. Each group may also have its own unique and special culture, and some students speak a dialect of English that is based on their socioeconomic background, their ethnic background, or the region of the country in which they live.

In developing a reading program for these students, Foerster (1976) suggests that materials be chosen carefully to reflect some of the differences that the children are experiencing; that teachers attempt to fill in gaps in the students' knowledge; that pictures and context clues be used abundantly; that skill development be emphasized after careful diagnosis; and that students be allowed to read orally frequently in order for the teacher to check their progress in pronunciation and intonation of standard English. These students may also profit from the use of a Language Experience Approach even though nonstandard English usually does not interfere with reading comprehension (Goodman & Buck, 1973; Rigg, 1978; Wolfram, 1979).

Handicapped Learners

Handicapped learners are those who have impaired vision, hearing, or speech. They may also be mentally retarded, emotionally disturbed, orthopedically impaired, or possess specific learning disabilities. Children who have such needs may be found mainstreamed into the regular classroom as a result of Public Law 94-142. Passed by Congress in 1975, this law requires that all children receive the most appropriate education in the *least restrictive environment*. This concept places children in a learning environment as close to the regular classroom as possible if it appears that they could benefit from such a placement. The placement in the regular classroom (mainstreaming) may be for a short or long segment of the school day. Mainstreamed students usually get support from a special teacher who assists them with the transition as well as with the work expected of them in the regular classroom.

When teaching handicapped learners, it is important that the regular classroom teacher prepare the students to receive the new class member by explaining the nature of the handicap and what the student's special needs will be. This will help the regular class members be able to accept the handicapped students and offer them support.

It is not unusual for mainstreamed students to read at a somewhat lower reading level than many of their classmates. To avoid instilling feelings of frustration and inadequacy, the regular classroom teacher may need to teach reading to the students on an individualized basis as described in Chapter 11. The teacher may also need to make special effort to allow handicapped students to excel in some other areas. The attitude of the teacher toward handicapped students is extremely important since it is often necessary to give handicapped students much understanding and encouragement.

When teaching reading to special students, teachers should be careful to present only a small amount of material at one time. For example, only one consonant digraph should be presented in a lesson, not several; only two or three vocabulary words should be introduced; just one comprehension skill or process should be presented. Each new skill or process should be given detailed direct instruction followed by a variety of practice activities as described in Chapters 6 to 8. Special students need to be instructed in materials appropriate for their reading level and move at a pace where they can be successful. These students may need to move more slowly with continuous teacher assessment in order to be successful in reading.

Gifted Readers

Gifted readers often have very advanced verbal skills for their age. They use advanced sentence structures and have command of a large vocabulary both in oral and written language. These students learn language skills much more rapidly than their regular classmates. Therefore, they often need to be challenged in order to forestall boredom and disinterest in school and reading. Gifted readers often display a great interest in books and reading. They may also have a wide range of interests and be capable of high-level abstract and/or creative thinking.

Students who are gifted readers still should have instruction in reading to help them continue to grow and acquire higher level reading and thinking skills. Most gifted readers do not need much instruction in the decoding process; rather they need to be challenged to greater understanding of the world around them. Often this can be accomplished through individualization and by (1) encouraging them to explore topics not normally included in the regular curriculum; (2) involving them in activities that require problem solving, critical thinking, investigation, and inquiry; and (3) requiring them to develop a product (Renzulli & Smith, 1980).

Teachers of gifted readers also need to provide a large supply of resource materials for use by these students. Care should be taken by teachers of gifted readers not to just give these students *more* work because the first was completed, but to get them involved with challenging activities that stimulate and retain their interest in reading.

THE ROLE OF THE TEACHER IN TEACHING READING

What is the role of the classroom teacher of reading?

In light of all this information about reading and the reading process, consider the role of a classroom teacher of reading. Throughout this text we will be defining this role and explaining how to teach reading. However, from the very beginning, teachers should have a basic understanding of their role and know what it is that an effective classroom reading teacher does.

The teacher is the most important factor in determining how students are going to learn to read (Rosenshine & Stevens, 1984). The teacher must create the conditions in the classroom that make it possible for students to learn to read and want to learn to read. Through the use of direct instruction, the teacher must *teach students how to read*. There is sufficient evidence to show that teachers who *directly* teach students how to read produce more effective readers than those who do not (Rosenshine & Stevens, 1984).

The effective classroom reading teacher exhibits four very important characteristics (McGreal & McGreal, 1984a,b; Rosenshine & Stevens, 1984). The teacher is *enthusiastic,* is *businesslike,* has *fast-paced lessons,* and has *varied lessons.* To become an effective reading teacher, one must develop an enthusiasm for reading and teaching reading. This is accomplished by learning how to teach reading and enjoying it.

In a classroom, teachers should have fun with students but always in a businesslike manner. This involves letting students know exactly what they are going to learn and clearly teaching them what they need to know. Effective teachers don't try to become one of the students; they are teachers.

As skill in teaching is developed, teachers should learn to make lessons fast-paced. Long, drawn-out lessons are boring for students and the teacher. Lessons should be clearly focused and directly to the point. Be prepared with the materials needed and be organized.

Finally, vary lessons. No one likes to do the exact same thing day after day. Effective teachers make their lessons exciting and vary their lessons and their routines.

These are the things that an effective reading teacher must do. The remainder of this text was written to help teachers learn the knowledge and skills needed to become effective classroom reading teachers.

CONCLUDING REMARKS

In this chapter reading and the factors that influence it for regular and special needs students have been discussed. Reading is a process of constructing meaning; clues from the text trigger meanings from the reader's prior experiences. In this way the reader interacts with the text to form meaning. Background experience and oral language are the foundations on which all reading is built.

The process of reading involves two components, decoding and comprehension, that operate within the effective reader simultaneously. Decoding is knowing the pronunciation of words, and comprehension is constructing meaning. No reading takes place unless comprehension occurs. The reader must learn to decode words automatically in order to be able to focus attention on comprehension.

PRACTICE EXERCISE

Directions
This series of exercises is designed to help you practice and check your knowledge of information presented in this chapter. Complete each exercise; then check your answers with those in the Answer Key at the end of the text.

Part I
In this chapter you encountered many terms which were probably new to you. Match the words in column A with the correct definition in column B.

Column A

_____ 1. decoding (as defined in this text)

_____ 2. oral language

_____ 3. reading

_____ 4. background experience

_____ 5. schema

_____ 6. comprehension

_____ 7. comprehension monitoring

Column B

a. an interactive process between the reader and the text whereby meaning is constructed.

b. listening and speaking

c. knowing whether one's reading is making sense

d. using clues from the text to construct meaning

e. structures of concepts stored in one's memory

f. associating sounds with letters which leads to orally pronouncing or silently thinking a word

g. all the things one has learned in life

Part II

For each of the following questions, circle the letter of one best answer.

1. Reading is an interactive process that builds on
   a. decoding and comprehension
   b. oral language and background experience
   c. schema and cognitive monitoring
   d. writing

2. To say that reading is an interactive process means that the reader
   a. can pronounce words
   b. gets meaning by calling words and looking them up in the dictionary
   c. uses clues from the text and relates them to prior experiences to construct meaning
   d. is able to write words from the text in a meaningful way

3. To say that reading is a process of constructing meaning means that the reader
   a. gets all of the meaning from the text
   b. develops meaning by using clues from the text and ideas from his or her background
   c. gets one idea after another in reading
   d. pronounces words and knows their meanings

4. Language arts consist of
   a. reading and writing
   b. decoding, comprehension, speaking, and listening
   c. speaking and listening
   d. speaking, listening, reading, and writing

5. The two foundation blocks for reading are
   a. oral language and background experience
   b. listening and speaking
   c. schema and decoding
   d. writing and listening

6. A student taking a trip to the zoo with friends and discussing it would be a good example of
   a. learning to decode
   b. building background and oral language
   c. effective classroom teaching
   d. none of the above

7. An effective reader must be able to decode words
   a. slowly and carefully
   b. with 100 percent accuracy
   c. quickly and accurately
   d. as fast as he or she comprehends

8. As a reader matures, his or her conscious use of the components of the reading process
   a. shifts from comprehension to decoding
   b. shifts from decoding to comprehension
   c. remains about the same
   d. depends completely on his or her oral language

9. A student who is able to tell that something that he or she is reading is not making sense and tries to correct this problem is using
   a. oral language
   b. decoding
   c. background experience
   d. comprehension monitoring

10. To say that reading is strategic means that the reader
    a. can decode words quickly and accurately
    b. is flexible and adjusts his or her reading to the purpose for reading
    c. uses oral language and background experience
    d. thinks carefully before reading each word or sentence

11. Reading is influenced by the reader's
    a. motivation for reading and physical status
    b. purpose for reading and social-emotional status
    c. both a and b
    d. none of the above

12. The effective classroom reading teacher
    a. is businesslike, enthusiastic, and has fast-paced and varied lessons
    b. is enthusiastic and has good use of oral language
    c. can identify the components of the reading process
    d. none of the above

Part III

Write a summary paragraph *in your own words* that indicates what you have learned in this chapter about the reading process. Ask yourself the following questions as you develop your summary:

a. What is reading?
b. What are its components?
c. What are the foundation blocks for reading?
d. What factors influence it?
e. How does the reading process work?

Part IV

Based on what you have learned about the reading process in this chapter, what types of activities and experiences do you think should be included in a good reading program?

Part V

List the students who are considered to have special needs in learning to read. Give at least two ways to help each group improve chances to be successful in learning to read.

1. _____
   _____

2. _____
   _____

3. _____
   _____

4. _____
   _____

2

Prereading

**Define prereading
and readiness.
How are they
related to reading?**

As discussed in this chapter, prereading relates to those factors necessary for the beginning stages of reading instruction. In Chapter 1, the factors involved in the overall reading process were discussed. Those same factors are important in all stages of reading development, from beginning readers to mature readers. For this reason, some of the same factors discussed in Chapter 1 will be discussed in this chapter since they are directly related to prereading.

Prereading is often called *reading readiness* by classroom teachers and in published materials. We choose to distinguish between reading readiness and prereading because we believe that readiness for reading is something that is required at all levels of reading, whereas prereading takes place during the beginning stages of learning to read.

Readiness refers to those skills and understandings that the learner must possess in order to successfully complete any reading task. For instance, if assigned to read a chapter in statistics, the reader would need to know something about basic math such as addition and subtraction and some basic concepts about various types of data as well as why it would be important to use statistics to report the data. This knowledge and information would comprise what is needed in order to be ready to read the chapter or have readiness for the chapter. Therefore, readiness is a factor that all learners must have at any level before they begin any task.

Prereading is a special type of reading readiness; it refers to those special abilities that a young child needs in order to be successful in the process of learning to read. Prereading development takes place from the day a child is born. For example, the desire to read and the love of reading are important parts of prereading development that come as a result of exposure to people who enjoy reading and make that enjoyment obvious. Even these factors can be influenced by school experiences. Therefore, lessons and experiences can be developed in kindergarten and first grade that will foster children's prereading development and will help them as they learn the reading process.

PREREADING FACTORS

What are the major prereading factors?

The prereading factors must be developed to help the reader be ready to translate printed messages into meaning. These factors are normally taught to young children in nursery school, kindergarten, in some homes where reading is valued, and perhaps in early first grade. They are thought to be prerequisite to formal instruction in reading (Durkin, 1980). The following prereading factors are necessary for beginning readers to integrate their new learnings with their previous learnings:

1. Oral language development
2. Experiential background
3. Auditory discrimination
4. Visual discrimination
5. Directionality

Oral Language Development

How does oral language development relate to reading?

Oral language is the language that a person is able to use effectively orally, in other words, listening and speaking. As a prereading factor, oral language refers to the ability to both understand the spoken language as well as the ability to speak the language.

Oral language development is a major factor in the ability to acquire and use word recognition skills. To read the written message with any degree of accuracy or understanding, it is necessary to understand that which it represents—the oral language. A reader is able to understand a written message to the extent that the reader has acquired the oral vocabulary and oral language patterns represented in the written message. Remember the story in Chapter 1 about Mingleup? Difficulty was experienced in understanding that selection because several of the words used in that story were not in the reader's oral language. Even though words may have been decoded, understanding of the message did not occur.

If the written word the reader attempts to decode is not in that reader's oral language vocabulary, the accuracy of the decoding cannot be checked and meaning cannot be constructed. The reader may be able to decode or sound out the word sufficiently well to pronounce it accurately; however, if the reader is not able to determine whether or not the word is correctly decoded, then there is no understanding, therefore, no reading! For example:

The pale blue dress was made of mull.

They went out to get mum.

Most readers would have no difficulty decoding these two sentences. However, when asked to describe what the dress was made of, or what they went out to get, many readers would have difficulty. The difficulty stems from not having the words *mull* and *mum* in their oral vocabulary. Even though the words have been accurately decoded, there is no comprehension, therefore, no reading! (By the way, mull is a soft, thin muslin, and mum is a strong ale or beer.) Oral language development is of great importance to the beginning reader both for word recognition development as well as for comprehension development.

If the sentence structure used in the written message is more complicated than the reader has mastered orally, the written message will not be understood (Ruddell, 1985). Consider the reader whose oral language patterns and sentence structure are limited to ones like ''I want to go'' or ''Can I have one?'' A reader with this level of oral language development is likely to experience difficulty with more complex sentence structures, even though all individual words are decoded correctly. For example:

Don't play in your good clothes.

If you have on your good clothes, Mother won't want you to play outdoors.

More young readers would readily understand the first sentence structure than they would the second. If the second sentence is not understood, even though the words have been correctly decoded, the reader does not have the oral language development necessary to read that sentence.

Oral language development is, therefore, a major factor in the reader's ability to acquire and use word recognition skills. It is only as the decoded word is in the reader's oral vocabulary that the decoding process is checked. To read printed material with accuracy and understanding, it is necessary for the reader to understand that it represents the oral message and for the reader to have the required oral language skills.

Most young children like to talk. Numerous opportunities for both speaking and listening are important aspects of the development of oral language in children as they prepare to learn to read. Children should be given many opportunities to engage in conversation with adults—parents, teachers, and friends. The development of oral language is enhanced by having children tell about their experiences; look at pictures and describe them; describe a pet, a toy, or favorite food; and listen to stories and poems read by adults. As a teacher, encourage parents to read aloud to their children and to discuss what has been read with their children. Refer parents to the *Read-Aloud Handbook* (Trelease, 1985) as a good source of suggestions for what to read aloud and how to assist their children as they read aloud. These experiences all aid the child in learning to use oral language, understanding the words and the sentence structures as well as developing their ability to listen.

Experiential Background

How is experiential
background related
to prereading,
and what are the
two kinds of
experience?

Background of experience, sometimes referred to as prior knowledge, is another major factor in the reader's ability to understand what has been read (Reynolds, Taylor, Steffensen, Shirey, & Anderson, 1982). Background of experience refers to the accumulated knowledge that a person has at any point in time. Obviously, background knowledge continues to change and grow as people gain experience. When a reader has not experienced the things that are being read about, it is much more difficult for the reader to understand the author's message. Readers need to be familiar with both the language used and the concepts presented in the printed material. The relationships between language development and experiences are more obvious when you recall the krashanky story read in Chapter 1. It is as a child experiences things that the oral language necessary to describe these things is developed. Children often need many experiences with one concept before that concept is clearly defined. The concept of Easter may have to be experienced more than once in order for the child to develop a schema that would allow an understanding of krashanky.

Experiences may be either real or vicarious. Real experiences are those that are "first-hand," or direct, where the child has actually participated in the experience. Many of the stories that young children are expected to read and understand are based on what the authors believe will be direct experiences of the readers. Language experience stories, developed by the children, and further explained in this text, may be used to enhance background experiences as well as for the development of all of the other prereading skills. It is not necessary for all experiences to be real, although young children are more likely to remember these. All learners can acquire some knowledge indirectly, or vicariously. Vicarious experiences are those where one learns about things through indirect means such as from TV, books, movies, pictures, or conversations with others.

Experiential background can be built in a prereading program in a variety of ways. If a reader does not have experiences in the physical and social environment that stimulate and provide meaning for the symbols of oral language (words), the speaking and thinking vocabulary and consequent sentence structure may not be developed. In this way, oral language development and background of experience become interrelated. It is possible for a child to live in an environment that is so restrictive in the experiences it provides that language development is also restricted.

The reading teacher has the responsibility of being familiar with the strengths and inadequacies of the students' background of experiences and must make provision to extend those experiences to include the ideas and concepts presented in the material they are expected to read. Every reading lesson must include building the students' background of experience for the particular selection to be read. Otherwise, a lack of experiences may prevent readers from comprehending.

The comprehension skills and processes that the reading teacher must help readers develop are those which will enable readers to associate their experiences with those of the author. The stimuli that evoke this meaning are the printed symbols on a page that act to trigger the meaning the readers have in their background of experiences. If the readers have had experiences that permit giving meaning to the printed symbols, then, and only then, is the reader reading. Without the meaning, the reader would simply be decoding, or calling, words.

Auditory Discrimination

What is auditory discrimination? Why is it important?

Auditory discrimination is the ability to hear likenesses and differences in basic sounds of words. The word recognition skill of phonics is based totally on the relationships of letters to their sounds. Therefore, if this word recognition skill is to be taught successfully, the learner must have developed auditory discrimination ability. If the learner cannot hear that the middle sounds of *pat* and *pet* are different, or that the beginning and ending sounds are the same, it is not possible to be certain that the correct associations will be made between the letter seen and the sound presented when phonics is taught. The learner should be able to or be taught to hear such discriminations as:

> *day, neigh,* and *play* all rhyme
> *dog* and *donut* do not rhyme
>
> *see, sandwich,* and *soap* all begin alike
> *may, ham,* and *candy* do not begin alike
>
> *set* and *gem* have the same medial sound
> *cap* and *cop* do not have the same medial sound
>
> *dig* and *bug* end alike
> *pet* and *pen* do not end alike

All auditory discrimination activities are done orally or by "thinking" or saying the sounds in one's head. The teacher should develop auditory discrimination ability in prereading and beginning reading students for all parts of words (i.e., beginning sounds, final sounds, and medial sounds) through a variety of ways, including experiences with language.

Auditory discrimination activities that require the discrimination of the sounds of living such as being able to tell the ring of the telephone from the ring of the doorbell, high notes from low notes, or other environmental sounds do *not* transfer to the auditory discrimination skills necessary for reading. It is necessary for teachers to teach the auditory discrimination of *letters* in their various positions in words in order for auditory discrimination activities to transfer to formal reading instruction.

Visual Discrimination

What is visual discrimination? What kinds of visual discrimination must be learned?

As a prereading skill, visual discrimination is the ability of the reader to see likenesses and differences in letters and words. It requires that the reader notice the shapes of letters and the position of letters within words. It is the ability of the learner to see that *was* and *saw*, or *on* and *no* are not the same, even though they contain the same letters. Also, the learner needs to see that *b, p,* and *d* are not the same because they are turned a different way or because the letters are in different positions.

Visual discrimination activities in reading are different from a child's prior experiences with visual discrimination. In all visual discrimination experiences prior to reading, the child has been taught that things are the same, no matter from which direction they are viewed. Mother is mother no matter if she is viewed from the front, back, or side, and whether sitting, standing, or lying down. Visual discrimination activities in reading require the learner to be able to tell subtle differences between letters and words.

It is important for learners to be able to tell, for example, that *horse* and *house* are not the same word. Even though the shape of the word is the same, the words have different pronunciations and different meanings. Much visual discrimination work takes place with the reader long before the letters or words can be identified specifically. The activity is merely for the learner to discriminate visually whether the letters and/or words are the same or different.

Activities that require the discrimination of general features, such as finding the duck with the missing leg or dealing with likenesses and differences in geometric shapes, do *not* transfer to the development of the visual discrimination abilities necessary for reading. The ability to tell if one house lacks a window that other houses being viewed have does not transfer to the ability to see likenesses and differences in letters and words (Aaron, 1971; Mangieri & Kahn, 1977).

In addition to providing visual discrimination activities in relation to language experience activities, some other examples of appropriate prereading activities for visual discrimination would be activities that use letters and words. Examples would include:

Circle the letter that is different from all the rest. (or circle all the letters that are the same)
M M M W M M M M
b b d b b b b b
Put an X on all the words that are like the first one. (or put an X on all the words that are different from the first word)
come   come   came   come   come
garden   garden   garben   garden

Directionality

What is direction-
ality? What kind
of skills must be
learned?

Directionality refers to the order in which the reading of a language takes place. Knowledge of directionality helps the reader know where to begin reading a book and in what order to proceed. Directionality has developed in readers who know the front of the book from the back, what order to turn pages of a book, the top of a page from the bottom, the left side from the right, and so forth. Directionality also refers to the sequence in which letters appear in words, words appear in sentences, and sentences appear on the printed page. In English, words and sentences are written from left to right, line by line, and from the top of the page to the bottom. Comprehension depends upon the reader's ability to read words and sentences in a left-to-right fashion, line by line. Skipping words or reordering the position of words could lead the reader to assign a meaning other than the intended one. Left-to-right progression is sometimes used as a synonym for directionality when the reading of English and other languages such as French, German, and Spanish are discussed.

However, not all languages are written this way. Hebrew, for example, is written from right to left.

Directionality is not an intuitive skill; it must be learned. The importance of learning this skill can be illustrated by considering the problems a reader would have if the reader perceived *snug* as *sung*, *on* as *no*, and *saw* as *was*. Such a reordering of the sequence of letters and the viewing of a word from right to left when reading in English results in errors that drastically interfere with word recognition accuracy. Though directionality is often learned informally, some students need practice in such activities before directionality becomes an automatic skill.

All teachers would want to discuss aspects of directionality with children as they show books or cards. This is frequently accomplished by the teacher moving her hand along under the words being read, allowing children to see the flow of the language, discussing where the writing begins, and showing where the book is opened, even allowing children to help by turning the pages of materials being read to them.

Other Factors Related to Prereading

**What other fac-
tors should be
considered in
prereading?**

Even though the major factors in prereading have been discussed, there are other factors related to preparing for formal reading instruction (Durkin, 1980). They are social and emotional development, physical well-being, cognitive development, and interest in reading. These factors are not easily taught or developed, but they must be considered in a prereading program. In whatever ways it is possible, teachers would want to encourage the development of these factors in young children.

Social and emotional development refers to how learners relate to other people and how learners react to success, failure, deviations from usual routine, separation from home and parent, and so forth. The social and emotional development of young children plays a role in how well they adjust to more structured or formal education. Children who experience difficulty relating to other children and adults may also experience difficulty in the school setting and instruction in prereading.

The physical well-being of children refers to how well the body's needs are being met. It is related to such things as having sufficient and proper nutrition, adequate rest, and relatively normal sight and hearing. It may also be affected by the lack of appropriate clothing for the weather. When children lack physical well-being, it is not unusual for them to experience difficulty in concentrating on learning tasks.

Cognitive development is related to the growth and development of the mind or mental abilities. Although cognitive ability cannot be totally separated from heredity, it can be enhanced by stimulation within the environment. Children who are exposed to varied experiences with accompanying oral language development will also develop cognitively. Most children who are encouraged to reason and think begin to use these skills independently. Cognitive development takes place in the home as well as the school setting.

Interest in reading and in learning to read often is a direct outgrowth of children seeing others read and perceiving a need for reading. If children have experienced pleasure from being read to, they are more likely to be interested in learning to read themselves. The desire to learn to read, like the desire to learn anything else, gives the child with this desire an advantage over the one who does not want to or see a need to learn to read.

The development of prereading skills and abilities forms the foundation of successful programs in teaching reading. Although Gates (1937) long ago determined that age or maturation alone was not sufficient for success in reading, he determined that a learner can be taught, beginning where that learner is. Teachers must assess the strengths and inadequacies of the learner at the prereading level, then proceed to develop oral language, experience background, auditory discrimination, visual discrimination, and/or directionality as it is needed by the learner. Teachers should also encourage and support parents in enhancing their role in the development of prereading factors in children.

PRACTICE EXERCISE

Directions
This series of exercises is designed to help you practice and check your knowledge of prereading skills. Complete each exercise; then check your answers with those in the Answer Key at the end of the text.

Part I
Respond to each of the following questions.

1. List the five major factors related to prereading.

   a. _____

   b. _____

   c. _____

   d. _____

   e. _____

2. Compare and contrast reading readiness with prereading.

3. Give two examples of things that are necessary for the physical well-being of children.

   a. _____

   b. _____

4. What are the two kinds of experiences that can be provided for children? _____

   _____

Part II

Identify the major prereading factors being developed by a teacher who is having children participate in the following activities.

1. Put an X on the top picture.

Major Prereading Factor _____

2. Underline all of the letters on the line that are like the first letter.

   C   M   C   P   G   C   O   C   T

   Major Prereading Factor _____

3. Tell me a word that rhymes with *run*.

   Major Prereading Factor _____

4. Describe the eating and living habits of the cat that has been brought to the classroom.

   Major Prereading Factor _____

5. Give words to describe an apple.

   Major Prereading Factor _____

Part III

Mark the following statements true (T) or false (F).

_____ 1. It is necessary for a word to be in the reader's oral language in order to check the accuracy of the decoding process.

_____ 2. It is important for the sentence structure of a passage read to be in the oral language of the reader in order for understanding to occur.

_____ 3. Teachers of young children should encourage them to talk.

_____ 4. Inviting a resource person to talk to the children is helpful in developing auditory discrimination.

_____ 5. Having children listen to environmental sounds will aid in developing auditory discrimination ability necessary as a prereading factor.

Part IV

Choose the best answer among the stated possibilities.

1. When teaching auditory discrimination, the teacher should work with
   a. speech sounds
   b. rhyming words
   c. initial sounds
   d. medial sounds
   e. all of the above

2. Which of the following is *not* a goal of a prereading visual discrimination activity?
   a. mark the one that is different: no   on   no
   b. mark all that are the same: f   f   t   f   p   f
   c. mark the one that is different: ()   ()   []   ()
   d. none. All of the above activities are fine.

3. Which of the following would be a good activity to develop background of experience in children?
   a. having a tasting party
   b. having children color
   c. having children write their name
   d. all of the above

4. Which of the following activities would be a good activity to enhance oral language development?
   a. finger plays
   b. choral reading
   c. action songs
   d. all of the above

5. Reading readiness is expected to be present in reading instruction at
   a. first-grade level
   b. fifth-grade level
   c. tenth-grade level
   d. all of the above

3
Comprehension

What should be
learned about
comprehension as
a result of
reading this
chapter?

Reading is a process of constructing meaning that is composed of two basic components: decoding and comprehension. This chapter will present:

1. More about what comprehension is.
2. The importance of different types of text to reading comprehension.
3. What elements should be included in comprehension.

This chapter will give the reader a basic understanding of comprehension; Chapter 7 will present how to teach comprehension.

COMPREHENSION DEFINED

What is compre-
hension, and
how are compre-
hension skills
related?

During the last ten years, educators have learned more about reading comprehension than has ever been known, which has led to the development of more effective teaching strategies. Much of this new information has focused on what comprehension is and how one comprehends during reading. The more that is understood about comprehension, the better teachers are likely to be at teaching students how to comprehend.

Comprehension is a process of constructing meaning from clues in the text and information in the reader's background of experience; this process of building meaning involves interaction between the reader and the text. *The meanings formed by the reader do not come from the printed page.* The meanings a reader constructs are dependent upon the reader's prior experiences, including language development. Read the following sentence:

> The completion of the run brought a loud cheer from everyone nearby.

What did you think of as you read this—a baseball game, a track meet, a marathon race, a dog run at a kennel, or a job on the computer? Certainly, there are not sufficient clues in the text to let a reader know the exact topic being covered. However, prior experiences with *run* lead a reader to form an understanding which may or may not have been similar to the author's. When reading this sentence, readers draw on their schema for *run,* which is the information relative to *run* stored in the reader's memory; the limited clues in the sentence helped the reader activate or draw from that schema to construct meaning for the sentence. If the text had given more clues and the reader had the needed schema, a different meaning may have been formed. For example:

> The PRP Corporation would save $200,000 if the job could be completed by noon. At last, the computer was working. The completion of the run brought a loud cheer from everyone nearby.

This text gave more clues, making it possible for readers to activate a specific part of their schema for *run.* If a reader didn't have a schema for computers and *run,* it wouldn't be possible to form the correct meaning for this paragraph. The schema readers have relative to a particular topic depends on their background of experiences.

Reading does not occur unless comprehension takes place. Therefore, reading is comprehension or developing understanding. Just being able to decode words is not reading. No reading has taken place unless meaning is constructed.

As the reader reads words, sentences, or longer text, meanings are constantly being constructed and changed. As in the example about *run,* a more specific meaning for the sentences was constructed as more information was provided in the text. In reading, the reader constantly uses the skills and processes of comprehension along with decoding to formulate meaning.

THE ROLE OF SKILLS IN READING

When teachers talk about the various reading skills or decoding skills or comprehension skills, they are referring to a number of specific parts of reading that students can be taught to perform. There is a great deal of controversy, misunderstanding, and misuse of the concept of different skills of reading (Rosenshine, 1980). There is no evidence to indicate that there is *one* right set of reading skills or that the teaching of any one skill will necessarily make a student a better reader (Rosenshine, 1980). Reading involves learning to use a process; therefore, learning one skill after another does not automatically mean that a student will be able to read; the sum of the parts in this case does not equal the whole.

Our point of view is that students must be taught the skills of reading in such a way that they *learn to use the process of reading*. Being able to do this in teaching involves knowing how to teach skills so that they are applied and used in the reading of natural text, as explained in Chapters 6, 7, 8, and 9. How skills and processes of reading are taught is the most important factor to consider in making certain that students learn to use reading as a process. If a student fails to learn any one skill, it may not be significant to learning the overall process of reading. This is especially true in reading comprehension.

TEXT TYPE AND READING COMPREHENSION

What are the two types of text, and what are the elements of each type?

Reading comprehension is influenced by all those factors that influence the overall process of reading. However, the reader's ability to use the skills and processes of comprehension is related in part to the type of text which is being read. Different types of text require the reader to use different skills and processes. There are two basic types of text, narrative and expository.

Narrative text presents information by telling a story. Narrative text always contains the elements of setting, characters, problem, action, resolution, and theme. The *setting* is the time and place where a story takes place. The *characters* are the people or animals who are in the story. The *problem* is the situation or conflict that exists in the story. The *action* is what takes place as a result of the problem; the action leads up to the outcome or resolution. The *resolution* is how the problem is solved. The *theme* is the overriding idea that runs throughout the story. These elements of a narrative are called the story line or the story grammar. When these items are depicted graphically, they are called a story map. Figure 3-1 presents a narrative selection, ''The Three Little Pigs''; Figure 3-2 shows a story map for this selection, illustrating all of the elements of a narrative.

FIGURE 3-1
"The Three Little Pigs"—A Narrative Selection

Once upon a time, there were three little pigs who lived in a little house with their mother. Two of the pigs played all day long every day. The third little pig always helped his mother with her work. One day the mother decided her children were old enough to take care of themselves, so she gave each of them a dollar and sent them out into the world to make their fortunes. The third little pig promised not to let the other two spend their money foolishly. Then off they all went out into the big world.

"First, we must have houses to live in," said the wise little pig, and he promptly bought a load of bricks to build his house. His brothers laughed, "Bricks are much too heavy!" And with that, the first foolish pig bought a load of straw with which to build his house, and the second foolish pig bought a bundle of sticks for his house. "When the wolf comes after you, he will blow your houses away with one puff," said the wise pig. But his brothers paid no attention to his advice.

The wise little pig was soon busy at work, building his house of bricks. "Oh, let's play a bit before we go to work," said his brothers, and so they spent the day playing,

FIGURE 3-1 (continued)
"The Three Little Pigs"—A Narrative Selection

while the wise pig worked away on his house. "You had better hurry," he warned his brothers. "Night is coming, and you'll be sorry when the big, bad wolf comes around looking for you."

Finally, the first little pig went off and built his house of straw. Then he settled down inside for a nap. But, presently, along came the big, bad, mean wolf, and he knocked loudly on the door, saying, "Little pig, little pig, let me come in!" The little pig, trying to sound as brave as he could, said, "Not by the hair of my chinny chin chin!" "Then I'll huff and I'll puff, and I'll blow your house in," said the wolf. So he huffed and he puffed, and he blew the first little pig's house right down! The little pig was so afraid that he ran off to find the second little pig.

The second pig had been busy building his house of sticks, and he had just finished when the first little pig arrived, all out of breath and crying, "The wolf is after me! Help!" Quickly, the two pigs popped inside the house and shut the door tight.

The big, bad, mean wolf soon arrived and he knocked loudly on the door, saying, "Little pig, little pig, let me come in!" And in a trembling voice the pig replied, "Not by the hair of my chinny chin chin!" "Then I'll huff and I'll puff, and I'll blow your house in," said the wolf. So he huffed and he puffed, and at last he blew down the house of sticks. Off ran the two little pigs as fast as their legs would carry them to their brother's house of bricks.

Now the wise little pig had finished his house and he was sitting outside when he saw his two brothers running with the wolf right behind them. Quick as a wink the three pigs popped into the house and slammed the door.

Now the big, bad, mean wolf was very angry indeed! He pounded on the door, saying, "Little pig, little pig, let me come in!" And the wise pig replied, "Not by the hair of my chinny chin chin!" "Then I'll huff and I'll puff, and I'll blow your house in!" shouted the wolf. So he huffed and he puffed, and he huffed and he puffed, but he couldn't blow down the house of bricks.

"I want to eat those three fat little pigs," said the wolf to himself, and with that he climbed up on the roof, planning to drop down the chimney and surprise the pigs. But the wise little pig saw the wolf climbing up to the roof. He quickly made a great hot fire in the fireplace, and he put on a large kettle to boil. Then, down fell the wolf into the boiling water.

"Now, foolish brothers," said the wise little pig, "let us all live here in my house of bricks, and we will never again have to be afraid of a wolf eating us up."

Expository texts present facts and information in a variety of ways, depending on the type of information being presented and the purpose for presenting it. Expository texts are the types of writing usually found in a science book, a social studies book, or a newspaper article. There is not one specific pattern for expository texts as there is with narratives. There are four types of expository writing commonly used: description, collection (sequence or listing), causation or cause-effect, and comparison (Meyer, 1975; Meyer & Freedle, 1984). Table 3-1 presents a definition and an example for each of these types of expository text. The reading of expository text is difficult for students for two reasons:

FIGURE 3-2
Story Map for "The Three Little Pigs"

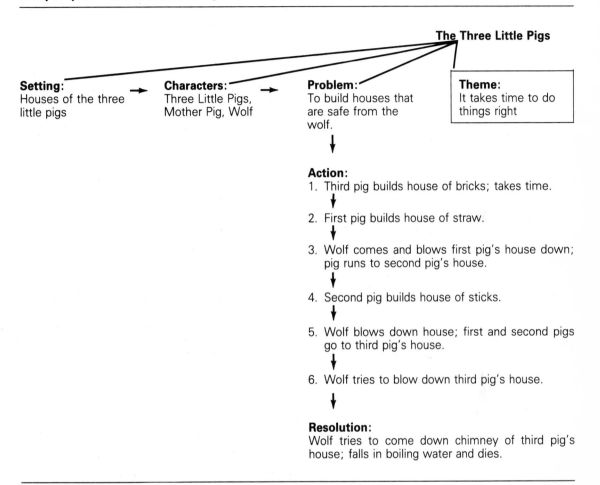

The Three Little Pigs

Setting:
Houses of the three
little pigs

Characters:
Three Little Pigs,
Mother Pig, Wolf

Problem:
To build houses that
are safe from the
wolf.

Theme:
It takes time to do
things right

Action:
1. Third pig builds house of bricks; takes time.

2. First pig builds house of straw.

3. Wolf comes and blows first pig's house down;
   pig runs to second pig's house.

4. Second pig builds house of sticks.

5. Wolf blows down house; first and second pigs
   go to third pig's house.

6. Wolf tries to blow down third pig's house.

Resolution:
Wolf tries to come down chimney of third pig's
house; falls in boiling water and dies.

1. Students have much more experience in reading narrative texts; many have heard stories all of their lives and are familiar with the elements of a narrative even though they don't call them by name.

2. Expository texts do not follow one consistent pattern as do narratives, and authors use several different patterns within the same text. Therefore, learning to comprehend expository texts requires focusing on several different text patterns at the same time.

Students must learn to read both kinds of text. Learning to read narrative text does not automatically transfer to expository text. As a part of learning how to comprehend, students must be shown how to read both narrative and expository texts.

TABLE 3-1
Types of Expository Text

Type	Definition	Example
Description	Give information about a particular topic; something is described.	Air travel is a very fast, efficient means of transportation. It saves you time and allows you to travel long distance in a short time.
Collection	Ideas are presented together as a related group. This is often called listing or sequence.	When you travel by air the first thing you must do is arrive at the airport early. Next, you check in at the ticket counter. Afterwards, you proceed to the gate to board your flight.
Causation	Ideas are presented to show that one causes another to happen. This cause-effect can be stated or implied.	There are often many problems associated with air travel. Heavy traffic going into the airport can make you late. Bad weather often prevents planes from landing on time. Overselling tickets frequently means that there are delays while airline personnel try to get volunteers to give up their seats and wait for a later flight.
Comparison	The likenesses and differences between two or more objects or ideas are presented.	Air travel and train travel of years past are both similar and different. Train travel and air travel were both the fastest means of transportation in the prime of their use. Both encounter problems and delays. Trains of long ago were slowed by animals blocking the tracks; airplanes are often slowed by weather conditions. Air travel and train travel are very different because airplanes move much faster than trains.

VOCABULARY DEVELOPMENT

What are the three elements of vocabulary development, and what skills must students learn to determine word meanings independently?

An important part of a reader's ability to comprehend is having an extensive meaning vocabulary (Davis, 1944; Davis, 1972; Johnston, 1981). An effective comprehender knows the meanings of many words in different contexts and also knows how to determine word meanings as text is being read. The reading program must make students conscious of words and their meanings and must constantly enrich and expand the reader's vocabulary. Meaning vocabulary for reading develops from the reader's listening and speaking vocabularies. Vocabulary development should include:

1. Teaching skills to determine word meanings independently.
2. Expanding and enriching vocabulary.
3. Teaching specific word meanings prior to reading text.

Determining Word Meanings Independently

Students must be taught the skills that will help them become independent in determining word meanings because it is not possible for readers to learn the meanings of each individual word that they will encounter in life. These skills include context clues, structural analysis, and the use of the dictionary.

Context clues involve the use of the words, sentences, or paragraphs surrounding a word to help determine the meaning of an unknown word. Context clues often give an approximate meaning for an unknown word rather than its specific definition. Context clues are one of the most effective clues the reader can use to determine word meanings.

There are several different types of context clues; four of the most commonly used are

• *Direct Definition*. This type of context clue directly gives the definition of a word in a sentence.

An *isthmus* is a narrow strip of land that connects two larger sections of land.

• *Appositive*. The definition of a word is given by a word or statement immediately following a word and is usually set off by commas. This is called an appositive or in apposition.

Larry's *jodhpurs,* riding pants, were a mess after the fall from the horse.

• *Synonym/Antonym*. A synonym or antonym is repeated for an unfamiliar word instead of using the unknown word. Usually this is done using a synonym rather than an antonym.

A strange, red liquid *oozed* from the crack in the wall; it **leaked** out slowly and covered the floor.

• *Surrounding Sentences*. Clues to the meaning of a word are given in several sentences surrounding it.

The speaker walked up to **the reading desk** and **placed his papers** carefully. As he prepared to speak, he adjusted **the slanted top** of the *lectern* so that he could easily **read his notes.**

As students read, they use context clues in conjunction with their other reading skills to help them determine word meanings. Context clues help readers determine both the meanings and pronunciations of words.

Structural analysis is the study of meaningful word parts; understanding the various parts of words will also help readers become independent in determining word meanings. Structural analysis helps readers determine both the meaning and pronunciation of words, as discussed in greater depth in Chapter 4.

There are several different elements students must be taught when learning to use structural analysis. These include base words, root words, prefixes, suffixes, inflectional endings, compound words, and contractions. All of these elements are defined and illustrated in the following chapter. Prefixes, suffixes, and inflectional endings are all known as affixes. Appendix A contains a list of common prefixes and suffixes, their meanings, and examples.

The reader who knows how to use structural analysis will be able to figure out the meanings of some words independently. Consider the following examples:

Spot came out of his *doghouse*.

The amount of work to be done was *unimportant* to the boss.

In the first example, the reader could use knowledge of compound words to determine the meaning of *doghouse* (*dog* + *house*). In the second example, the meaning of the base word *important* and the prefix *un* (*not*) could be used to determine the meaning of the word *unimportant*.

A final tool which helps the reader become independent in determining word meanings is the *use of the dictionary*. The dictionary not only contains the meanings of words, it also helps the reader determine the pronunciation of words (decoding) and is a valuable study tool. Therefore, the dictionary must be viewed as a tool that can help the reader in decoding, comprehension, and studying. The dictionary is discussed in depth in Chapter 5.

Expanding and Enriching Vocabulary

Why is expanding and enriching vocabulary important to comprehension, and what can be taught to aid expansion of vocabulary?

An important part of helping the reader develop an extensive meaning vocabulary is that of constantly making the reader aware of words. A part of this process is helping readers see how words are related to each other. As these relationships are developed, students also expand their backgrounds and their schemata. Think back to the example about *run*. If a student only thought of *run* as something associated with a sporting event, learning about *run* as related to computers would help the student see the relationship between run and computers; this would help expand the student's background and schema for future reading.

As a part of vocabulary expansion and enrichment, students need to learn about six types of word relationships: synonyms, antonyms, homonyms/homophones/homographs, denotation/connotation, multiple meanings, and analogies.

• *Synonyms*. Words that mean the same or nearly the same are called synonyms. In the sentence, "The *frightened* girl ran through the house as the *scared* dog hid behind the chair," the words *frightened* and *scared* are synonyms because they mean nearly the same.
• *Antonyms*. Words that have opposite or nearly opposite meanings are called antonyms. In the sentence, "Billy *closed* the back door but his brother, Mark, *opened* it," *closed* and *opened* are antonyms because they have opposite meanings.
• *Homonyms/Homophones/Homographs*. These terms are frequently used differently by various authorities in reading. Technically, *homonyms* are words which have the same oral *or* written form. Within the category of homonyms, there are homophones and homographs. *Homophones* are words with the same pronunciation, whether or not they are spelled the same; they have different meanings.

bear—the big *bear*
bare—the *bare* baby
bear—to *bear* the cost

Many authorities refer to these as homonyms. *Homographs* are words which have the same spellings whether or not they are pronounced the same.

wind—the *wind* blew
wind—*wind* the watch

• *Denotation/Connotation*. Readers need to learn the difference between a word's denotation and connotation because this helps them construct meanings more effectively. *Denotation* refers to a word's exact meaning; *connotation* refers to the feelings, emotions, or shades of meaning suggested by a word. Read the following sentences:

The man placed his dog in a *pen* to keep him from running away.
The *pen* on the desk was out of ink.

The denotations for the two italicized words in these sentences are different even though the visual forms of the words are the same. Therefore, words may have more than one denotation; these are called multiple meanings.

Now read the following two sentences:

The old woman *walked* down the road.
The old woman *trudged* down the road.

The two italicized words in both of these sentences indicate that the old woman moved down the road. The second sentence, however, makes you feel very different about how the old woman moved down the road. *Trudged* elicits different feelings or thoughts than *walked*. This is an example of a word's connotation. Examples of other pairs of words that illustrate different connotations would include:

boat—yacht
automobile—limousine
cried—wailed

• *Multiple Meanings*. Most words have more than one meaning, and some very commonly used words have a large number of meanings. For example, the word *run* has hundreds of different meanings ranging from ''to go by moving the legs rapidly'' to ''the extreme after part of a ship's bottom.'' Words with more than one meaning are called multiple meaning words. In the sentence, ''I will *run* to the machine and make it *run* efficiently,'' the word *run* has two different meanings. The reader must learn that words have different meanings in order to be able to select the appropriate meaning to fit a particular contextual situation.

• *Analogies*. Analogies compare two or more things point by point to show how they are similar. Learning analogies helps students expand and enrich their vocabularies. Johnson and Pearson (1984) suggest thirteen analogy categories to use in developing vocabulary:

1. Opposites in Sensation. *ice cream : pickle :: sweet : sour*
2. Object/Function. *wine : bottle :: crackers : box*
3. Characteristics. *rain : wet :: sun : dry*
4. Part/Whole. *leaf : tree :: feather : bird*
5. Whole/Part. *cup : handle :: clock : hands*
6. Location. *teacher : classroom :: sailor : ship*
7. Action/Object. *run : track :: swim : pool*
8. Agent-action or Object. *teacher : students :: doctor : patients*
9. Class or Synonym. *smell : sniff :: see : look*
10. Familial. *uncle : nephew :: aunt : niece*
11. Grammatical. *hear : heard :: look : looked*
12. Temporal or Sequential. *fifth : first :: twenty-fifth : fifth*
13. Antonyms. *smile : happy :: frown : sad*

Readers must be taught synonyms, antonyms, homonyms/homophones/homographs, denotation/connotation, multiple meanings, and analogies as a part of vocabulary expansion and enrichment. Students should be taught lessons using each of these categories to help them develop a broader meaning vocabulary.

Learning Specific Word Meanings

The final component of vocabulary development is the learning of specific word meanings. In order for students to internalize the word meanings into their meaning vocabulary and relate them to their existing background, the meanings of words should be taught in relation to text that is going to be read or an area to be studied. Therefore, before students read a selection the words that relate most directly to the key concepts or story line should be taught in written context.

By helping students learn specific word meanings before a selection is read, independently determine word meanings, and expand and enrich their vocabulary, you will help develop their meaning vocabulary, a significant part of comprehending more effectively.

IDENTIFYING RELEVANT INFORMATION IN TEXT

What is involved in teaching students to note important information in the text, and how is it related?

In addition to developing their meaning vocabularies, readers must be taught to use various processes in order to comprehend texts effectively. One of these processes involves learning to identify the relevant information in the text that is being read. Many times reading specialists refer to this as *literal comprehension* because it involves identifying the specifically stated information in the text.

When authors write, they provide readers with a certain amount of specifically stated information. In order to learn how to comprehend, readers must be taught how to identify this information and learn to see how the ideas presented are related to each other. This involves teaching students the process of noting important details and recognizing the relationships among the ideas.

Noting Important Details

Details are the specific facts or ideas that the author provides in the text. Readers must be taught to identify these and then to recognize those which are important to the text. Teaching students to identify the important details involves helping the reader recognize the topic of the material being read and then seeing how the details presented relate most directly to the topic. Teaching students to identify and remember important details involves teaching them to:

1. Recognize the details given by the author.
2. Identify the topic of what is being read by noting what most of the sentences are about.
3. Identify which details relate most directly to the topic.

Readers must learn to identify the important details in sentences, paragraphs, and longer text. The details tell about the topic, ideas, or events of the text, including such things as the traits of the various characters in a story or narrative text. Read the following sentence:

Marsha was a happy, friendly girl.

The details of this sentence tell about Marsha's character traits. She is a happy, friendly girl. The author has stated this information directly. Being able to identify details is important to a reader in both narrative and expository texts.

Noting How Information in Text Is Related

As a part of learning how to comprehend, readers must also learn the process of recognizing how the details or ideas in text are related. The process of doing this involves recognizing the *sequence* of ideas, *cause-effect relationships,* and *comparisons and contrasts.*

Sequence.   Sequence refers to the order in which an author presents the ideas in text. Read the following paragraph:

Larry and his family were going on a trip to visit his aunt. Larry's father said that each person could take only one suitcase because the van didn't have much extra room with all the other boxes. Larry thought about what he would take. Then he packed his suitcase. After Larry was finished packing his suitcase, he helped his father pack the van.

In this paragraph, the topic is the family trip to visit an aunt. All of the details presented are relevant to the topic, but in this situation the sequential relationship of the details or events is also important to understanding what happened.

Sequence is important in both narrative and expository texts. In narrative texts, being able to identify the sequence helps the reader determine the events that lead up to the resolution. In expository texts, sequence is important in understanding the order of events in such areas as history.

Following directions is a special form of sequence. Students must be taught to follow written directions and see how important it is to perform the steps in the order given. This is an especially important process to be taught in learning to follow directions given in school and in such activities as putting things together, completing job applications, or cooking.

Teaching students to use the process of sequencing involves:

1. Showing them how and why the order of events in a paragraph or longer text influences the meaning that is constructed.

2. Teaching clue words that are likely to denote a sequential relationship of ideas in text. These can include *first, second,* etc. . . ., *next, after, before, prior, following, then,* and *last.*

3. Showing students how to identify the sequence of relevant details in both narrative and expository texts.

Cause-Effect Relationships.   Authors frequently present relevant details so that they show a cause-effect relationship where one thing causes another one to happen. Readers must be taught to recognize and understand these relationships. Read the following sentence:

Martha went to school early because she wanted to help with the class project.

In this sentence, the cause is that Martha wanted to help with the class project, and the effect is that she went to school early. In this example, the clue word *because* alerts the reader to a cause-effect relationship. Notice that in this example the effect was given before the cause. This is not always true but students must be taught to recognize that this often happens, especially when authors use clue words to indicate the relationship.

Cause-effect relationships can be found in both narrative and expository texts. In narrative texts, cause/effect often shows how one action caused another to happen. Look back at the story "The Three Little Pigs." In the fourth paragraph, "[the wolf] huffed and he puffed, and he blew the first little pig's house right down" is cause/effect in a narrative text.

The following paragraph shows an example of cause/effect being used in expository text:

We observed the tiger from our vehicle as he stalked the herd of deer. *As a result of* the slight noise from our running camera, the tiger turned and knew we were there. This didn't stop him from returning to his intended prey. Slowly and carefully he moved forward, not making a sound. The deer were initially unaware of his presence but *because of* the shifting winds, they caught the tiger's scent. This was enough to scare them away. (Cooper, 1986)

The author of this paragraph has clearly used cause/effect in the second and fifth sentences to report what happened with the tiger and his prey.

Teaching readers to use the process of cause/effect involves:

1. Teaching them to recognize how relevant details are presented in a cause-effect relationship.

2. Teaching clue words that are likely to denote a cause-effect relationship such as *because of, since, therefore, so, as a result,* and *because.*

3. Teaching students to use cause-effect relationships in narrative and expository texts to construct meaning.

Comparisons and Contrasts.   Comparisons and contrasts require the reader to learn to recognize and remember how an author shows the likenesses and differences between characters, events, or other relevant details in the text. In comparing, the author shows how things are alike. In contrasting, the differences between things are shown. Read the following paragraph.

> People live and work in the city and in the country. City and country dwellers *both* have jobs to do. City dwellers often travel some distance to work. *On the other hand,* people who live in the country often work on their own farm.

The first sentence shows how city and country dwellers are alike—they are compared. The second sentence contrasts city and country dwellers and shows how they are different. Notice that in both instances the clue words (in italics) help the reader note the comparisons or the contrasts. Some of the commonly used words are

> comparison—both, same, alike, same as, similar, like
>
> contrast—on the other hand, different from, unlike, but, although, rather than

Authors use comparisons in both narrative and expository texts. For example, in a narrative an author might use a comparison to show how two characters are different:

> Queen Ida is charming and friendly but her sister Princess Ann is rude and withdrawn.

In an expository text, the author might show how two events are similar or different:

> Northside's victory last week was much like that of Central High in 1943. In 1943, Central needed a win to bring them out of their long losing streak. Northside was in the same situation this year.

Teaching students to use the process of comparison and contrast requires teaching them:

1. To recognize how authors directly state comparisons and contrasts.

2. How clue words will alert them to comparisons and contrasts.

3. To use the process of recognizing comparisons and contrasts in both narrative and expository texts.

INFERENCING

What is inferencing, and how is it influenced as one reads?

Another process that readers must learn to use as a part of becoming effective comprehenders is that of inferencing. When inferencing, readers use the details provided by the author plus their own prior experiences to determine information that is not stated by the author. Read the following passage:

Mr. Edwards was walking to his car, carrying his two bags of groceries. The eggs were sticking out of the top of one of the bags. As he leaned over to attempt to unlock his car, the bag with the eggs tilted. Ten minutes later, he returned to his car with another carton of eggs which he carried carefully in a bag by itself.

In order to read and understand this paragraph, one must use inferencing. The paragraph states:

1. Mr. Edwards was carrying two bags of groceries.
2. The eggs were sticking out of one of the bags.
3. The bag with the eggs tilted as he leaned over to unlock the car.
4. He returned to the car later with another carton of eggs.

From experience one knows that:

1. Eggs break easily if dropped.
2. Carrying two bags of groceries and trying to unlock the car can be awkward.
3. This same experience has happened to many people.

By using the clues in the text in combination with experiences, a reader is able to tell that Mr. Edwards dropped the eggs and broke them. This is the process of inferencing. Good readers use it continuously as they read to determine ideas and information that the author does not directly state.

As students learn to use the process of inferencing, they must also learn that as they gain more information from text, their inferences may change or be proven incorrect. Now read the next paragraph in the story about Mr. Edwards.

When Mr. Edwards walked into the house, the first thing his wife said was, "Did you remember the two dozen eggs?" "Oh, yes," he replied. "But only after I nearly dropped the first dozen as I unlocked the car. You can sure bet I was more careful with the second dozen."

Mr. Edwards didn't break the eggs, but he almost dropped them. Now a reader can infer something else; one can tell that the incident at the car with the first dozen eggs caused Mr. Edwards to remember the second dozen eggs and return to the store to buy them. In this instance the reader is inferring a cause-effect relationship. Many times as one reads one can infer details, sequence, cause and effect, comparisons and contrasts and also make predictions about what is likely to happen next and draw conclusions. In all of these situations readers are using the same process of inferencing, where inferences are based on the details provided in the text in combination with prior experiences.

As students are taught to use the process of inferencing, they must learn that the ideas they infer are based on the details given plus their own prior experiences. The inferences students make as they read must be supportable from the details that are given by the author in order for them to be logical and correct.

Teachers often have difficulty in teaching inference because they expect students to give one right answer to inference questions. However, in many instances there are several supportable answers. Sometimes in text it is not possible to verify the exact answer. Therefore, all defensible possibilities must be accepted by the reader and the teacher.

The use of inference is required in both narrative and expository texts. However, it is more likely to be required in narrative text because the author is telling a story rather than presenting factual information as is the case in expository text. Even in expository text authors often use inference if they are trying to get the readers to form their own thoughts or to sway them to think a certain way. This will be discussed more in "Criticial Reading/Thinking" later in this chapter.

MAIN IDEA

What is the main idea and how may it be presented in the text?

Determining the main idea of paragraphs and longer text is another process students must be taught as a part of teaching them how to comprehend. Main idea refers to the central thought or idea that is represented in a paragraph or longer text. Read the following paragraph:

> A baby deer, wolf, or lion is referred to as a cub. A newly hatched fish is called a fry. A young kangaroo is called a joey. There are many different names for young animals.

The main idea of this paragraph is that there are many different names for young animals. This main idea is stated in the last sentence and could be called a literal main idea. All of the other sentences in this paragraph present important details supporting the main idea. Many times the main idea will be the first or last sentence, *but it can come at any point in the paragraph.*

The main idea of a paragraph or longer text is not always directly stated. Many times it is necessary for the reader to infer the main idea by using the relevant details in a paragraph to determine the central thought. Read the following paragraph:

> The Alakai Swamp in Hawaii is known as "the swamp in the sky" because it is located within the crater of an ancient volcano on the island of Kauai. The swamp is one of the world's rainiest spots; rain falls there nearly every day. The dense plant life and numerous animals make the Alakai Swamp a fascinating place for nature studies. Many scientists go there to observe rare birds not found in most other parts of the world. Because the Alakai is such an unusual swamp, the state of Hawaii has laws to protect it.*

In this paragraph, there is not one sentence clearly stating the main idea. The reader must infer the main idea by using all of the important details provided in the paragraph to determine that the main idea is that the Alakai Swamp is one of the most unusual swamps in the world.

An important part of learning to determine the main idea of paragraphs or longer text is being able to determine the topic of the material being read. For example, the topic of the first paragraph presented in this section was the names of young animals. The topic for the paragraph presented above was the Alakai Swamp. The topic for a paragraph is the one thing that most of the sentences are about. The main idea is a statement that sums up what most of the sentences are telling about the topic; the main idea can be stated in the paragraph or it may have to be inferred by the reader.

---

*From *Triumphs,* Teacher's Edition (p. 110) by William K. Durr et al., 1986, Boston: Houghton Mifflin Co.

What are the
four parts of the
process for
determining the
main idea?

Teaching readers to use the process of determining the main idea of paragraphs and longer text involves four systematic steps (Cooper, 1986):

1. Read the material and determine the general topic. This is done by teaching students how to identify the important details and how they are related to each other.
2. Look for a sentence that seems to summarize the related details of the text. This sentence may appear at any point in the text. If this sentence exists in the text, it is likely to be the main idea.
3. If there is not one sentence summarizing the related details, look to see what ideas are irrelevant to all the others. These should be ignored.
4. Use the related details to formulate a main idea in your own words.

By teaching students to use a process for determining the main idea, teachers provide them something that can be easily generalized to both narrative and expository texts. Main ideas can be found in both types of text but many times they are more important to the reader in reading expository texts. While specific paragraphs of texts usually have main ideas, it is often possible to identify the main idea of an entire text. In narrative texts the main idea and the theme are very similar. Teaching main idea as a process will also help readers see that the important details of a paragraph or text support the main idea whether it is stated or inferred.

CRITICAL READING/THINKING

What are criti-
cal reading and
thinking, and
why are they
discussed to-
gether and some-
times not taught?

Reading and thinking are processes that an individual uses simultaneously. A part of teaching students to be effective comprehenders is to teach them the processes involved in critical reading/thinking.

Critical reading/thinking requires the reader to make an evaluative judgment about something that has been read. This judgment is based on the reader's own values, prior experiences, and knowledge, and/or it may be based on a set of criteria provided by another source such as a teacher or an employer who is asking that you read something and evaluate it. Critically reading and thinking are what effective, mature readers should be doing constantly while reading. Readers should be judging and evaluating as they read.

Barriers to Critical Reading/Thinking

Unfortunately, critical reading/thinking is a comprehension process that does not always receive the degree of attention it should in reading instruction. In fact, many teachers devote little time to helping students develop this level of comprehension. This omission results from several causes, primary of which may be that many teachers do not understand critical reading/thinking, do not practice the process themselves, and, therefore, do not attempt to teach it.

Other significant factors obstruct the development of the process of critical reading/thinking as a part of a school's reading program. In our schools there is a predominance of emphasis and stress placed on facts; students are expected, and become conditioned early in their school careers, to regurgitate facts. Teaching critical reading/thinking promotes open-ended responses for which there are often no right or wrong answers. Importance is placed upon the logic the reader uses to defend a judgment. It is difficult to assign a letter grade to this response, and our schools have traditionally been geared to the evaluation of student progress by a rating system of some sort. The use of critical reading/thinking makes evaluation difficult to do and defend by a numerical score.

Schools tend not to expose students to controversial issues that might cause overtones of disagreement or adverse reactions from parents. This attitude has been prompted by angry confrontations among parents, school boards, school administrators, and teachers when controversial issues were made part of the classroom instructional program.

Quite frequently only one source of information or a single text is used in teaching the content subjects. This does not permit the students to make comparisons and become aware of author bias as well as reader bias in dealing with written information in various formats.

What to Teach in Critical Reading/Thinking

What are the elements involved in teaching students to become effective in critical reading/thinking?

Teaching students to be effective critical readers involves teaching them to recognize certain elements of critical reading/thinking and then showing them how to use a process that will allow them to apply their critical reading to all types of reading situations. While it is necessary for readers to read critically in all types of material, critical reading becomes most important when students read expository texts where factual material is presented.

Fact/Opinion.   Readers must learn to recognize facts and opinions. Facts are statements that can be proven. Opinions are statements of what an individual or group thinks, feels, or believes. There can be many different opinions on the same subject. Read the following statements:

> O'Hare International Airport in Chicago is one of the world's busiest airports.
>
> The best airport in the world is Chicago's O'Hare International Airport.

The first statement is a fact. One can verify or prove this. The second statement is an opinion. It indicates how someone feels about the airport. There is no real way to verify or prove this statement.

Bias.   Many times authors will indicate in their writing that they are in favor of something or are opposed to it; this is showing bias. Authors do this to try to influence the reader to think one way or another. Biased writing can be recognized by the fact that the author takes a stand on the topic and will frequently use emotion-laden words to get the reader to be for or against a topic or issue. Read the following statements:

> The new fire laws are sure to make our community a safer, more secure place to live.

The new fire laws will take effect next month; the city officials will be watching to see their impact.

The new fire laws are going to be an expensive burden for many businesses and families in the community.

The first statement illustrates bias in favor of the new fire laws. The words *safer* and *more secure* show this. The third statement illustrates bias against the laws; the words *expensive burden* indicate a negative feeling about the laws on the part of the author. The second statement simply presents information about the fire laws in an unbiased manner.

Assumptions.   Assumptions are statements accepted as true at the time they are made without being proven. For example, look at the following sentence:

If Mark Anderson becomes a mayor, citizens will pay more taxes and get fewer services than they have ever had.

This statement is an assumption. The individual making it is assuming that it is true, and there is no way at the time it was made to prove or disprove it. Authors frequently make assumptions in their writing. A part of reading and thinking critically is being able to recognize when assumptions are being made.

Propaganda Techniques.   Another element involved in becoming an effective critical reader is recognizing when an author is using propaganda. Propaganda is the spreading or presenting of ideas and information designed to persuade someone to be for or against something. There are eight commonly used types of propaganda.

• *Bandwagon.* This technique encourages the reader or listener to go along with something because everyone else is doing it.

Try Marvello Skin Cream, the cream that keeps the world young.

• *Compare and Contrast.* The author compares or contrasts similar products or ideas to convince the reader that one is better than the other. The claims which are made for the better product or idea are difficult to prove.

Green Gro was good for your lawn, Green Gro Plus was better, but new Green Gro Spray is best for keeping your lawn green. Try new Green Gro Spray.

• *Emotional Words.* The author selects words that are designed to arouse the reader's feelings rather than inform the reader of information.

Linda Marlow is a dynamic, confident, intelligent politician. Vote for Marlow for mayor.

• *Faulty Cause/Effect.* The author says or implies that one thing causes another when there is no real evidence that this is true.

Buy your groceries at Shop and Save and watch your bank account grow.

• *Name Calling.* With this technique the author uses belittling names to describe an individual or group in a way that makes them look bad.

That monster, Mr. Motor, thought he would win the fight. The worm never had a chance.

• *Repetition.* The author repeats a particular name or word over and over again in hopes of making you remember it.

Improve our schools—Elect Smith
Lower taxes—Elect Smith
Have better roads—Elect Smith
Howard Smith for Mayor

• *Testimonial.* The author using this technique has a famous individual recommend a product or idea in hope that the reader will buy it or accept it.

Track star Leo Flag says, "I always wear Fleet Fast Shoes. They made me a winner."

• *Transfer.* The author using this technique usually shows an individual or individuals and expects you to believe that whatever has happened to them will happen to you.

A weight loss clinic shows an ad with a before and after photograph of an individual who has lost 50 pounds. The caption reads "The New You."

A Process for Critical Reading/Thinking

What are the steps in the process of critical reading?

Simply teaching students to recognize the elements of critical reading/thinking is not sufficient to help them become critical readers and thinkers. Students must be taught to use a process that helps them pull together all aspects of comprehension (Cooper, 1986). This process involves four basic steps which must be systematically taught to students after they have learned the elements of critical reading/thinking described earlier. These four steps include:

1. During reading, try to get a general idea of what the author is saying and what the author is trying to persuade the reader to think.
2. Look for elements that might lead to questioning what the author is saying. Has the author
—used bias?
—made assumptions?
—used propaganda techniques?
—mixed facts and opinions?
3. Compare the information being read with what is already known or look for more information in another source.
4. Evaluate what is read. Decide whether the information is important. If it is not, simply store it in memory for future use. If it is valuable, evaluate it in terms of Steps 1 to 3 and take one of the following actions:
a. Accept what the author says.
b. Consider what has been read but wait for more information to make a judgment.
c. Reject what was read because of a conviction that the information is not fair or correct.

Students must be taught each of the steps in the process of critical reading and thinking. By focusing comprehension instruction on the process of critical reading rather than just teaching each separate part, readers will learn to use critical reading abilities rather than just identify different elements of critical reading such as fact/opinion.

COMPREHENSION MONITORING

What is metacognition, and how does it relate to reading?

Teaching students to comprehend effectively also involves helping them learn to be aware of whether what they are reading makes sense; this is called comprehension monitoring and was introduced in Chapter 1. Monitoring is a part of the metacognitive processes that effective readers are able to use. What exactly is metacognition, and how does it relate to reading?

Metacognition and Reading

Metacognition refers to the knowledge and control that individuals have over their own thinking and learning (Brown, 1980). The prefix "meta" means going beyond and "cognition" means thinking. Therefore, metacognition means going beyond thinking to the point of understanding how thinking and learning take place. Metacognition involves two basic processes (Baker & Brown, 1984b):

1. Knowing the processes and skills needed to complete any task successfully.
2. Being able to tell whether or not one is performing a task correctly and being able to make corrections during the task if needed; this is monitoring or comprehension monitoring.

There are many things in life that one does without stopping to think about them—driving a car, typing, playing a musical instrument, writing, reading a newspaper to find sales, and so forth. Each of these tasks is performed without thinking about the skills and processes needed to do them. In all of learning, individuals must know what skills and processes they need to use to perform successfully whatever task they are undertaking.

Reading is no different. Effective readers need to know what processes and skills they need to use as they read and perform any reading task. Therefore, an important part of teaching students to use the processes and skills of reading is to help them see how and where to use what they are being taught in actual reading (Mier, 1984).

The second part of metacognition, *monitoring*, involves helping learners tell whether their reading is making sense *as they read* rather than waiting until they complete their reading to discover that they don't understand it. Effective learners know how to correct or approach their lack of understanding.

Think about reading this text. If an effective reader reads a section of a chapter that doesn't make sense, he or she stops and tries to clarify it while reading. Several different actions may be taken:

1. Reread the part that doesn't make sense.
2. Look up unknown words in the dictionary.
3. Read on to see if it is explained more fully.
4. Ask someone to explain it.

As readers do these things they are monitoring their reading. They know it doesn't make sense and take some type of action to clarify it. This is comprehension monitoring.

Research evidence indicates that poor readers do not know how to monitor their comprehension, but they can be taught to do so (Palincsar & Brown, 1984a, 1984b). Teaching students to monitor their comprehension involves teaching them a process that they are able to use while they read.

A Process for Monitoring

The process of comprehension monitoring presented here is the one which has been studied by Palincsar and Brown (1984). Current evidence indicates that it is an effective one in helping students learn to monitor their comprehension (Palincsar & Brown, 1984a, 1984b; Baker & Brown, 1984a, 1984b).

There are four steps to this monitoring process:

1. Summarize
2. Clarify
3. Question
4. Predict

In the *summarize* step, the reader stops at a designated point in reading and tells what has been read. At this stopping point, the reader *clarifies* by asking the question, "Is this clear to me?" If something is not clear to the reader, attempts are made to clarify it by rereading or discussing with someone else. Next, the reader asks a *question* that a test or teacher might ask over this segment of the text. Finally, the reader *predicts* what is likely to happen in the next part of the reading. The reader then reads on to the next designated stopping point and repeats the process.

DEVELOPING LITERARY APPRECIATION

What is literary appreciation, and what are some types of literature?

Teaching students to comprehend also includes helping them develop an appreciation for what they read. In many reading programs this is called literary appreciation or literary skills. Literary appreciation can be divided into two broad categories: types of literature and styles and techniques of writing.

Types of Literature

Students must learn to recognize different types of literature. There are two broad categories, fiction and nonfiction.

Fiction is the type of material that comes from the author's imagination and is not true. Within this category there is *reality* or *realistic fiction,* which is about people or events that could exist. *Fantasy* is the type of fiction that is composed of make-believe characters such as those in the story of "The Three Little Pigs."

Besides realistic fiction, there are many other types of fiction that students will encounter in their reading:

Folktales. Stories that come from tradition and are eventually written down.
Fables. Stories that teach a lesson called the moral.
Myths. Imaginary stories that tell how certain things in nature came to be.
Legends. Stories that are often connected with a national hero or event and may or may not be based on truth.
Tall Tales. Stories about imaginary characters that use humor and exaggeration.
Historical Fiction. A story based on an historical event.
Biographical Fiction. A fictionalized story based on the lives of real people.
Science Fiction. A story that uses scientific facts but projects into the future.
Mystery Stories. Stories of suspense, usually involving some type of crime.

Nonfiction tells about real people and events. Included in this category are informational articles, biographies, and autobiographies.

Students should also learn to read and understand plays and poetry.

Styles and Techniques of Writing

What are the different styles and techniques of writing?

Appreciating literature requires the understanding of different styles and techniques of writing. Included in this category is *figurative language,* those phrases in our language that have one meaning literally but have an interpretation that is different from this literal form. These phrases help the reader visualize more clearly. For instance, the reader is able to visualize a more vivid picture when reading "Her tears flowed like wine" than when reading "She cried."

There are seven types of figurative language or figures of speech. One example can often represent more than one type of figurative language. The *hyperbole* is an exaggeration or overstatement that is not meant to be taken literally. The sentence, "The two men decided to bury the hatchet," does not mean that two men were actually going to dig a hole and bury a hatchet.

A *simile* occurs when one thing is compared or likened to a dissimilar thing. The comparison generally involves the use of the words *like, as,* or *than* and results in such sentences as "He eats like a pig," or "She is as silly as a goose," or "My cat is sillier than a clown." In simile, the comparison is explicit.

A *metaphor* resembles a simile in that it, too, is a comparison between two different things; however, it differs from a simile in that it is implied rather than explicitly stated. It is accomplished by using a word or phrase that is generally used when speaking of one thing and applying it to something different. The phrase, "All the world's a stage," is an example of a metaphor.

Satire involves the use of irony, ridicule, and sarcasm as a means of exposing, attacking, or deriding. When a professor says the class "really did a *great* job on the exam'' when in reality the class did very poorly on the exam, satire, as a means of attacking the group, is being used.

Personification is a procedure for giving personal characteristics to inanimate objects or abstract ideas. An example of personifying an inanimate object would be ''The teakettle sang a merry tune.'' Giving a personal characteristic to an abstract idea is also the skill of personification. For example, ''Time flies'' or ''The idea for the new invention jumped to the foremost part of his thoughts.'' In each of these examples, note that a nonhuman was attributed a characteristic possessed by humans.

Using words whose pronunciation suggests the natural sound associated with the object of action discussed is the application of *onomatopoeia*. For example, the sentence, ''Buzz, buzz, went the alarm clock,'' uses the word *buzz* to indicate the sound the alarm made.

Euphemism involves the substitution of a mild or indirect expression for one that is considered harsh or offensive. The aim is to be more tasteful. In many instances, a euphemism becomes a glorification of something that has come to be considered commonplace. For example, euphemisms present the terms ''sanitation engineer'' for a garbage collector, ''maintenance engineer'' for a janitor, and ''facilitator of learning'' for a teacher.

One of the techniques capitalized on by comedians is known as *malapropism*. This technique is derived from Mrs. Malaprop in Sheridan's play, *The Rivals*. It represents a ridiculous misuse of words. Reference to the Internal Revenue Service as the ''Infernal Revenue Service'' is an example of a malapropism.

In addition to learning to recognize and interpret figurative language, readers must also learn to recognize that authors use different techniques to make their writing interesting and exciting. Included in these techniques are point of view, repetition, foreshadowing, and flashback.

Authors write from different *points of view*. This means that they either tell the story themselves or have one of the characters tell the story. When the author tells a story using ''I,'' this is called first person. When the story is told about characters, this is third person.

Repetition is a writing technique where the author repeats sounds, words, phrases, sentences, or ideas over and over again to create suspense or to emphasize certain sounds or points. This is used in stories but also is used frequently in poems. Remember the poem, ''Hickory-Dickory Dock''? This poem uses repetition.

Foreshadowing is the technique that an author uses to hint at what is to come. This is done to build suspense and excitement in writing. For example, when a character in a story says, ''Little did the boys know about what would follow,'' the author is letting you know that something is going to happen. This is foreshadowing.

Flashback is the technique that an author uses to interrupt the current scene in a story to tell about something that happened earlier. For example, a character in a story is on a long trip through the mountains. The character then remembers about his childhood days and tells about it and relates it to the current scene. Sometimes authors tell an entire story as a flashback. This helps to add interest to an author's writing and provides the author a way to bring in additional background.

WHEN SHOULD COMPREHENSION BE TAUGHT?

> ❧ Why doesn't a reader ever completely master comprehension, and when should comprehension be taught?

Comprehension is a very complex and involved process. To become effective comprehenders, students must learn to use many different processes and skills. Comprehension is a process that a reader never completely masters because at different levels of difficulty and in different types of text, readers must use their comprehension skills and processes differently. The reader's background and schemata also expand and change.

Comprehension instruction begins at the prereading level and continues throughout all levels of the reading program. At the prereading level, the development of oral language builds the foundation for the teaching of meaning vocabulary and the processes of comprehension such as noting relevant details and their relationships, inferencing, determining the main idea, critical reading, and appreciating literature. The development of background and experiences at this level helps readers develop the schemata needed for effective comprehension.

Throughout all other levels of the reading program students must be taught the specific skills and processes of comprehension. It is necessary to repeat the teaching of some of the same skills and processes at all levels because of the differences in the difficulty levels of the text and the broadened background knowledge of the reader. As texts become more complex, the use of the various comprehension processes also becomes more complex. Therefore, the teaching of such processes as inferencing will need to be repeated at nearly all grade levels.

PRACTICE EXERCISE

Directions
This series of exercises is designed to help you practice and check your knowledge of comprehension. Complete each exercise; then check your answers with those in the Answer Key at the end of the text.

Part I
Select the best answer for each of the following questions.

1. Comprehension is a process where the reader
   a. orally calls words
   b. constructs meaning using clues in the text and background
   c. reads orally after having read silently
   d. gets the meaning of text from the text

2. The meanings which readers form as they read text will vary most according to
   a. their background and language
   b. the length of the text
   c. the author's style
   d. the author's attitude

3. For students to become effective comprehenders, they must
   a. be taught each individual skill of comprehension in isolation
   b. learn all the comprehension skills before the end of second grade
   c. be taught the skills of comprehension so that they use them in the process of reading
   d. learn that all meaning comes from the text

4. The type of text which tells a story is called
   a. inferential text
   b. expository text
   c. narrative text
   d. critical text

5. Narrative text always contains
   a. cause-effect types of passages
   b. setting, characters, problem, action, and resolution
   c. inferences, main ideas, cause-effect relationships, and comparisons
   d. comparisons and contrasts

6. Narrative text is easier than expository text for students to read because
   a. narrative text is usually shorter than expository text
   b. students have less experience with narrative text
   c. expository text is more consistent than narrative text
   d. narrative text always follows a consistent pattern

7. When readers are inferencing, they are using
   a. only the information provided in the text
   b. details from the text and prior knowledge
   c. only the information stored in their schemata
   d. a literal skill

8. When readers are evaluating and judging as they read, they are
   a. reading and thinking critically
   b. noting the sequence of events
   c. identifying the details of text
   d. using literary appreciation

9. When readers are able to tell whether what they are reading makes sense and know what to do if it doesn't, they are using
   a. inferencing
   b. critical reading
   c. monitoring
   d. sequencing

10. Comprehension instruction should be
    a. provided at the prereading level
    b. provided primarily in the intermediate levels
    c. provided at all grade levels
    d. discontinued after the sixth grade

Part II

As students read, they use many different comprehension skills and processes simultaneously. Read the following paragraphs and then identify places where readers could be using each of the comprehension skills and processes listed. The sentences have been numbered to help you identify your examples. There can be more than one answer for some of the items.

[1] I could see the strange figure moving through the dark. [2] It wore a top hat and carried a walking stick. [3] As it moved out of the fog into the dim glow of the street lamp, I could see a mustache on its face. [4] At least I could now tell who I was following; the face of this character was as ugly as a Halloween monster.

[5] After walking for several more blocks in the dense fog, I had to stop. [6] The fog was so thick I could hardly see. [7] The strange figure ahead of me had stopped, too. [8] Following this character for so long was like following a ghost; first it was in one place and then it was in another. [9] I knew I would catch this demon. [10] I had always been successful before on these hunts.

1. Noting important details _____

_____

_____

2. Noting sequence _____

_____

_____

3. Noting comparisons _____

_____

_____

4. Main idea _____

_____

_____

5. Inferencing _____

_____

_____

6. Critical reading _____

_____

_____

7. Fact/opinion _____

_____

_____

8. Context clues _____

_____

_____

9. Monitoring _____

_____

_____

10. Literary appreciation _____

_____

_____

Part III
Match the items in the two columns below. Each item in column B can only be used once.

Column A

_____ 1. homonym

_____ 2. metacognition

_____ 3. synonym

_____ 4. story map

_____ 5. narrative text

_____ 6. prefix

_____ 7. suffix

_____ 8. base word

_____ 9. cause/effect

_____ 10. contraction

_____ 11. multiple meanings

_____ 12. metaphor

_____ 13. repetition

_____ 14. bandwagon

_____ 15. inferencing

Column B

a. a bound morpheme that is added to the end of a base or root word to change its meaning

b. a technique for swaying the reader to think a certain way *or* repeating a statement over and over for effect

c. the picture or outline of the parts of a narrative text

d. using clues from the text and prior knowledge to determine information that is not stated

e. *can't, won't, isn't*

f. two words that are pronounced the same but have different meanings and spellings (e.g., *bare, bear*)

g. Mark hit the ball and it flew over the fence.

h. a free morpheme that is the major meaning carrier of a word

i. *Charlotte's Web*

j. knowledge and control that individuals have over their own thinking

k. Buy new Barko for your dog. All dog lovers are using it.

l. two words that mean nearly the same

m. bound morphemes that are added to the beginning of a base or root word to change meaning

n. I tried not to *slide* on the ice. Mark went down the *slide*.

o. making a comparison without using *like* or *as*

Part IV
Each of the following groups go together in relation to reading comprehension. Briefly explain why.

1. using a single text in class; emphasis placed on facts; no encouragement of open discussions

2. fiction, fables, biographies, legends

3. summarize, clarify, question, predict

4. compare/contrast; emotional words; name calling; testimonial

5. direct definition; appositives; synonym/antonym; surrounding words

4

Word Recognition Skills

How are oral and written language related?

Language is a system of oral symbols used to communicate. The spoken message is considered to be the primary system of human communication. The written language system represents the oral system. When people are taught to read, they are taught to translate written language into meaningful oral language. Even though this chapter deals with systems of attacking words in an attempt to pronounce them, the desired end product of reading instruction is much greater than the pronunciation of words. The act of reading is an exceedingly complex process and requires much more than the mere pronunciation of words.

Written English uses the alphabetic principle. Letters of the alphabet represent speech sounds. The letters of the alphabet are combined into specific patterns (written words) representing patterns of oral sounds (spoken language). This process is referred to as decoding or cracking the code. The skills used are called word recognition skills.

What are the word recognition skills?

The word recognition skills are those skills used by readers to help them pronounce printed words. These skills are sometimes called decoding skills, word analysis skills, word attack skills, and/or word identification skills. In this chapter, five word recognition skills are discussed:

1. Sight vocabulary
2. Context clues

3. Phonics
4. Structural analysis
5. Dictionary

Word recognition skills are merely a set of tools used toward the ultimate goal of comprehension. Even if all words have been pronounced correctly by the reader, if the written message has not been understood, *no reading has taken place*! Readers vary in their ability to use each of the word recognition skills. Some learners need more (or less) work in each skill category. Slow learners are more likely to need more work with the type of decoding process that works best for them, for example, building sight vocabulary. Most readers do not use any one word recognition skill exclusively; instead, they use a combination of skills in rapid succession (Anderson, Heibert, Scott, & Wilkinson, 1985).

SIGHT WORDS

What are sight words, and when are they taught as whole words?

There are two important definitions of sight vocabulary. The first definition is those words that are instantly recognized by the reader. In the sense of this definition, any and/or all words may be, or become, sight words for the reader. These are words that do not need any analysis by the reader, but are just known immediately by sight. The ultimate goal of all word recognition is that the reader will have a very large group of words that are instantly recognized; that is, a large sight vocabulary. All other word recognition skills are taught as tools toward this goal and to aid the learner in acquiring sight vocabulary independently.

A second definition of sight words is those words that are taught or learned as whole words. Again, any word could be taught or learned as a whole word. However, teaching words as whole words usually is done only under the following circumstances:

1. When the word to be taught has an irregular spelling pattern, therefore defying analysis using regular phonic or structural generalizations. Examples: *have, come, said*.

2. When the reader needs to know the word, but hasn't yet learned the generalizations that would apply to its pronunciation. Examples: *old, find, night, car*. In the case of these words, the students would not have learned the exceptions to the short vowel generalization; therefore they would not be expected to know that all of these vowel sounds are governed by another set of generalizations.

3. When the word must be learned for success in reading because it occurs so frequently in printed material. These words form a special category of words often known as *basic sight words, structure words*, or *high-frequency words*. There are several published lists of such words. When such a list of words is known by the reader, approximately two-thirds of all words met in reading are known (Ekwall & Shanker, 1985). The best known of these lists is the Dolch List (Dolch, 1942). A more recent list is the Johnson Basic Vocabulary (Johnson & Pearson, 1984). Examples: *the, be, at, of, and, this*.

It is important for readers to develop large sight vocabularies in the process of learning to read. All readers need to instantly recognize words as they read, rather than having to apply some type of analysis skill. All students need work with developing a large sight vocabulary. Some special students who have learning difficulties need to have more emphasis on sight vocabulary development than many of the other word recognition skills. When the teaching of other word recognition skills is not producing successful readers, teaching whole words will often produce some degree of success. The problem with teaching sight words, to the exclusion of the other word recognition skills, is that it does not lead to independence in attacking new words.

CONTEXT CLUES

What are context clues, and how can they be used?

The use of context clues as a word recognition skill means that the reader will use other words in the sentence to determine the pronunciation of an unknown word. In the sentence, "The horses galloped across the field," if the unknown word is *galloped,* the context is "The horses _____ across the field." In order for a reader to use context clues in an attempt to pronounce the unknown word, it is necessary to have the word *galloped* in the background of experience and the oral vocabulary of the reader. With prior knowledge of the ways in which horses might move across a field, and some knowledge of beginning sounds, the reader has the possibility of using context to determine the unknown word.

As with some of the other word recognition skills, it is difficult to separate the use of context clues for word recognition from the use to aid understanding. Ideally, context clues are used by the reader for both purposes of word recognition and meaning at the same time. Consider the following sentence:

Please be sure to record attendance.

When a reader encounters this sentence, it is necessary to determine meaning at the same time the reader pronounces the word *record,* since the word may be pronounced more than one way. In this case, an incorrect pronunciation also produces an incorrect meaning. Context clues must be used to ascertain the correct pronunciation.

Because a word must make sense in a sentence, considering context when encountering an unknown word can drastically limit the possibilities as to what the unknown word might be. For example, in the sentence, "The little girl _____ happily down the street," the reader, calling on background experiences and considering context, can limit the possibilities from any word known, to the few that make sense, such as *ran, walked,* and *skipped.*

It is obvious from the example that context clues alone cannot ensure correct recognition of an unknown written word. Usually more than one word can logically fit, so context clues must be used in conjunction with other word recognition skills.

Context clues may be used in a variety of ways, including:

1. To check the pronunciation of a word
2. To augment other word recognition skills

3. To anticipate the appropriate word
4. To see if the word makes sense in the sentence
5. To determine the meaning of an unknown word

PHONICS

What is phonics?

Phonics is the study of the relationships between the speech sounds and the letters that represent them. The speech sounds of a language are commonly referred to as phonemes. The letters representing speech sounds are commonly referred to as graphemes. The letter *m* in the word *most* is a grapheme. This grapheme represents the phoneme /m/. The written representation of a speech sound is often represented between slash marks. Any letter may be a grapheme. In English, all graphemes do not have a consistent phoneme; the graphemes may represent more than one phoneme, and two or more letters may represent just one phoneme. For example, in the word *phone,* the *ph* is a grapheme representing /f/, the *o...e* is a grapheme representing the long *o* sound, and the *n* is a grapheme representing /n/. In *cough,* the *c* is a grapheme representing /c/, the *ou* is a grapheme representing /aw/, and the *gh* is a grapheme representing /f/. Phonics is the study of the relationships between phonemes and graphemes or sounds and the symbols that represent them in various spelling patterns in the English language.

Any speech sound is a phoneme. In English, all phonemes do not have consistent graphemes; in other words, the same phoneme may be represented by more than one grapheme. The following are examples of two phonemes and their various graphemic representations:

Phoneme	*Graphemic Variations*
/f/	*ph*one
	*f*ork
	pu*ff*
	rou*gh*
/e/	*ea*t
	s*ee*
	p*ie*ce

Phonics is sometimes called decoding. It is the actual sounding out of unknown words. Since there is no one-to-one consistency of phonemes and graphemes in English, phonics is a highly abstract and difficult word recognition skill to learn. The amount of phonics instruction needed by individual learners varies greatly according to their ability.

Phonics produces *only* pronunciation of the unknown word. The pronounced word must be in the reader's oral language, both to check the accuracy of the decoding process and to check the meaning of the word in its contextual usage. For example,

Pitta are almost extinct because of acid rain.

Although readers may be able to say "pitta," they may not understand the above sentence. No real reading has taken place unless the meaning of the author has been conveyed to the reader, even if the decoding was perfect! (By the way, pitta are brightly colored birds found in southern Asian and Australian forests.)

Consonants

What is a consonant, and what sounds are expected for *c*, *g*, and *s*?

A consonant is a speech sound (phoneme) in which the flow of breath is constricted or stopped by the tongue, teeth, lips, or some combination of these. The letters (graphemes) representing such speech sounds are also called consonants. Most single consonants are regular in sound, and usually they represent only one sound no matter where they appear in a word.

boy	ta*b*	ra*b*id	(*b*s all sound alike)
dog	ha*d*	ra*d*ar	(*d*s all sound alike)

There are several notable exceptions to consistent single consonant sounds. The grapheme *c* is expected to have its hard sound when it is followed by the vowels *a*, *o*, *u*, or by any consonant. The hard sound of *c* is the sound usually associated with the letter *k*.

*c*at   *c*ot   *c*ut   *c*lass   al*c*ove

The soft sound of *c* is expected when it is followed by the vowels *e*, *i*, or *y*. The soft sound of the *c* is the sound usually associated with the letter *s*.

*c*ent   *c*ity   *c*yclone   a*c*e   bi*c*ycle

The hard and soft *g* generalization is not as consistent as the hard and soft *c* generalization. The grapheme *g* is expected to have its hard sound when it is followed by the vowels *a*, *o*, or *u* and in the final position of a word or syllable. The hard sound of *g* is the guttural sound that is heard in the words:

*g*ate   *g*ot   *g*um   *g*lad   ra*g*

The soft sound of *g* is expected when it is followed by the vowels *e*, *i*, or *y*. The soft sound of *g* is the sound usually associated with the letter *j* as in the following words:

*g*iant   *g*entle   *g*ym   *g*arage

The letter *s* has four different sounds. There is no generalization covering when the reader should expect each sound. The sounds represented by *s* are illustrated by:

*s*ee—the /s/ phoneme

*s*ure—the /sh/ phoneme

ha*s*—the /z/ phoneme

trea*s*ure—the /zh/ phoneme

The following exceptions to consistent single consonant sounds are far less common than those noted above. They are presented here to illustrate that there are other exceptions, and as a caution to teachers to think before requiring learners to decode irregularly sounded words.

> The *f* in *of* has a /v/ phoneme.
> The *x* in *exit* has a /ks/ or /gz/ phoneme.
> The *x* in *xylophone* has a /z/ phoneme.
> The *x* in *xray* has a /eks/ phoneme.
> The *qu* in *antique* has a /k/ phoneme.
> The *qu* in *quiz* has a /kw/ phoneme.

What are consonant clusters, and what else may they be called?

Consonants may also appear in *clusters* in words; that is, more than one consonant may come before a vowel or between vowels in a word. Some materials for reading instruction refer to all groups of consonants as consonant clusters. Other materials divide them into two categories: digraphs and blends.

Consonant Digraphs.   A consonant digraph is two consecutive consonants in a word or syllable that represent one speech sound. In other words, two graphemes make just one phoneme. The word digraph means (di) two (graph) letters. It also contains the digraph *ph*. There are essentially three kinds of digraphs:

1. Those consonant digraphs that represent a whole new sound that is unlike the sound of either of the single consonants. This type of consonant digraph may have more than one sound.

Digraph	*Example Word*
sh	*sh*ut
th	*th*is (voiced *th*)
	*th*in (unvoiced *th*)
wh	*wh*en
	*wh*o
ch	whi*ch*
	*ch*asm
	*ch*ef

2. Those consonant digraphs that represent the sound of one of the single consonants contained in the digraph.

Digraph	*Example Word*
ck	ki*ck*
kn	*kn*ot
wr	*wr*ite
gn	*gn*at
pn	*pn*eumatic
gh	*gh*ost

3. Those consonant digraphs that represent the sound of another grapheme.

Digraph	*Example Word*
gh	lau*gh*
ph	*ph*one

Other consonant clusters often referred to as digraphs include *nk* as in ba*nk*; *ng* as in si*ng*; and double consonants as in mi*tt*en, su*mm*er, and ru*dd*er. Only the most common consonant digraphs have been identified in the previous lists.

Consonant Blends.   A consonant blend is two or three consonants clustered together in a word or syllable before a vowel, where all consonant sounds are heard. The phonemes merge in speech sounds. The reader produces a speech sound for each consonant seen. The word blend contains two blends, *bl* and *nd*. There are three major categories of blends.

1. Those blends that begin with the letter *s*:

str	*str*ong	sc	*sc*ab	sn	*sn*ail
spl	*spl*ash	sk	ri*sk*	sp	wa*sp*
scr	*scr*eam	sl	*sl*ow	st	la*st*
spr	*spr*ing	sm	*sm*og	sw	*sw*an

2. Those blends that conclude with the letter *r*:

br	*br*oth	fr	*fr*esh	tr	*tr*out
cr	*cr*owd	gr	*gr*ass	spr	*spr*ay
dr	*dr*aft	pr	*pr*ove	str	*str*aw

3. Those blends that conclude with the letter *l*:

bl	*bl*ue	gl	*gl*ass	cl	*cl*ose
pl	*pl*ace	fl	*fl*ip	sl	*sl*ave

The *lp* in he*lp,* the *tw* in *tw*in, the *dw* in *dw*arf, and the *nd* in sa*nd* are all examples of other consonant blends. It is important to remember that whenever a cluster of consonants can all be heard, it is called a blend.

Why are consonant sounds important?

Consonant sounds, either single or in clusters, are the most consistent sounds of our language. There is less deviation in the sounds of consonants, whether they are single or in clusters, than in any of the other phonetic sounds of our language; therefore, they should be taught first. It is also possible for words to be read when only consonants are presented. Consonants give the most accurate clues to an unknown word. For example:

Wh-ch d-y n-xt w--k sh-ll w- g- sh-pp-ing?

Even without vowels, but with the context, this sentence can be read.

Vowels

What is a vowel, and what are the categories of their sounds called?

A vowel is a speech sound in which the flow of breath is unobstructed. The letters representing such sounds are also called vowels. The vowel letters are *a, e, i, o, u,* and sometimes *y* and *w*. The categories of vowel sounds are short vowels, long vowels, vowel digraphs, diphthongs, the schwa sound of vowels, exceptions to expected vowel sounds, and *y* and *w* functioning as vowels.

Short Vowel Sounds.   The short vowel sounds are sometimes referred to as unglided sounds. There are five short vowel sounds in English, as represented in the following words:

ăt   Ĕd   ĭt   ŏx   ŭp

The breve, or curved line over the vowel (ă), is the diacritical marking often used to indicate the short vowel sound in phonetic respellings.

Two other vowel sounds that are also referred to as short vowel sounds are the /aw/ sound as represented by the *a* in c*a*ll, the *ou* in c*ou*gh, the *au* in c*au*ght, and the *aw* in l*aw;* and the short *oo* sound as in l*oo*k and g*oo*d.

Long Vowel Sounds.   The long vowels are those in which the name of the letter is heard. These sounds are sometimes referred to as the glided sounds. There are five long vowel sounds in English, as represented in the words:

āt̸e   ē̸at   īc̸e   ō̸pen   ūs̸e

The macron, a straight line over the vowel (ā), is the diacritical mark used to indicate the long vowel sound in phonetic respellings (the slash mark indicates no sound). Another vowel of this type is the long *oo* sound as heard in r*oo*m and c*oo*l.

Vowel Digraphs.   Vowel digraphs, like consonant digraphs, occur when two adjacent letters produce only one speech sound; that is, two vowel letters only produce one phoneme. Obviously, these two vowels must be in the same syllable. The most frequently occurring vowel digraphs are

Vowel Digraph	*Example Word*
ee	s*ee*d
oa	g*oa*t
ea	s*ea*t
ai	p*ai*n
ay	d*ay*

The most usual sound of these vowel digraphs is the long sound of the first vowel. However, not all vowel digraphs represent the long sound of the first vowel, as can be seen in such words as *bread,* where the first vowel represents the short *e,* or *piece,* where the second vowel in the digraph has its long sound.

Diphthongs.   In some reading materials, diphthongs are called vowel blends. Diphthongs, like consonant blends, consist of two vowels where both sounds are heard. The vowels forming a diphthong must be in the same syllable. The most frequently occurring diphthongs are

Diphthong	*Example Word*
oi	*oi*l
oy	*oy*ster

There are two sets of vowels that regularly have two different sounds. Sometimes they form a digraph; sometimes they form a diphthong. These sets are *ou* and *ow*. The *ou* may be sounded as in *out*, or as in br*ou*ght. The *ow* may be sounded as in n*ow,* or as in sh*ow*. When teaching the phonemes to be associated with these graphemes, it is necessary to teach that they each have two distinct sounds.

ou

Digraph	*Diphthong*
c*ou*gh	c*ou*ch

ow

Digraph	*Diphthong*
sn*ow*	c*ow*

Schwa.   The schwa sound of a vowel is known as the softened or indeterminate sound. It sounds like a short *u* and frequently occurs in the unstressed or unaccented syllable of a word. The diacritical mark representing the schwa sound is often an upside down and backwards *e* (ə).

Vowel	Example of Schwa Sound	
a	above	(əbove)
e	craven	(cravən)
i	beautiful	(beautəful)
o	committee	(cəmmittee)
u	cherub	(cherəb)

The schwa sound may be represented sometimes by two vowels as shown with the *io* in the word port*io*n (portən).

Explain the exceptions to the expected vowel sounds.

Exceptions to Expected Vowel Sounds.   Short vowel sounds are the most common vowel sounds in words. The short vowel is expected in a closed syllable, a syllable (or word) ending with a consonant. For example, *cat* and *at* are closed syllables, ending in a consonant. There are four standard exceptions to the expected short vowel sounds in a closed syllable.

1. When a vowel grapheme is followed by r, the vowel sound will not be expected to be short; rather, it will be called an r-controlled vowel.

ar c*ar*	er h*er*	ir f*ir*
or f*or*	ur f*ur*	

Notice that the *er*, *ir*, and *ur* all sound the same. The *ar* sounds like the letter name *r*, and the *or* sounds like the word *or*.

2. When the vowel grapheme *a* is followed by *l*, it usually represents the /aw/ phoneme.

sa*l*t   ta*l*k   ba*l*l

3. When the vowel grapheme *o* is followed by *lt* or *ld,* it will have the long *o* phoneme.

b*olt*   g*old*

4. When the vowel grapheme *i* is followed by *gh, ld,* or *nd,* it will have the long *i* phoneme.

n*igh*t   s*igh*   w*ild*   m*ind*

When do *y* or *w* serve as vowels?

Y as a Vowel.   When the letter *y* functions as a vowel, it will represent either the short or long sounds of the letter *i,* or it will be part of a digraph or diphthong. The short *i* sound of *y* is expected in a closed syllable.

g*y*m   g*y*p   s*y*mbol

The long *i* sound of *y* is expected in an open syllable; that is, one ending with a vowel, in this case *y.*

m*y*   d*y*namic   p*y*thon

When *y* is preceded by the vowels *a* or *e,* it functions as the second vowel of a vowel digraph.

d*ay*   th*ey*

When *y* is in the final position in words of two or more syllables, it usually represents the short *i* sound.

part*y*   assembl*y*

Note: In some dialects, this final *y* sound is the long *e.* Many dictionaries mark its pronunciation both ways. There are two infrequent patterns in which *y* also represents a vowel. These are when *y* is preceded by *u* or followed by *e.*

g*uy*   b*ye*

W as a Vowel.   The letter *w* only functions as a vowel when it is in combination with another vowel. The grapheme *w* functions as a vowel as part of a digraph when preceded by *a, e,* or *o* and as part of a diphthong when preceded by *o.*

W as Part of a Digraph	*W as Part of a Diphthong*
p*aw*	cl*ow*n
bl*ow*	n*ow*
gr*ow*	

What generalizations govern vowel sounds? Illustrate each.

Vowel Sound Generalizations.   There are no hard and fast rules for the expected vowel sounds, only generalizations. The generalizations are quite interrelated. Only those generalizations determined to be the most consistent and applicable are presented in this text (Bailey, 1967; Clymer, 1963; Emans, 1967). Because of the complexity of the vowel generalizations, many reading authorities recommend that the consonant sounds be taught first.

The most common vowel sound generalization relates to the short vowel sound. This sound is expected in a closed syllable, one ending with a consonant. This kind of syllable is sometimes referred to as the CVC pattern (C = Consonant, V = Vowel, C = Consonant). The consonants may be single or in clusters, and it is not mandatory to have the first consonant in such a syllable or short word. All of the following words follow the CVC pattern:

rag   (CVC)

shot   (CCVC)

wish   (CVCC)

at   (VC)

The CVC generalization is useful in pronouncing one- and two-syllable words as well as individual syllables of polysyllabic words. When this pattern exists, the expected sound is the short vowel sound. This is the most commonly used vowel sound generalization. The following words all contain closed syllables with a short vowel sound:

hamlet   *ham*-let

fancy   *fan*-cy

section   *sec*-tion

There are three generalizations related to when to expect long vowel sounds. The first of these is the sound expected in an open syllable, one ending with a vowel. It is sometimes referred to as the CV pattern (C = Consonant, V = Vowel). There may or may not be a consonant before the vowel. The following words and syllables follow the CV pattern:

me   *o*-pen   *ho*-tel   *mu*-sic

The CV generalization is useful in pronouncing one- and two-syllable words as well as individual syllables of polysyllabic words. The expected vowel sound in an open syllable is the long sound. The following words all contain open syllables with long vowel sounds:

Uranus   *u-ra*-nus

premolar   *pre-mo*-lar

romance   *ro*-mance

Titantic   *ti*-tan-ic

meter   *me*-ter

A long vowel sound is also expected with certain vowel digraphs. When the vowel digraphs *ee, oa, ea, ai,* and *ay* are in the CVVC pattern, the first vowel often represents its long sound, and the second vowel is not sounded. The number of consonants preceding or following the two vowels may vary. All of the following words follow the CVVC pattern:

b*oa*t   s*ay*   str*ai*n   *ea*t   s*ee*

c*oa*st   del*ay*   p*ai*nt   tr*ea*t   sl*ee*p

The third time when a long vowel sound is expected is in the CVCe pattern. This is sometimes referred to as the final *e* pattern, and the *e* is usually a lowercase letter as shown. The final *e* is not sounded, but serves to indicate that the preceding vowel should represent the long sound. It occurs most frequently in one-syllable words. All of the following words follow the CVCe pattern:

ate   make   rebate   stroke   dune   fine

It is important to remember that when the word recognition skill of phonics is used by the reader it will only have real value if the decoded word is in the reader's oral language. Once phonic generalizations have been applied to an unknown word, the reader has to have that word in his or her oral language in order to recognize whether the decoding process has resulted in a recognizable English word. The reader will also need to use context clues to decide whether the decoded word makes sense in the sentence.

Phonics is only one of a group of word recognition skills to be taught to students who are learning to read. Phonics is not the ultimate goal of reading instruction; it is merely an aid or crutch towards the ultimate goal of understanding what has been presented in print. Some learners experience difficulty with learning phonics. When this is true, other word recognition skills should be taught as the primary means of reaching the ultimate goal of reading instruction, which is comprehension.

STRUCTURAL ANALYSIS

What is structural analysis?

Structural analysis is a word recognition skill in which knowledge of the meaningful parts of words aids in the identification of an unknown written word. Structural analysis may be used by a reader either as an aid to the pronunciation of an unknown word or as an aid to understanding the meaning of an unknown word. Structural analysis, like the use of context clues, may be considered both a word recognition and a comprehension skill. As with the use of context clues, it is difficult to separate the use of structural analysis into either a word recognition skill or a comprehension skill without some discussion of its other use. In reality, a mature reader may use structural analysis for both purposes simultaneously. Structural analysis requires the reader to look at meaningful units or parts of words in order to decode a word or to decide what a word means. The diagram on page 69 may be helpful to the reader when trying to see the relationships of the parts of structural analysis.

What are morphemes, and what two types of morphemes are there?

The meaningful structural parts of words are called morphemes. A morpheme is the smallest unit of meaning in a word. Any unit of meaning in a word is a morpheme.

> *Cat* is a single morpheme.
>
> *Cats* is two morphemes.

The *s* added to the word *cat* means more than one cat, so it is a second meaning unit added to the meaning unit *cat*.

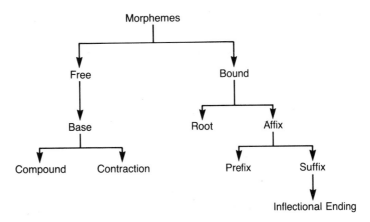

There are two kinds of morphemes. They are bound morphemes and free morphemes. A bound morpheme must be attached to another morpheme in order to carry meaning. A free morpheme can stand alone, as a word, in the English language. The *s* in *cats* has no meaning unless it is attached to a word. It is a bound morpheme. The word *cat* does have meaning without any additions. It is a free morpheme. The following words illustrate bound and free morphemes.

> *Unhappy* has two morphemes. (*un* is bound; *happy* is free)
> *Redoing* has three morphemes. (*re* and *ing* are bound; *do* is free)
> *Disagreeable* has three morphemes. (*dis* and *able* are bound; *agree* is free)
> *Desk* has one morpheme. (it is free)

Root Words and Base Words

What are the components of structural analysis? Illustrate each one.

Every word has a main morpheme; that is, the part of the word that carries the major meaning of that word. This part of the word may be either a bound or a free morpheme. The main morpheme is called either a root word or a base word. Root words come from or are derived from another language and will not stand alone in English. They are bound morphemes. Base words are English words and will stand alone without other morphemes. They are free morphemes.

Root Words

con*tain*	de*tain*	re*tain*
re*fer*	con*fer*	de*fer*
con*cede*	re*cede*	

Notice that *tain, fer,* and *cede* are the major meaning-bearing parts of these words, but are not English words. An English word is formed only when other bound morphemes are added to these roots. Each of the above words contains two bound morphemes.

Base Words

Girl	*girl*s
comfort	un*comfort*able
mark	re*mark*ing

Notice that the base word remains a free morpheme even when one or more affixes have been added to it.

Even though, technically, base words and root words have different meanings, they are sometimes both referred to by either name or the terms are used interchangeably.

Affixes

A second group of bound morphemes is called *affixes*. Affixes are prefixes, suffixes, and inflectional endings. An affix is any morpheme added to the main meaning-bearing part of a word. An affix may precede or follow the root or base word. Base and root words may have more than one affix. Root words must have at least one affix.

A *prefix* is a bound morpheme added to the beginning of a word. Prefixes add to and change the meaning of the base or root word.

Prefix	Meaning	Example
dis	not	disable
	remove, to make not	disappear
	undo, reverse	disassemble
ex	out	exhale
	beyond	expand
re	back	revert
	again	remake

A *suffix* is a bound morpheme added to the end of a word. Suffixes add to or change the meaning of the base or root word.

Suffix	Meaning	Example
er	one who has to do with	laborer
	resident of	southerner
	performs an action	worker
ness	condition of being	fullness
less	without	powerless
	beyond the range of	sightless

The preceding are only a few examples of prefixes and suffixes. Since they are important to both the pronunciation and meaning of words, a more comprehensive list is presented in Appendix A.

Words formed by the addition of prefixes or suffixes to base or root words are known as *derived words*, or derivatives. A different meaning has been derived, or obtained, from the meaning of the original root or base word.

Inflectional endings are a special set of suffixes. They, like other suffixes, are added to the end of a base or root word. Inflectional endings, unlike other suffixes, change the root or base words in terms of number, tense, case, form, or gender.

Number:	cats	more than one
Tense:	helped	past tense

Case:	child's	shows ownership
Form:	taller	compares two things
Gender:	hostess	changes to female

Inflectional endings change the number, case, or gender when added to nouns; tense when added to verbs; and form when added to adjectives and adverbs. The following are the most common inflectional endings:

1. *s* when affixed to nouns to indicate plurality, as in *toys*, and to verbs to indicate agreement with third-person singular nouns, as in "Mary works."
2. *'s* when attached to nouns to indicate possession, as in "John's ball is red."
3. *s'* to indicate plurality and possession, as in "It is the girls' recess time."
4. *es* when attached to nouns to indicate plurality, as in *dresses*.
5. *ed* and *ing* when attached to verbs to indicate, respectively, past tense and present participle, as in *walked* and *walking*.
6. *er* and *est* when affixed to adjectives or adverbs to indicate, respectively, comparative and superlative forms, as in *faster* and *fastest*.
7. *ess* when attached to nouns to indicate change of gender, from *steward* to *stewardess*.

Inflected Forms

When new words are formed by the addition of inflectional endings, they are called inflected forms of the words. A reader must understand that inflectional endings are so named because of the type of change they make in the base or root word. Therefore, the *er* in *taller* is an inflectional ending since it changes the form of the word, but *er* in *helper* is not an inflectional ending because it does not change the tense, case, number, form, or gender of the word.

It is possible for a word to be both derived and inflected. Any word that has had a prefix or suffix added to it is a derived form of that word. Only the addition of an inflectional ending produces the inflected form.

Independent is a derived form of *depend*. (prefix *in* + *depend* + suffix *ent*)

Unhappier is both derived and inflected. (prefix *un* + *happy* + inflected ending *er*)

Compound Words and Contractions

There are two other types of words formed by the combination of meaningful structural units or morphemes. They are known as *compound words* and *contractions*. Compound words are a combination of two free morphemes. The meaning of the new word must retain elements of both meanings and pronunciation of the two previous morphemes in order to be classified as a compound word. *Dollhouse, racetrack,* and *bathroom* are compound words: *office, target,* and *together* are not compound words.

Contractions are formed by combining two free morphemes into a shortened form by the omission of one or more letters and the insertion of an apostrophe where those letters were omitted.

> *are + not* form the contraction aren't
>
> *they + are* form the contraction they're
>
> *he + will* form the contraction he'll

Without the use of context clues, confusion may arise with the use of *'s* with singular nouns. The word *boy's* could be the contracted form of *boy + is*, or it may be a change of case and the possessive form of boy.

> John's sister can't say what John's going to do.

In this sentence, the first *John's* is possessive while the second one is the contracted form of *John is*.

Structural Changes and Spelling

What are the important structural changes in a word that influence spelling?

Structural analysis is a word recognition skill when knowledge of the meaningful parts of words helps the reader to identify, or say, the unknown word. Sometimes beginning readers find the addition of a structural part to a known word changes the look of the word enough that they are unable to recognize the derived word. This is especially true when a spelling change occurs in the base word. Therefore, the following generalizations should be taught to aid in the reader's recognition of such base words as well as to aid in the spelling of such words.

1. When a word ends with *e*, the *e* is dropped before adding an inflectional ending that begins with a vowel.

> *bake + ing* becomes *baking*
>
> *hope + ed* becomes *hoped*

2. When a word ends with a single consonant, that consonant is doubled before adding *ing* or *ed*.

> *hop + ed* becomes *hopped*
>
> *begin + ing* becomes *beginning*

3. When a word ends with *f* or *fe* (with a silent *e*), the *f* is usually changed to *v* before the ending is added.

> *calf + es* becomes *calves*
>
> *wife + es* becomes *wives*

4. When a word ends in *y* preceded by a consonant, the *y* is usually changed to *i* before endings are added, unless the ending begins with *i*.

> *dry + ed* becomes *dried*
>
> *party + es* becomes *parties*
>
> *sorry + est* becomes *sorriest*
>
> *cry + ing* becomes *crying*

5. When a word ends with *y* preceded by a vowel, no change is made in the base word before adding endings.

boy + *s* becomes *boys*

stay + *ed* or *ing* becomes *stayed* or *staying*

6. When the base word ends with *s, ss, ch, sh, x, f/fe* changed to *v*, or *y* changed to *i*, the inflectional ending *es* is added, rather than *s*.

focus becomes *focuses*

mess becomes *messes*

lunch becomes *lunches*

dish becomes *dishes*

box becomes *boxes*

half becomes *halves*

cry becomes *cries*

Syllable Generalizations

What is a syllable, and how does knowledge of syllables aid in word pronunciation?

A syllable is an oral language unit in which a vowel sound is heard. There are as many syllables in a word as there are vowel sounds. In written English, there are only clues as to possible syllabic divisions. A syllable may or may not contain a consonant sound.

a   my   ate   dog   boat   (these are monosyllabic words)

dis-con-tin-ue   re-lat-ed   (these are polysyllabic words)

One kind of syllable is known as an open syllable. The vowel sound in an open syllable is expected to be long.

mu-sic   *ba*-con   *a*-ble   *me*

Another kind of syllable is known as a closed syllable. It is one that ends with a consonant or consonant cluster. The vowel sound in a closed syllable is expected to be short.

desk   *it*   *con-cept*   *that*

There are other kinds of syllables that are neither open nor closed in terms of expected vowel sounds. The -VCe is one such type of syllable where the first vowel is expected to be long and the final *e* silent.

ni-*trate*   *bake*

A syllable's vowel sound may also be represented by a vowel digraph or diphthong. Still another type of vowel sound within a syllable may be determined by the letter that follows the vowel. The sound may be controlled by the letters *r, l, u, w, gh, ld, lt,* and *nd.*

The only justifiable reason for teaching or learning how to divide words into syllables is to give the reader clues to the possible pronunciation of vowel sounds in unknown words. The consonants are relatively consistent in sound; it is the vowels that have great variability.

What are the generalizations concerning syllable division?

Generalizations for syllabic division of words give the reader possibilities to try when encountering an unknown word. In order to be sure the division and the pronunciation of the word are correct, the decoded word must be in the reader's oral language. The oral language is the reader's check on the accuracy of the generalizations that have been applied to the unknown word.

The first four generalizations for syllables deal with the structural parts of unknown words. Whenever readers are being taught to divide words into syllables, they should be urged to look for meaningful chunks of the unknown word, that is, bases, roots, and affixes.

1. The structural elements of the word usually take precedence over phonic generalizations. In the word *reconstitute*, the prefix *re* would be separated before any other generalizations for syllable division take place.

2. Almost all affixes form separate syllables. In the word *rewrite, re* is a separate syllable; in the word *useless, less* is a separate syllable. Exceptions to this include the inflectional endings *'s, s,* and *ed* except when *ed* is preceded by *d* or *t*.

> *books* is one syllable
> *Sue's* is one syllable
> *chained* is one syllable
> *wanted* is two syllables
> *loaded* is two syllables

3. The two words of a compound word form separate syllables, even if there are additional syllables in one or both of the words used to form the compound word.

> *cowboy* has two syllables   cow + boy
> *lumberjack* has three syllables   lum - ber + jack
> *policewoman* has four syllables   po - lice + wo - man

4. The contracted form of two words usually produces just one syllable because it is a vowel that has been deleted to form the contraction.

> *can't* is one syllable
> *they'll* is one syllable

The next five syllabication generalizations deal with phonic generalizations.

1. When two consonants occur between two vowels, the syllabic division is usually *between the two consonants*. (Consonant digraphs and blends are treated as single consonants. Do not divide these.) This pattern is known as the -VCCV- pattern. There may or may not be other consonants preceding or following this pattern.

> bargain   bar-gain
> circus   cir-cus
> enter   en-ter

2. In the -VCCV- pattern, if the two consonants form a blend or digraph, do not divide between them. Instead, usually divide *before or after the blend or digraph*. (Many experts believe that double consonants are digraphs.)

letter   lett-er

graphic   graph-ic

doctrine   doc-trine

3. When one consonant occurs between two vowels, the syllabic division may put the consonant with *either the first or second vowel*. This is known as the -VCV-pattern. There may or may not be other consonants preceding or following this pattern.

a. When the consonant goes with the first vowel, it forms a closed syllable, and the first vowel sound is expected to be short (VC-V).

riv-er   ex-it   liz-ard

b. When the consonant goes with the second vowel, it forms an open syllable and the first vowel is expected to be long (V-CV).

ma-jor   ho-tel   ba-con

c. There are a few words in our language with the -VCV- pattern that actually divide both ways. (These words are called homographs.) The contextual usage of the words and the reader's oral language are the only checks on the correct pronunciation.

record (rē-cord rĕc-ord)   Be sure to record record low temperatures.

present (prē-sent prĕs-ent)   Will you present the present to our guest?

When a reader encounters an unknown word with the -VCV- pattern, it may be necessary to try pronouncing the word with both divisions. If the first division does not produce a recognizable English word, the second division should be tested for the production of a recognizable word.

4. When a word ends in *le* preceded by a single consonant, the final syllable usually consists of the *consonant plus the le*.

cradle   cra-dle

trifle   tri-fle

If two consonants precede the *le*, usually divide *after the second consonant* to prevent splitting blends and digraphs.

rattle   ratt-le

ankle   ank-le

5. The vowel sound in an unstressed or unaccented syllable is often the schwa sound. Any vowel may have the schwa sound, which sounds like the short *u*.

com-mit'-tee   *a*-gain'   dem'-*on*-strate

The division of unknown words is not governed by rules, rather generalizations or possibilities. It is important to note that these generalizations must be used in conjunction with each other and phonics. Even then, there are many words in the English language that are not phonetically regular. Sometimes it is both necessary and desirable to check the pronunciation of a word in the dictionary, since it is the final authority on word pronunciation. Teachers need to use caution when requiring students to sound out words in lessons, always being sure that such words do follow accepted generalizations for their pronunciations.

DICTIONARY

What skills are necessary for dictionary use?

Dictionary use may be viewed as a word recognition skill, a comprehension skill, or a study skill, because the reader may use the dictionary for different purposes. Therefore, the skill of dictionary use, like the use of context clues and structural analysis, cannot truly be separated from its use in other aspects of reading. The dictionary serves as an excellent aid in both reading and spelling, but in order to use it effectively, there are several skills that must be learned. These skills will be presented in Chapter 5. Here, the main emphasis of skills necessary for dictionary use will be directed toward its use for pronunciation.

The reader needs to be able to locate words in the dictionary by using the various levels of *alphabetical order*. Readers also need to be able to use *entry* and *guide words*. Once the unknown word has been located, it is necessary that the reader be able to use the *phonetic respelling* of the word. This is the important word recognition skill as related to the dictionary.

The symbols and markings used to represent the sounds in the phonetic respelling are given in the pronunciation key. These markings are called diacritical marks. The key to these markings is usually printed at the bottom of every other dictionary page or in the front of the dictionary. Markings vary from dictionary to dictionary, so teaching this skill needs to be dictionary specific.

Another useful skill to the end of using the dictionary to aid in the pronunciation of an unknown word is understanding accent marks. These are the marks following a syllable that indicate where stress or force is given in the pronunciation of the word. There are two kinds of accent marks: primary and secondary. *Primary accent marks* indicate the syllable receiving the major stress; *secondary accent marks* indicate the syllable receiving less stress. Usually the accent mark (a slanted line) is darker or bolder for primary accent and lighter for secondary stress.

Often the dictionary is taught apart from the other reading skill areas since it overlaps with all other areas. It is important to remember that dictionary use is a contributing skill in word recognition, but not one of the fundamental skills.

COMBINING WORD RECOGNITION SKILLS

How and why should word recognition skills be combined while teaching?

When children enter school, they come from a wide variety of backgrounds. They have had a variety of experiences and represent many levels of physical, emotional, and intellectual development. No teacher can expect that one skill approach for teaching reading will be successful with all learners; some will be more visually oriented to learning, while others may learn better auditorily or kinesthetically. The diversity of learners widens as they progress through formal education. For these reasons, it is important for teachers to use numerous and combined methods in an attempt to meet the individual needs of all students.

The ability of a student to recognize words is of obvious importance in the teaching of reading. Although some understanding can take place without the correct pronunciation of every single word, little understanding is obtained if very many words are not correctly identified. Although word recognition is necessary to reading, it is not sufficient, since the ultimate goal of reading is comprehension or understanding of what was read.

In early reading instruction, all skill approaches to decoding should be introduced because students may not have developed preferences, and their most successful mode of learning may not be obvious. As the teaching/learning process continues, however, strengths and weaknesses of the learner often become more apparent. Phonics may be very difficult for learners with poorly developed auditory discrimination skills or speakers of another language; learners with good auditory discrimination skills, native English speakers, and gifted students may be very successful with the decoding skill of phonics. Learners not visually oriented may have trouble with whole-word strategies, whereas those who are visual learners or who have learning disabilities may find this a helpful word recognition tool.

Some learners seem to be successful no matter how the teacher presents new material. Others seem to experience difficulty under the same circumstances. Some of the word recognition skills are simpler than others; however, some are more valuable in leading the reader to independence than others. The keys to teaching these skills lie with the teacher's abilities, the needs of the students, and the skill with which the teacher is able to combine these.

SEQUENCE OF WORD RECOGNITION SKILLS

Generally, in what order are the word recognition skills taught?

The sequence of word recognition skills refers to the order in which they are taught. There are no "hard and fast" rules for the order in which these skills should be taught. Some school systems incorporate the sequence used in the basal readers. Other school systems have the teachers, or a curriculum committee, develop a sequence that will be used. Whichever way the decision concerning the sequence of skills is made, a rationale can be built to suggest that the following sequence is beneficial to developing efficient readers (Durkin, 1980).

1. Students should become competent with the prereading skills; that is, they should develop auditory discrimination abilities, visual discrimination abilities, have knowledge of directionality, and have reasonable oral language development based on experiences.

2. Students should learn some basic sight vocabulary. This may be accomplished in a variety of ways, including the use of pictures and configuration.

3. The use of context clues should be introduced, asking students what word would make sense in oral and written sentences. Along with context clues, basic sight vocabulary should continue to be developed.

4. Phonic instruction should be begun with initial consonants for the following reasons:

    a. Consonants are more consistent in sound.

    b. About 85 percent of words begin with consonants.

    c. Initial consonants plus context are very helpful.

    d. Consonants provide more visual clues to words.

    e. Consonant placement can influence vowel sounds.

Consonants are usually taught in the initial position of a word first, then the final position of a word, then in the medial position of a word.

5. The phonic skill of consonant clusters should be introduced. Usually some consonant digraphs are taught before working with blends, followed by the less common digraphs, including silent letters.

6. Structural analysis work with inflected endings should be introduced as sight vocabulary increases. The endings *s, ed*, and *ing* are usually introduced first, followed by *'s, er*, and *est*. Accompanying spelling generalizations must be noted.

7. Structural analysis elements of simple compound words and simple contractions are taught.

8. Work with short vowels in the medial position follows as students gain competence with the skills listed above.

9. Work with long vowel sounds begins. The VCe pattern is often introduced first, then the most regular vowel digraphs such as *ee, ea, oa, ai*, and *ay*.

10. Vowel sound controllers such as *r, l*, and *w* are introduced.

11. Dictionary work is introduced. Here, again, it should be noted that dictionary skills are sometimes taught apart from other reading skills. This level of introduction assumes some prior work with alphabetical order and perhaps exposure to a picture dictionary earlier in the school experience.

12. Phonics instruction continues with work on diphthongs and long and short double *o*.

13. Structural analysis work continues with study of prefixes, suffixes, and base words.

14. Vowel generalizations are stressed, reviewing VCe and others, but adding the concepts of open and closed syllables.

15. Syllabication generalizations are introduced. At this point the schwa sound of vowels must be taught as well as accents.

16. Higher level dictionary skills are introduced, such as using the pronunciation key, along with the phonetic respelling of words.

17. Use of appropriate word recognition skills is encouraged by the teacher to help the student find a lifelong means of unlocking unknown words.

Word recognition skills are important in the process of teaching reading only to the extent that they serve to enhance the reader's ability to interact with the message on a printed page. The goal of reading instruction is to produce individuals who not only *can* read and understand, but readers who *do* read and *enjoy* it!

PRACTICE EXERCISE

Directions

This series of exercises is designed to help you practice and check your knowledge of word recognition skills. Complete each exercise; then check your answers with those in the Answer Key at the end of the text.

Part I

Classify the italicized letters in the following words as (a) diphthong, (b) vowel digraph, (c) consonant digraph, or (d) consonant blend. Write the correct letter in the blank to the left of each word.

_____ 1. *bl*ack   _____ 11. *gn*aw

_____ 2. *oy*ster   _____ 12. *p*ai*l*

_____ 3. *sh*ine   _____ 13. br*ou*ght

_____ 4. t*oi*l   _____ 14. wre*ck*

_____ 5. *br*ight   _____ 15. t*ow*

_____ 6. *dw*indle   _____ 16. thi*ng*

_____ 7. *pn*eumatic   _____ 17. cra*ft*

_____ 8. g*oa*t   _____ 18. n*ee*d

_____ 9. *ea*se   _____ 19. *str*ing

_____ 10. h*ow*   _____ 20. l*ay*

Part II

From among the four words in each list, select the one that does not conform to the phonics generalization that the other three do. Write the letter of the exception on the line to the left. Then write the generalization to which the other words conform on the next line. If all words conform, choose "e," no exception.

Example:

__*c*__   a. bait   b. sail   c. said   d. bail   e. no exception

_____ *CVVC generalization — ai digraph* _____

_____ 1. a. rate   b. line   c. mete   d. one   e. no exception

_____

_____ 2. a. gin   b. gift   c. gym   d. gem   e. no exception

_____

_____ 3. a. cup   b. pin   c. slur   d. get   e. no exception

_____

_____ 4. a. eat   b. seat   c. coat   d. seem   e. no exception

_____ 5. a. be   b. no   c. music   d. me   e. no exception

_____ 6. a. fir   b. fur   c. order   d. me   e. no exception

Part III
From column B select the synonym, example, or definition that best fits a word recognition term in column A. Then write the letter of the synonym, example, or definition on the line to the left.

Column A

_____ 1. grapheme

_____ 2. morpheme

_____ 3. derived word

_____ 4. phoneme

_____ 5. digraph

_____ 6. compound

_____ 7. phonics

_____ 8. basic sight word

_____ 9. affixes

_____ 10. base word

_____ 11. possessive

_____ 12. diphthong

_____ 13. contraction

_____ 14. inflected word

Column B

a. can't
b. blended vowel sound
c. inhospitable
d. letter
e. clues provided by sentence meaning
f. speech sound
g. merging consecutive consonant sounds, each retaining its own identity
h. meaningful structural unit
i. meaner
j. two letters representing a phoneme
k. tablecloth
l. women's
m. study of phoneme-grapheme relationships
n. an
o. major meaning-bearing unit
p. prefixes, suffixes, inflectional endings

Part IV
Divide each of the following nonsense words in syllables, and mark the vowels with diacritical marks. State your reasons for syllabication and for vowel sounds. Where two possibilities for division exist, give both.

1. ekon
2. roashing
3. whochment
4. sluppelgug
5. presilnapishment
6. drackle
7. mastle
8. kromsul
9. bleting

Part V
Choose the best answer among the stated possibilities.

1. The study of the phoneme/grapheme relationship in English is called
   a. phonetics
   b. phonics
   c. linguistics
   d. both a and b

2. The word pronounced by the use of phonics must be in the reader's oral language in order to
   a. check the accuracy of the pronunciation
   b. check the accuracy of phonics rules
   c. check the contextual meaning of a word
   d. all of the above

3. The sounds of *c* and *g* may be identified as
   a. hard and soft
   b. short and long
   c. hiss and guttural
   d. none of the above

4. Which of the following words contains a digraph?
   a. blind
   b. must
   c. kick
   d. gram

5. Which of the following words contains a consonant blend?
   a. wash
   b. letter
   c. ship
   d. stripe

6. The sounds of *s* may be
   a. c, st, sh, s
   b. s, sh, z, zh
   c. k, c, z, s
   d. gz, ks, s, c

7. Which of the following groups of words contains exceptions to vowel generalizations?
   a. sir, cat, bake
   b. colt, see, out
   c. car, find, old
   d. vie, sigh, my

8. Which of the following words would you *not* expect to see on a list of basic sight words?
   a. the
   b. play
   c. with
   d. certainly

9. Which of the following words is probably correctly divided into syllables?
   a. mis-thez-ment
   b. bomn-y
   c. ci-mtor
   d. ba-tmle

10. Which of the following words contains a schwa?
    a. again
    b. cart
    c. book
    d. below

5
Study Skills

What are the study skills, and how does the reader use study skills with other reading skills?

When students study, they use basic skills of reading to gain knowledge, information, or skills that will help them take a test, write a report, or complete a similar task (Anderson & Armbruster, 1984). In addition to the basic reading skills, a number of skills such as locating information, interpreting graphic and pictorial materials, and organizing information are also used to study. These skills are known as study skills, survival skills, or life skills. This chapter discusses the study skills and what students must learn in order to know how to study. These skills can be divided into four broad categories:

1. Locating information
2. Organizing information
3. Interpreting graphic and pictorial materials
4. Study habits and techniques

The exact order for teaching study skills is an arbitrary decision. Study skill instruction usually begins after students have developed a fairly good grasp of the basic reading skills and processes. However, it is appropriate to teach some of the more basic study skills at the very beginning stages of reading instruction.

LOCATING INFORMATION

What are the five ways of locating information, and what should be learned about each one?

In order to locate information effectively, there are some specialized skills which must be learned. They are discussed below.

Alphabetical Order

Materials in various sources are arranged differently. However, arrangement by *alphabetical order* is the most common mode of organization. Dictionaries, directories, card catalogs, indices, encyclopedias, and many other materials are arranged this way.

Students need to know the alphabet in order to be cognizant of where to look for a piece of information arranged alphabetically. The first step in learning to use alphabetical order is learning the alphabet and being able to put the letters in their correct order. The next step is to arrange words by their first letter and later by their second letter and beyond. Finally, students need to learn to arrange titles and names in alphabetical order.

Students must learn that when arranging names alphabetically, the last name is presented first (e.g., Carter, Mark). When arranging or locating a title the words *a, an,* or *the* are not used when they are the first word in the title; instead, the next word is used for locating or arranging the material.

Using Parts of a Book

Every book has a variety of aids designed to assist the user in locating and evaluating information within it. The *title page* in the front of a book gives the title of the book, the authors and their location, and the publisher and its location. This information may be used by the reader to obtain additional information from the authors or the publisher.

The *date of publication page* follows the title page. It gives the copyright date and the name of the person or company who holds the right to reproduce the material. Also included are the place and date of printing and the Library of Congress card number.

The *table of contents* follows the date of publication page and presents the sequential listing of chapters and sections of the book; these are presented in numerical order with the page number where they begin. The table of contents may be viewed as an outline of the book's contents. This section of the book would be used by the reader to see what is in each chapter and how the book is organized.

In some books, lists of *tables, maps, illustrations,* or *charts* presented in the text will follow the table of contents. These listings would generally appear only in books in which such items were used in sufficient detail to explain or further enhance the text.

The *preface* or *foreword* usually precedes or follows the table of contents. This section of the book gives the author's purpose for writing the material and explains for whom the book was intended. In some instances, a summary and limitations of the book are presented.

The *glossary*, located following the body of the book, is a kind of dictionary that contains an alphabetical listing of terms important to the text. Using the glossary requires the reader to use the same skills needed when using a dictionary. The pronunciation of the term and its definitions as used in the text are given.

Also located in the back of a book is another valuable tool, the *index*. The index provides an alphabetical listing of topics covered in the text and all the pages where the topic is discussed or presented. Some books contain both author and subject indexes.

There are two related skills that are important to using an index; these are classifying topics and cross-referencing. Since a particular subject may be discussed under several headings, a student must first learn the *classification of topics*; that is, under what other categories might the information be located. A topic listed in the index with all of the sources where it may be found in the book is called *cross-referencing* or *cross-listing*. Such an entry would be followed by "*see also* _____."

The *appendix* is another section of the book that students need to know how to use. This section is also located in the back and contains material that explains or expands the content of the text but is not necessary to the main text.

Students need to know how to use a *bibliography*. This is a listing of books, articles, or materials referred to or used in the text. Bibliographies are usually arranged alphabetically by author or editor. Bibliographies may be presented at the end of an entire book or at the end of each chapter.

Footnotes are the explanatory notes usually presented at the bottom of the page and keyed by number to a specific item on the page. Footnotes may also give credit to another source of information for material used or explain a needed point. In some books, footnotes are designated by a number in parentheses, which corresponds to a listing in the bibliography.

Dictionaries

There are different types of dictionaries. A picture dictionary or pictionary shows a word with a picture. This type of dictionary is often used in beginning reading. At the elementary and junior high levels there are abridged dictionaries containing the types of information appropriate to the level. The unabridged dictionary is considered a complete dictionary in that terms and definitions have not been omitted.

The first skill necessary for use of a dictionary is *alphabetical order*, which has already been discussed. Next, the student must learn to use the *guide words* which are printed at the top of the dictionary page. The guide words are the first word of the left-hand column and the last word of the right-hand column. Guide words are also used in encyclopedias and sometimes in indices. In these references the guide words would represent the first and last topic presented on the page. When using guide words, a student can tell whether or not a particular word or topic appears on the page. The student must use knowledge of alphabetical order, especially using the second, third, or fourth letter, to use guide words.

Learning to use the dictionary also requires the student to know what *entry words* are. The entry words are the words presented and defined in the dictionary. In most dictionaries they are printed in bold type and broken into syllables.

The entry word precedes the *phonetic respelling* which gives the accepted pronunciation or pronunciations of the word. The symbols and markings used to represent the sounds in the phonetic respellings are given in the *pronunciation key*. These markings are called *diacritical marks* and are explained in the key which is usually printed at the bottom of every other page or in the front of the dictionary.

To be able to interpret phonetic respellings completely, students must understand and be able to use *accent marks*; these are the marks following a syllable that indicate where stress or force is given in pronunciation. Most native speakers of English know which part of a word to accent from their oral language.

Once students have learned to locate a word in the dictionary and figure out its pronunciation, they must make use of one last skill. That skill is *selecting the appropriate meaning to fit the context* in which the word is used.

Special References

Encyclopedias are valuable sources of information that persons may use throughout their lives. An encyclopedia is a single book that treats a great many specific topics or a series of books in which the topics are arranged alphabetically. The series normally has an index appearing in a separate volume, usually the last.

An *atlas* is a collection of maps bound together. Many times social studies books and encyclopedias will have a section called the atlas, or an atlas may be a separate book. The maps presented in an atlas are usually arranged alphabetically by title or topic. All the sections normally found in a book are also found in the atlas to aid a student in finding materials.

Certain special references are published on a regularly recurring basis. These materials are referred to as *periodicals* and include almanacs, yearbooks, directories, newspapers, and magazines.

An *almanac* is published annually. It may include data related to the year immediately past as well as predictions and guides for the following year in such areas as weather and crops.

The *yearbook* is an annual publication designed to update a series of books in existence or to present a particular topic in depth. Encyclopedias usually publish a yearbook to update their materials. Some organizations publish a yearbook covering a particular topic in depth or presenting a summary of the organization's activities for the year. This type of publication is also referred to as an *annual*.

Another periodic source of information is *directories*, including telephone directories, city directories, or directories of organizations. Directories are generally arranged alphabetically and require students to make use of many of the same skills used in locating information in other books.

Newspapers are periodicals students will continue to use after completing school. In using the newspaper, students need to learn the various parts and their purposes. A newspaper contains news items, editorials, features, columns, and advertisements.

Each part of the newspaper provides a different type of valuable information. Knowing what can be found in each part will help a student make the most effective use of the newspaper.

Magazines are organized like books but are published more frequently. These periodicals present changing points of view, current events, special stories, and many other features. Magazines usually have a table of contents and some publish an annual index. Each magazine usually has a volume number and an issue number that appear on the front or inside cover. Each volume is made up of all issues printed during a given year.

The key to locating and using material in magazines is the *Readers' Guide to Periodical Literature*. This is a special reference which serves as an index to many published magazines. The front of the guide indicates the magazines indexed and the abbreviations used. Materials are indexed alphabetically by subject, author, and title.

A *thesaurus* is a special reference listing synonyms and antonyms for words. The most commonly used thesaurus is *Roget's International Thesaurus*, and there are various thesauruses published for various grade levels.

Three additional types of reference materials are becoming more widely used and should be given attention when teaching students to use special references. These include *audiovisual recordings, microfilm,* and *microfiche.*

With the expanded use of television and other types of audiovisual media, students need to have the opportunity to learn to use these sources of information. Microfilm and microfiche are widely used in storing large quantities of printed material. Microfilm presents material on a continuous roll of film; microfiche presents this material on a film card. Both types of film require a special machine for reading.

Using the Library

The library, a lifelong information source, may be used effectively when one knows how it is organized. The key to locating material in the library is the *card catalog*, an alphabetical listing of all materials in the library. An *author, subject*, and *title* card for each piece of material in the library is filed in the card catalog. Each card includes the call number, the author's name, the title, the publisher, and the copyright date.

The *call number* is the number by which a book is shelved in the library. It is found on the card catalog card and on the spine of the book. The type of call number used depends on the classification system used by the library, either the *Dewey Decimal System* or the *Library of Congress System*.

The Dewey Decimal System consists of ten numerical categories for filing materials in the library. Most libraries in the United States are changing from this system to the Library of Congress System, used by the Library of Congress in Washington, D.C. This system has twenty categories, each of which is designated by a letter followed by numerals. Changing to the Library of Congress System allows publishers of materials to categorize books when they are printed and also produces consistency in filing materials in libraries across the country. The latter system also allows for more call number combinations since it uses both letters and numerals.

In many large libraries, the computer is being used to organize and store information formerly stored in the card catalog. Use of the computer to store information is much more efficient than the card catalog and requires less time and effort to maintain. Most school libraries, however, still use the card catalog.

In addition to teaching a student each of these specific skills for using the library, the teacher must direct the student in drawing upon previously learned skills (e.g., alphabetical order and use of special references) as they are needed.

ORGANIZING INFORMATION

What are the parts of organizing information, and how do they relate to comprehension?

Once an individual has located information, it becomes necessary to organize it so that it may be useful. Organizing information, the second broad category of study skills, includes classifying information, identifying main idea and supporting details, ordering information, summarizing, synthesizing information, taking notes, and outlining. These skills not only overlap with each other but also with comprehension. This is the one study skills area that has the most in common with comprehension.

Classifying Information

Good organization of anything depends upon putting together those things that go together or work well together. Therefore, the first subskill of organizing information is *classifying information*. In learning to use this skill, the reader must begin by learning to classify objects that go together; for example, apple, orange, and pear all go together because they are fruits, they can be eaten, or they grow on trees. Next, readers need to learn to classify words, then sentences and larger ideas. Learning this skill helps readers relate ideas and begin to organize ideas so that they will be more easily remembered and used.

Identifying Main Idea and Supporting Details

Classification of information is the first step in learning to identify the *main idea and supporting details*. Even though this is comprehension, it becomes very significant in study skills because the reader must be able to identify the main idea and the details that support it in order to outline. The main idea is the central or most significant thought of the paragraph or piece of material. The supporting details do just that; they support the main idea. Much of the time when the reader is identifying the main idea, inferential skills are being used because the main idea itself is not stated in the material. The details are given, but these must be used to infer the main idea.

In some materials the main idea is stated in a topic sentence, and the details supporting it are given in the surrounding sentences. Teaching students to read and identify the main idea and supporting details involves teaching the processes and skills discussed in Chapter 3.

Ordering Information

Ordering or *sequencing* ideas is a skill that is important to readers as they learn to outline. Readers must not only be able to recognize the logical sequence of ideas but must also be able to read material and recall or recognize the ideas in their correct sequence. Using this skill becomes very important in following directions, studying history, and carrying out experiments.

Summarizing

The skill of *summarizing* requires learners to state briefly what has been read or heard. This sophisticated skill requires the reader to identify the topic of what is being read by using five basic tasks (Brown & Day, 1983):

1. Read the material to be summarized and identify ideas that are redundant; these ideas should be deleted and reduced to a single statement.
2. Identify ideas in the material that are trivial or are irrelevant to the topic; delete them.
3. Look for lists of ideas that fit a given category; replace the list with the category. This is known as identifying a superordinate for the list.
4. Select a topic sentence for the paragraph. If more than one paragraph is being read, select one for each passage.
5. If a topic sentence does not exist for each paragraph, formulate one based on the most repeated ideas.

These five tasks can be systematically taught to students (Day, 1980), but it must be remembered that learning this process is developmental; each step must be built upon the other.

Synthesizing Information

Synthesizing information is the skill of summarizing applied to several sources of material and involves the use of the process described above. This skill is needed when a student is writing a report or doing any task requiring the use of several sources of information. The development of this skill would not begin until the student has good use of the other skills in this category.

Taking Notes

Research has shown that *note taking* can be a very effective study technique (Anderson & Armbruster, 1984). Note taking becomes a significant skill for learners to use in order to remember certain points and details from reading or listening. Note taking requires that the reader be able to recognize the main idea and the important supporting details, to summarize, and to order ideas sequentially.

Notes may be taken in a variety of forms—key words, phrases, sentences, paragraphs, or outlines. Students should learn to adjust note-taking procedures according to the purpose for taking the notes. Students should be taught that when taking notes, the title of the source and pertinent facts about it such as pages, publisher, and copyright, or the name, date, and topic of a speaker should be recorded.

Outlining

The skill of *outlining* requires the reader to identify the main ideas and supporting details in their correct sequence from the text. This skill helps the reader organize the material so that it may be more easily remembered and understood. Outlines may be prepared in several forms: phrases, sentences, or paragraphs. It is necessary that the student be taught a format for outlining because this, too, aids in seeing the organization of material.

INTERPRETING GRAPHIC AND PICTORIAL MATERIALS

What skills are included in graphic and pictorial materials?

The organization and explanation of text material is enhanced by pictures, charts, and graphs. In order to get the most from materials in which such devices are used, the reader must be able to interpret graphic and pictorial materials. This category of study skills includes interpreting pictures; political cartoons; timelines; tables, charts and diagrams; graphs; and maps and globes.

Pictures

Pictures not only add interest to the text but also clarify concepts, assist with comparisons, and bring new experiences to the reader. For the nonreader, less capable reader, or bilingual reader, pictures may become a major source of information. For pictures to be of value in improving the understanding of text, the reader must be taught to focus on them and see how they enhance the text. If this is not done, pictures can mislead the reader and cause misunderstanding of what is being read (Schallert, 1980).

Political Cartoons

Political cartoons are a special type of picture used in newspapers and magazines. Generally, political cartoons are important in critical reading because they often depict satire in relation to a particular government event. If taken literally, these cartoons are likely to have a very different meaning from the one intended by the author. Therefore, the reader must be given instruction in interpreting these materials.

Timelines

A *timeline* is a type of graph that arranges events in their order of occurrence. Timelines are used in many reference books to summarize or clarify material and to show the relationship of events in sequence. A timeline may be arranged vertically or horizontally. Figure 5-1 presents an example of each type. The timeline allows the reader to make comparisons and visualize events in relationship to each other. Each space on the timeline represents the same designated amount of time.

Tables, Charts, and Diagrams

Tables and charts are a concise way to organize data for comparative purposes. These terms are often used synonymously. Figure 5-2 presents an example of two types of tables. Note that they may be single column, multicolumn, vertical, or horizontal.

Diagrams are drawings that are used to illustrate the parts of something; for example, Figure 5-3 shows the diagram of a computer with the important parts labeled. Students must be taught to use these drawings to help them understand as they read.

FIGURE 5-1
Sample Timelines

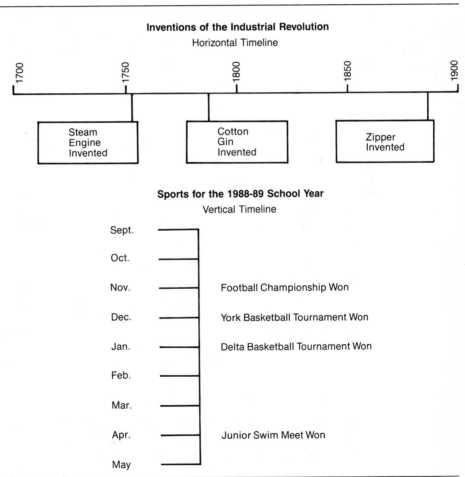

Inventions of the Industrial Revolution
Horizontal Timeline

1700   1750   1800   1850   1900

Steam Engine Invented

Cotton Gin Invented

Zipper Invented

Sports for the 1988-89 School Year
Vertical Timeline

Sept.

Oct.

Nov. — Football Championship Won

Dec. — York Basketball Tournament Won

Jan. — Delta Basketball Tournament Won

Feb.

Mar.

Apr. — Junior Swim Meet Won

May

FIGURE 5-2
Sample Tables

TABLE 1
Foods Eaten in One Week

DIRECTIONS: Make a tally mark for every food eaten during the week.

	Bread	Meat	Fish	Green Vegetables	Yellow Vegetables	Sweets
Monday						
Tuesday						
Wednesday						
Thursday						
Friday						
Total						

TABLE 2
Ice Cream Cones Sold by Girls

Girls	Ice Cream Cones
Mary	6
Ann	8
Sue	19
Wendy	5

FIGURE 5-3
Diagram of a Computer

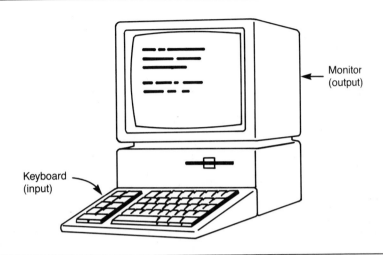

Monitor
(output)

Keyboard
(input)

Graphs

Graphs, like other aids discussed in this section, serve to organize material visually for easy comparison. There are four basic types of graphs: circle, line, bar, and picture.

The *circle graph* allows easy comparison of the parts to the whole. Figure 5-4 is an example of this type of graph. Each division of the circle represents a portion of the whole.

FIGURE 5-4
Circle Graph

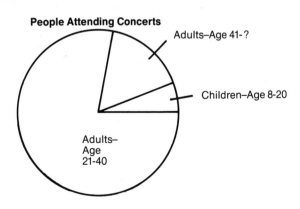

People Attending Concerts

Adults–Age 41-?

Children–Age 8-20

Adults–
Age
21-40

Line graphs, bar graphs, and picture graphs are different from circle graphs in that they have axes. *Axes* are the lines going vertically and horizontally along the edges of the graph. Each line represents a different variable in the graph. The axes can be seen in the graphs in Figures 5-5, 5-6, and 5-7. Each of the types of graphs presented may be made vertically or horizontally. The line graph and bar graph are two-axis graphs, and picture graphs are single-axis graphs.

The *line graph* presented in Figure 5-5 is the type of graph used to show the progress of a trend over a period of time or series of items. The *bar graphs* in Figure 5-6 show comparisons by the length of the bars. In both the line graph and bar graph, each space represents a designated amount.

FIGURE 5-5
Line Graph

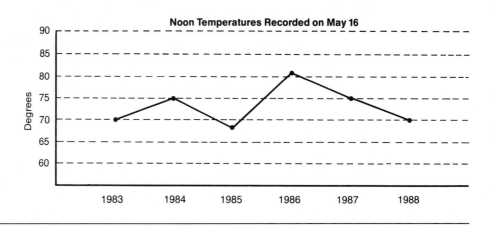

The picture graph shown in Figure 5-7 is a single-axis graph in which a picture represents a given item or quantity. In some cases, the symbol used is divided to represent only a portion of the quantity represented by the picture.

Maps and Globes

Maps and globes are a representation of the features of a particular area of the earth's surface. *Maps* are usually flat and depict the entire area of the earth's surface or a selected portion. *Globes* are spherical and represent the entire earth's surface. Learning to interpret maps and globes depends upon learning to use certain basic skills.

Representation is the use of certain symbols to represent particular characteristics and features on the map, globe, or graph. A student must have the concept that certain symbols represent specific things. These symbols may be pictures or designs that may be colored or noncolored. Figure 5-8 shows examples of how representation would be used to depict certain features on a map or graph.

FIGURE 5-6
Bar Graphs

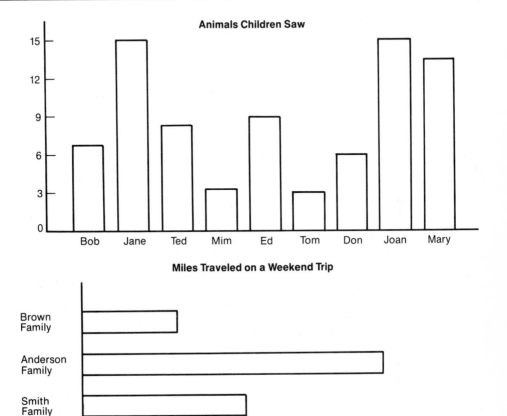

Orientation skills help the reader know how to locate directions on a map or globe and be able to locate points in relation to each other. The directions *north, south, east,* and *west* are designated on a map by a symbol usually presented near the key. Normally, north is at the top, south is at the bottom, east at the right, and west at the left as a map is faced. If no information is given concerning directions on a map, it should be assumed that north is at the top. A student must learn not only to interpret north, south, east, and west, but also must learn to recognize the intermediate directions such as northeast and southwest.

FIGURE 5-7
Picture Graph

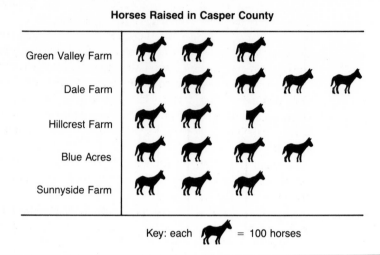

Horses Raised in Casper County

Key: each 🐴 = 100 horses

FIGURE 5-8
Examples of Representation Used on Map or Graph

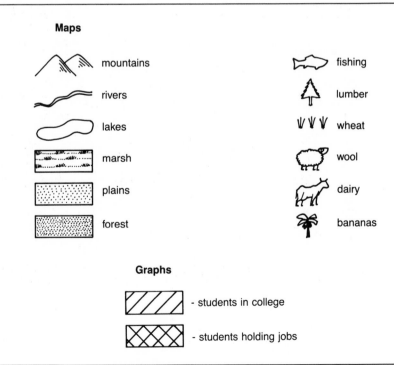

Maps

mountains   fishing

rivers   lumber

lakes   wheat

marsh   wool

plains   dairy

forest   bananas

Graphs

- students in college

- students holding jobs

Locating places on a map or globe also depends on being able to use the *lines of latitude and longitude*. The lines of latitude are the imaginary lines extending east and west, representing distances north and south of the equator. These lines are also called parallels. The equator is the zero parallel.

The lines of longitude are imaginary lines extending north and south representing distances east and west of the prime or zero meridian. The prime meridian passes through Greenwich, England. These lines are also called meridians.

The unit of measure used to designate the distances between the lines of latitude and longitude is the degree. The *degree* is 1/360 part of a complete circle. Each degree may be broken down into 60 parts called *minutes*. The symbol for degree is ° and for minute is '. Figure 5-9 shows a map with the lines of latitude and longitude marked.

Distances on maps are generally measured by a *scale*. The scale tells the distance on the map which is equalled by a given measure. Figure 5-10 presents two maps that use different scales.

Finally, the last skill needed in reading and interpreting maps and globes is the ability to read the *legend* or *key*. This is part of the map or globe where the symbols and their representation and the scale are presented.

FIGURE 5-9
Latitude and Longitude

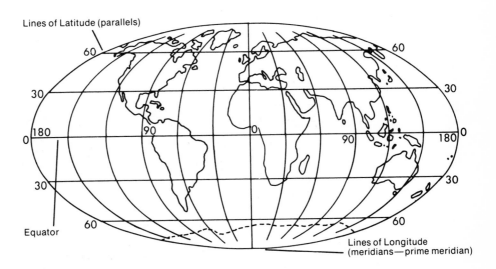

Source: Wayne Otto and Eunice Askov, *The Wisconsin Design for Reading Skill Development* (Minneapolis: National Computer Systems, 1971), Study Skills, Level G. Reprinted by permission.

FIGURE 5-10
Map Scales

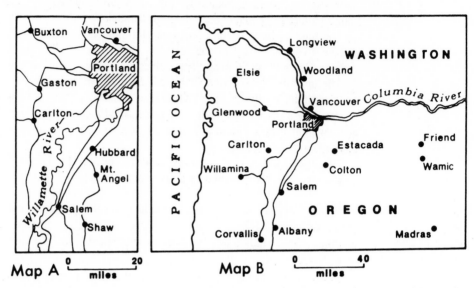

Source: Wayne Otto and Eunice Askov, *The Wisconsin Design for Reading Skill Development* (Minneapolis: National Computer Systems, 1971), Study Skills, Level F. Reprinted by permission.

STUDY HABITS AND TECHNIQUES

What must students be taught to help them be flexible and adjust their rate of reading?

This chapter has discussed the specific skills involved in studying various types of reading material. In addition, students must be taught certain procedures that will help them learn *how to study*, including flexibility and adjustment of rate and different study systems and techniques.

Flexibility and Adjustment of Rate

Flexibility and adjustment of rate pertain to readers being able to adjust their rate according to the purpose for reading. Certainly, the important factor is not just being able to read an increasingly higher number of words per minute. Research has shown that lasting improvement of rate depends upon the reader's being able to comprehend (Harris, 1968).

One of the first skills to teach the reader when teaching flexibility is to *set a purpose for reading*. This means that the reader is looking for something during reading. A mature reader is able to adjust the rate of reading according to this purpose. Rate and flexibility are affected by many factors:

1. The reader's purpose for reading
2. The reader's use of basic skills

3. The difficulty of the material

4. The reader's attitude, interest, and motivation

Another skill that assists the reader in adjusting rate is *skimming*. Skimming occurs when the reader is trying to get a general overview of what the material is about. The reader would use this skill when:

1. Reviewing materials previously read

2. Getting a general idea of the content of the material

3. Determining whether certain material is pertinent to a particular topic

The last skill to be taught in rate and flexibility is that of *scanning*. When readers use this skill, they are looking for a specific item. This skill is different from skimming; when skimming, the reader is trying to get a general idea or overview, whereas in scanning a specific fact or answer is sought.

Study Systems

What are the important study techniques?

A part of teaching students how to study involves showing them how to approach the reading of the chapters in their textbooks. Of the many different study systems that can be taught, three are described below. All are ways of helping the student to set purposes before reading and then to read to accomplish them. The use of these systems in conjunction with note taking will also help students develop good study habits.

SQ3R Study System (Robinson, 1962)

Survey

1. *Make a quick survey of the assignment to get the main ideas.* Notice the title, read the introduction, look through the assignment for main sections, and read the summary.

Question

2. *Turn headings into questions.* The questions will make important points stand out. If there are no headings, make up questions. The heading "Natural Regions of South America" could be changed to the question, "What are the natural regions of South America?"

Read

3. *Read to answer questions.* Read to the end of the headed section. Rate depends upon purpose and difficulty of the materials. Make use of the italics and boldface type, topic sentences, summaries, and graphs and charts.

Recall

4. *Recall the answer to questions.* After reading the first section, look away from the book and try to *answer the question.* If possible, use an example. If necessary, reread the section. Then write down *key phrases* in outline form in a notebook. Make these notes brief. *Then repeat steps 2, 3,* and *4 for each succeeding headed section. Turn the heading into a question, read to answer that question, restate the answer, and outline. Read this way until the lesson is completed.*

Review

5. *Review the material.* Look over notes to get a bird's-eye view of the different ideas brought out in the lesson. Cover up the notes and try to remember the main points. Then uncover the main points and try to remember the subpoints. Go over notes or outline just before a test.

Several variations of SQ3R (Robinson, 1962), have been suggested by other authorities in the field. These include PQRST (Spache, 1963) for science and SQRQCQ (Fay, 1965) for math. These systems are very similar to SQ3R but are aimed at specific content areas. The following outlines present the steps of each technique.

PQRST Study System (for Science) (Spache, 1963)

<u>P</u>review	Rapidly skim the total selection.
<u>Q</u>uestion	Raise questions to guide the reading.
<u>R</u>ead	Read the selection, keeping the questions in mind.
<u>S</u>ummarize	Organize and summarize the information gained.
<u>T</u>est	Check your summary against the selection.

SQRQCQ Study System (for Math) (Fay, 1965)

<u>S</u>urvey	Read the problem rapidly to determine its nature.
<u>Q</u>uestion	Decide what is being asked by the problem.
<u>R</u>ead	Read for details and interrelationships.
<u>Q</u>uestion	Decide what processes should be used.
<u>C</u>ompute	Carry out computation.
<u>Q</u>uestion	Ask if the answer seems correct; then check the computation against the problem facts and the basic arithmetic facts.

Underlining, Note taking, Outlining

Underlining, note taking, and outlining are all techniques that have value in helping students learn to understand text more effectively (Anderson & Armbruster, 1984). It is probably the process of deciding what should be underlined that really helps students understand and remember materials better rather than the actual underlining itself. Note taking and outlining are also important study techniques that students must be taught how to use when studying various kinds of content materials.

Planning Study Time

An important element in teaching students how to study involves teaching them to plan their study time and place. Working out a schedule will help them make efficient use of their time. Showing students how to make a list of school tasks and work out a short-term and long-term schedule will help them learn to plan their time more effectively.

How to Take Tests

Students need to be taught how to study for tests and focus on the points the teacher has emphasized in class. They should be taught to develop sample questions of their own as a technique for trying to predict the type of information that will be included on a test. Studying for a test may involve such techniques as:

1. Using SQ3R when reading chapters.
2. Answering questions provided in chapters.
3. Writing summaries and/or outlines of chapters.
4. Making lists of key terms and definitions from chapters.

Students should be taught how to study for a variety of types of tests. These include short answer, matching, fill-in-the-blank, multiple choice, and essay.

WHEN TO TEACH STUDY SKILLS

When should study skills be taught?

Study skill instruction should begin as soon as students have developed some use of their basic reading skills and have a need for study skills. Usually this will begin around the end of second or beginning of third grade. However, in some programs the simpler study skills may be taught earlier if students have the need for them. The bulk of study skill instruction will take place in fourth through eighth grades.

Study skill instruction should not only be provided during reading but also during science, social studies, and other content areas. Each content area requires the use of different reading skills. Therefore, it is often more effective to teach many of the reading skills, including study skills, when the various subject areas are taught.

PRACTICE EXERCISE

Directions
This series of exercises is designed to help you practice and check your knowledge of study skills. Complete each exercise; then check your answers with those in the Answer Key at the end of the text.

Part I
In each of the following categories, one item does not belong. Draw a line through this item and tell why it does not belong in the category. The first one has been done for you.

1. Advertisements, features, political cartoons, headlines, ~~Library of Congress~~

   All others are newspaper parts.

2. Comprehension, main idea, outlining, ordering events, alphabetical order

3. Almanac, atlas, globe, orientation, representation

4. Phonetic spelling, glossary, bar graph, diacritical marks, entry word

5. *Readers' Guide*, alphabetical order, title card, thesaurus, Library of Congress

Part II

Match the items in column A with the correct item in column B. Some items from column B may be used more than once. Some items in column A may match more than one item from column B.

Column A

_____ 1. dictionary

_____ 2. table of contents

_____ 3. SQ3R

_____ 4. 3°, 2′

_____ 5. NE, NW

_____ 6. picture graph

_____ 7. directory

_____ 8. yearbook

_____ 9. preface

_____ 10. appendix

_____ 11. classification of topics

_____ 12. key

_____ 13. synthesizing material from several sources

_____ 14. bar graph

_____ 15. pronunciation key

Column B

a. limitations of the book

b. vertical

c. annual update

d. summarizing

e. outline of contents

f. representation

g. method of study

h. â—*care, air*
   ü—*rule, move*

i. organization of information

j. intermediate directions

k. degree and minute

l. supplementary material

m. listing of names and the locations

n. alphabetical

o. horizontal

p. comparison of material

Part III

Select the one best answer for each of the following questions.

1. Study skill instruction usually begins
   a. in prereading development
   b. as soon as students have developed some of their basic skills
   c. after comprehension has been mastered
   d. as a part of phonics

2. Helping students learn to take tests involves
   a. giving students experiences with different types of tests
   b. teaching them how to study for a test
   c. having students answer chapter questions
   d. all of the above

3. Underlining helps students
   a. remember what was read
   b. read faster
   c. decode words more accurately
   d. all of the above

4. In the SQ3R study system, the first R stands for
   a. recall
   b. recite
   c. review
   d. read

5. Lines running east and west on a map are called
   a. lines of longitude
   b. axes
   c. lines of latitude
   d. meridians

6. The one type of graph which does not have axes is
   a. circle graph
   b. picture graph
   c. line graph
   d. bar graph

7. Which of the following would be most useful in helping students learn to identify the names of bicycle parts?
   a. a picture graph
   b. a diagram
   c. a chart
   d. the index

8. Learning to summarize is a process that involves
   a. deleting redundant material
   b. identifying trivia
   c. identifying superordinates for lists
   d. all of the above

9. The key to locating materials in many libraries is the
   a. *Readers' Guide*
   b. computer
   c. card catalog
   d. b and c

10. Which of the following book parts would be most helpful to the reader in critical reading?
    a. preface
    b. glossary
    c. index
    d. a and b

6

The Directed Reading Lesson—
An Overview

What will you learn in this chapter?

Most students do not learn to read on their own; rather they are taught to read. The average citizen does not feel competent to teach a student how to read. In fact, preservice teachers are sometimes heard to say that they have no idea how to teach students to read. The previous chapters presented *what* is involved in the reading process. This chapter presents the *how* of a reading lesson.

The reading lesson structure is sometimes called a Directed Reading Activity (DRA), a Directed Reading/Thinking Activity (DRTA), or a Directed Reading Lesson (DRL). In this text, the structured reading lesson is called a Directed Reading Lesson (DRL). The four chapters that follow this one present detailed descriptions of specific teaching strategies that may be used in carrying out a DRL. Therefore, this chapter, and the four that follow it, are interrelated, and must be used together. In this chapter, a Direct Instruction Model used in the DRL is also presented.

What are the parts of a DRL, and how does a DRL relate to basals?

The process of learning to read is complex. Although there is a body of skills that a learner *may* need to learn in order to read, *the reading process is more than the learning of a multitude of isolated skills*. There is some danger that the separation of reading skills from the complete reading lesson indicates that the reading skills are separate from the process of learning to read. There is no such intention here; the skills of reading should be an integral part of the total process of learning to read. *Much emphasis should be placed upon the importance of the learner using the skills* that have been taught in a reading situation rather than just learning them in isolation.

Usually the DRL consists of four integrated parts:

1. Skill development
2. Background and vocabulary
3. Reading and discussing the selection
4. Enrichment or follow-up

Reference is made to these parts of a DRL in the teachers' editions of most basal readers, although the names of the lesson parts may vary among basals. Since basal readers are the most common materials used for the teaching of reading, teachers should be familiar with the parts of a reading lesson, as they will most likely be presented in the materials used for reading instruction.

Most students are taught to read using basal readers, and most teachers have access to the accompanying manuals in which abundant teaching suggestions are provided. Often it is necessary for teachers to be selective in choosing activities from teachers' editions in order to best meet the needs of a particular group of students. The suggestions contained in the manuals can be used to advantage within the instructional model that will be presented in this chapter. The extent to which these suggestions can be used will depend upon the teacher's ability to see the relationship between the manual's suggestions, the various parts of the Direct Instruction Model, and the needs of the students.

The four parts of a DRL are outlined below. Notice the terms *teach, practice*, and *apply* in the outline. These are parts of the Direct Instructional Model. This model will be described immediately following the outline, then each part of the DRL will be explained, showing how the Direct Instruction Model fits into a DRL.

- **Skill development**
  Teach a skill
  Practice a skill
  Apply a skill (under some circumstances)
- **Background and vocabulary**
  Teach words (using previously taught skills)
  Practice words
  Build background and motivate
- **Reading and discussing selection**
  Apply skill that was taught (usually)
  Apply vocabulary that was taught (always)
  Guide silent reading with purposes
  Get answer to purpose question(s)
  Engage in discussion
  Check application of skill
  Check application of vocabulary
  Ask extension questions
  Elicit oral rereading with purposes (when appropriate)

- **Enrichment**
  Extend concepts
  Build good attitudes
  Provide enjoyment

THE DIRECT INSTRUCTION MODEL

What are the parts of the Direct Instruction Model?

Research evidence clearly shows the advantages of teaching reading using some type of direct instruction (Baumann, 1984; Hansen & Pearson, 1983; Hunt, 1976; Meyer et al., 1983; Rosenshine & Stevens, 1984). Direct instruction is a process of teaching, where the teacher (1) clearly shows, demonstrates, or models for students, (2) provides opportunities for students to use processes, and (3) provides corrective feedback and monitoring to students.

The Direct Instruction Model is composed of three major parts, each contributing significantly to the likelihood of a learner's success in reading. Although the three parts of the Direct Instruction Model will be discussed as separate entities, there is a blending of the three parts in actual classroom work with students. The three parts of the model are Teach, Practice, and Apply. First, students are taught what they need to know in order to be successful. Then they are given opportunities to practice whatever was taught, and finally they are given opportunities to apply or use what was taught and practiced.

The Direct Instruction Model can be illustrated by the diagram presented in Figure 6-1. The parts of the model overlap and repeat in the process of learning. Teaching may be considered an ongoing process for a period of instructional time; guided practice is a part of the teaching component. At any point in direct instruction, it may be necessary to reteach and provide additional guided practice with corrective feedback. The independent practice activities may be begun following the guided practice, but the teacher may need to return to teaching, depending on how well the students complete the independent practice. Ultimately, teaching and reteaching

FIGURE 6-1
Interrelationships of the Direct Instruction Model

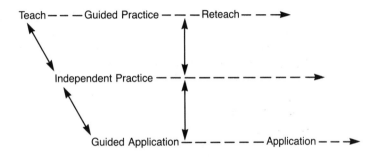

cease, independent practice may continue, and independent application begins. Finally, students are expected to apply independently, after a long period of direct instruction.

Teach

In the teaching phase, the teacher presents the skill to be developed. The teacher may be a person (the teacher or aide) or a teacher substitute such as a tape with a tape recorder, a computer, or material used with any of a number of other pieces of hardware or machines. Some of the programmed printed materials or software that are used in education are also teacher substitutes.

The teaching act may include a variety of activities such as explaining, guiding, showing, demonstrating, clarifying, drawing analogies to show the relationship between an unknown concept and a known one, and/or asking clarifying questions. Other synonyms for teaching might include leading, directing, or telling. The act of teaching is helping the learner to be able to do something as the result of the teacher's acts. As a result of teaching, something is known or understood, or the learner is able to do something. Teaching implies systematic and direct instruction to develop a particular faculty or skill. The teaching aspect of the Direct Instruction Model includes the following:

Introduce the Lesson.   The teacher lets students know what is to be learned in the lesson and relates the lesson to the students' background knowledge and/or prior learnings.

Instruction.   The teacher explains and models whatever is to be taught (specific steps are given in Chapter 7 for specific skill modeling procedures). Many times teachers do more than one kind of activity as a part of the modeling act. A teacher might show a student how to divide words into syllables at the same time the teacher is telling the student about the process that is being used to divide the word.

Guided Practice.   The teacher has students participate in doing that which was just modeled by the teacher. Guided practice is under teacher direction and provides immediate corrective feedback to the students. Corrective feedback means that the teacher lets the students know whether they were right or wrong in their responses. If students are having difficulty, the teacher reteaches on the spot or at the beginning of the next lesson.

Summary.   The teacher gets the students to verbalize what has been learned, and a discussion of when and how it is to be used follows. When students have difficulty with verbalizing a summary, reteaching and review will be necessary immediately or in future lessons.

Often it is necessary for teachers to reteach or review the same lesson or skill, using these same elements, over an extended period of time. Many students do not learn the lesson the first time it is presented; repetition is essential to learning. In a DRL, direct teaching takes place twice; once in skill development when a comprehension, word recognition, or study skill is taught, and again when the vocabulary is taught.

Practice

What is practice?

During this phase of Direct Instruction, the students practice alone. An independent practice activity is one directly drawing attention to exactly the same skill or process that has just been taught. Different types of practice activities include matching, multiple choice, fill-in-the-blank, or manipulative and gaming-type activities. Practice emphasizes the skill or process with much direct work on that particular skill or process. The major emphasis of the instruction has shifted from the teacher to the student. Sometimes the practice leads to mastery; other times it leads to continued growth in using the skill or process.

Many of the comprehension skills and processes require continuing practice. Recall the earlier discussion in Chapter 3 related to factors affecting a reader's ability to comprehend, and it becomes clear that many of the other factors related to this ability continue to grow, such as language and experience. As a reader matures, the basic elements of comprehension are learned, but the reader must continue to understand, infer, and evaluate what has been read in the light of new sources of information that exist because of broader language and experience background. A young reader may find materials being read very difficult, or the reader may not be interested in the material being read. As the reader matures, and understands more concepts, that same material may become less difficult and/or more interesting. In these senses, comprehension, even though practiced all along the path of becoming an able reader, must continue to be practiced at higher levels during all of one's life.

A teacher should expect students to learn a number of sight words. These words would have been taught in separate lessons over a period of time. Each time new words were taught, they were also practiced. This kind of practice aims toward a time when no more practice will be needed; the student will know the words every time they are encountered. The words are mastered. Some students seem to know words from today's lesson today, but tomorrow, they have forgotten them. Practice, in this case, is not yet completed, and it is necessary for the teacher to reteach or to give additional guided and/or independent practice with the words until such time as they are truly remembered over time. The connotation of completed practice should not be one where mastery would be expected in one lesson. Most skills and processes of reading need intense practice for a fairly long period of time before they are permanently learned. The initial practice activities need guidance from the teacher as a part of teaching; later practice may be completed independently by the learner.

In the DRL, the independent practice phase of the Direct Instruction Model should occur twice; once in practicing the skill or process and again in practicing the vocabulary. Notice that guided practice takes place during the teaching phase of direct instruction while independent practice forms the second phase of the model.

Apply

Application occurs when the student is given the opportunity to use the skill that has been taught and practiced in a *new* situation. Application is reading words, sentences, or longer text, depending on what skill or process is being applied. This application should be in the real world of reading. In other words, the student should apply what has been taught and what has been practiced in contextual reading rather than in isolation. In order to account for metacognitive development as described in Chapter 3, there should be a reminder from the teacher of the process or skill to be applied. This is especially true when working with beginning readers and those who are experiencing difficulty with reading. Opportunities to use the reading skill should be amply included in a paragraph, story, or book to be read where the student is expected to use the skill or process under consideration. The learner should see the purpose and the use of the skill or process, and how proficiency or continued growth in the skill will be helpful in the long-range goals of reading, whether it is to decode a word, understand a main idea, outline a chapter, or any other skill or process that has been taught.

While learning to read, application is guided by the teacher. During this phase of the lesson, the teacher should ask the students questions to help guide them in their use of the skill as they read. These questions are comprehension questions related to the content of the story where it is necessary for the reader to use the new skill or process. Mature readers make their own decisions related to the appropriate times for utilizing the skills they possess. This is called independent application as opposed to earlier guided application when the teacher helped the reader know how and/or when to use a particular skill or process.

Mastery.   The Direct Instruction Model in some ways infers that, for most learners, there comes a time when the particular skills or process can be appropriately applied and that no additional work on that particular skill or process seems necessary or desirable. This concept is frequently referred to as the *mastery* of a skill. As the Direct Instruction Model is used, many teachers will find that it is necessary to teach most skills or processes more than once because the students do not completely understand the skill or process taught, or they cannot apply it independently. Such teachers are attempting to have their students master a particular skill or process before teaching emphasis on that skill has ceased.

Many educators use the term mastery to mean that a skill has been learned to a certain level; for example, 90 percent accuracy. Materials that have been mastered at a specified level will not usually be retained at that level unless used frequently by the learner. Because a student masters a skill or process during a given group of lessons does not mean that mastery will necessarily be retained unless there are opportunities for the student to continue to use the skill or process. This is one of the reasons for skill review. In the Direct Instruction Model, teach might become reteach or review in some lessons. The following discussion presents an explanation of each of the four parts of the DRL and explains their relationship to the Direct Instruction Model.

THE DRL AND DIRECT INSTRUCTION

Skill Development

How does the Direct Instruction Model fit into the skill development phase of a DRL?

In the skill development phase of the DRL, students are taught any of the reading skills and processes of comprehension, word recognition, and/or study skills. When teaching the skills or processes of reading, it is important to present only a small amount of new skill work in any given lesson. For example, only one short vowel sound would be appropriately presented in a given lesson, not all short vowel sounds. Only one blend or digraph, not all blends or digraphs. Most often it is necessary to reteach or review skills and processes that have been presented. For example, a single short vowel sound would probably need several lessons devoted directly to work on that particular sound before a new short vowel should be introduced. After all short vowel sounds had been presented in individual lessons, and retaught as necessary, then and only then would it be appropriate to have a review lesson covering all of the short vowel sounds.

In the skill development phase of a DRL, the teacher would first choose an appropriate skill to be taught. Often the teacher's edition of a basal reader makes several suggestions as to which skill(s) should be taught along with the particular story or selection. It may be necessary for the teacher to select from those suggested skills to be taught, or it may be appropriate for the teacher to work with several skills during this phase of instruction if all of the skills have been taught previously and only need to be reviewed in this particular lesson.

In the process of teaching, the teacher should follow a specific set of steps to accomplish the teaching phase of skill instruction. First, the teacher should *introduce* the lesson, making sure that the students understand what they will learn and why they will need to know it. Next, the teacher should *model* the use of the skill or process, essentially "thinking aloud" for the students as the teacher goes through the steps or processes necessary for the skill. Then, the teacher leads the students through the same process, this time talking them through the process in *guided practice*. Finally, the teacher elicits from the students what has been learned and when it will be useful to them. The final part of the teaching, then, is a *summary* of what has gone on during the lesson. No one set of teaching procedures will be totally successful with every learner; therefore, teachers need to know a variety of teaching procedures that might be used to teach skills. Selected strategies for skill teaching are presented in Chapter 7.

Following the teaching of the reading skill or process, the teacher should prepare one or more independent practice activities that will provide the learner with the opportunity to reinforce that which was taught. The practice should be the exact same skill that was taught. Practice should require the learner to repeatedly do that that was taught. The practice activities might be workbook pages, ditto-page activities, games, puzzles, or other manipulative activities. Suggested types of practice activities are listed in Appendix B as well as in teachers' editions of basal readers and books that have been published to provide such ideas.

Whenever possible, the application of the skill or process that has been taught should occur *during* the actual reading of the selection. In many basal reading programs, the materials are coordinated in such a manner that this is possible. The teacher needs to examine the story to ascertain if it will be possible for the students to use the skill as they read. If application is not possible during the guided reading of the lesson selection, then it becomes desirable for the teacher to provide sentences or a paragraph wherein the skill can be applied. The teacher-prepared materials would then be used as the final part of the skill development phase of the DRL. It is, however, much more desirable to have application as a part of reading and discussing the selection, than as a separate component of the skill development part of the DRL. Ideally, all application comes during the third part of the DRL rather than at the conclusion of a single component of the lesson. One notable exception to this is that phonic and structural analysis skills that have been taught should be applied (used) as students are introduced to new vocabulary. A type of guided application should occur wherein the teacher reminds the students to use context, phonic, or structural generalizations previously learned in order to decode the new vocabulary.

Assume for a moment that the skill lessons deals with one sound of *ow*. The skill was taught and practiced. Which of the following groups of sentences would be appropriate for application?

Set A: The cow went down the hill.
How did the cow go down?
The cow went down fast.
Now the cow sits and rests.

Set B: It is time for bed.
Go to bed at nine.
Then you will be rested for school.

Set A contains several *ow* words; therefore, if the student were going to read a story of this type in the basal reader, no separate application would be necessary. If the basal story were the Set B type where there is no opportunity for the application of the *ow* skill taught, then it would be desirable for the teacher to devise a few sentences for application within the skill phase of the lesson. In either case, it would be necessary for the teacher to build a bridge between the teaching and the practice to the application by reminding students of the skill they need to apply, or use, as they read the selection. In the case of the Set A selection, the words *cow, how, down,* and *now* would not have been used in the teaching phase of direct instruction; they would be new to the student when encountered in the selection, but the lesson would have dealt with this particular sound of *ow* with words such as *bow, owl,* or *howl*.

The application step is always preceded by the teacher asking a question that requires attention to be drawn to the skill or process that was taught. This is a *comprehension question*, not a question such as "What words do you see that contain the new sound?" The students read the application material silently and then answer the teacher's question. This may be followed by some additional discussion related to the materials read. In the case of the sentences in Set A, the teacher might ask the student to read to find out what animal this story is about and what the animal did in the story. If the student can read the words *cow* and *down,* and therefore correctly answer the teacher's question, it may be assumed that, at least in this instance, the student could apply the skill that had been taught. In added discussion, the teacher could ask how the cow went down the hill and what the cow did next. This discussion might also be used to check the reader's application of the *ow* skill lesson.

All teaching in the area of reading is designed to make mature readers, not students who are proficient in completing workbook pages or isolated skill activities. If a student is able to perform as a mature reader, separate skill teaching is not necessary. The skills are not an end in themselves, but a means to an end. There is a danger that segmented skill instruction will provide segmented readers who are unable to apply the skills to the real world of reading for pleasure and information. The division of the DRL into a skill section is not intended to put undue emphasis on the teaching of reading skills, but to show the integrated relationship of the reading skill lessons to the total reading lesson. When students are able to use the reading skills without the detailed lessons related to the specific skills, then obviously the skill lessons are no longer necessary since the students are now applying them in the real world of reading. Too much emphasis on skill work can kill the joy of reading. It is important that students be given ample opportunity to use their knowledge of how to read for pleasure and information.

Background and Vocabulary

How do background building and vocabulary development relate to the Direct Instruction Model?

The second phase of the DRL is the part in which teaching efforts are directed to the preparation for reading a story or some piece of material. The vocabulary and background phase of the DRL is the part of the lesson that provides the learner with the necessary readiness for the reading of a particular selection, as discussed in Chapter 2. This part of the DRL includes teaching or reviewing necessary vocabulary (applying word recognition skills when appropriate), practicing that vocabulary, building background for the reading of the selection, and motivation for the reading.

Often it is a good idea to relate the teaching of vocabulary and the background building. As the background is built, necessary vocabulary is introduced, or as the vocabulary is introduced, background is inserted. It is during this part of the DRL that the teacher is attempting to assure that the students have a reasonable chance for success in the given lesson. Most basal manuals provide some suggestions for preparing students to read the selection. Almost all basals indicate what the new vocabulary for the lesson is as well as some suggestions for motivation and background building. Since the authors of basals are not familiar with any particular group of students, it is difficult for them to suggest precisely the necessary vocabulary, background, or motivation for every group of students who will read the selection. For example, the authors would not know if the students were urban or rural. They would not know if vocabulary is new or not since vocabulary listed to be taught in the basal is only new in the sense that it has not been introduced in the particular basal series before this particular point. Conceivably, different groups have had different experiences, and it would be necessary for the teacher to draw from what the particular students have experienced in order to choose vocabulary for instruction, build background, or motivate the students for the particular reading.

Building background is relating known experiences of the students to those topics that will be read. This is the phase of the lesson where the student develops a schema for the selection, as discussed in Chapter 1. For example, assume that the students will read about a dog show; many students have not experienced a dog show. They may have, however, experienced other types of judged contests. In building background, the teacher would lead the students to discuss the kinds of experiences that they have had and relate these experiences to the dog show concept. Some students may have experienced county fairs where items were judged and given blue, red, or white ribbons. This could be related to ribbons given in dog shows. Other children may have watched a beauty contest on television and that experience could be related to the judging of dogs in each classification. This type of background building is topical in nature; in other words, a schema is built about the topic of the selection.

Research evidence has clearly demonstrated the importance of a second type of background development for helping students comprehend selections more effectively (Beck, 1984; Beck, Omanson & McKeown, 1982). For example, the selection may concern the feelings of the main character about fair play in contests or the resultant feelings of winning or losing a contest. Both of these types of background may need to be developed in order to give the reader the broadest schema in which to interpret the selection. The important thing is for the teacher to relate the past experiences of the students to the concepts to be developed in the material to be read.

Motivation is simply causing the students to want to read the material. Although by definition motivation is simple, it is frequently highly complex in an actual classroom. Pictures, art objects, records, or filmstrips can be used to motivate. Sometimes conversation, questions, or discussion will suffice to motivate students. Occasionally the topic of the material itself is sufficient motivation, in which case very little teacher effort would be needed for the lesson. Often background building can be used in conjunction with motivation. For example, sharing a model of an octopus might serve to heighten interest in reading about an octopus as well as show the children what an octopus looks like if they had never seen one. The vocabulary necessary for the reading is very likely the same vocabulary that you would need to use in the discussion about the octopus and its habitat; therefore, there can and should be a blending of these components of the DRL.

Vocabulary development for success in the reading of a particular story or selection is an important part of the DRL. Students vary in their proficiency with vocabulary—some needing more or less work in this area. When students have extensive vocabularies, less emphasis would be placed here; when students are weak in vocabulary, more emphasis would be given. Care should be taken that both pronunciation *and* meaning are clear to the students in this part of the lesson.

A set of specific steps should be used when presenting new vocabulary. The same steps involved in the teaching phase of direct instruction should be used in this part of the DRL. Selected specific strategies to be used in teaching vocabulary are presented in Chapter 8. The new vocabulary should be completely taught, one word at a time, using one of these strategies.

Following the teaching of the new vocabulary, it should be practiced. During practice, students should be able to pronounce the word as well as know the meaning of the word. Practice activities may be pencil and paper tasks, manipulative activities, and/or oral activities with the words taught. Oral activities dealing with the vocabulary words might also take place during the teaching phase of Direct Instruction as part of the guided practice. Then the manipulative activities and paper and pencil tasks might be used as independent practice. Selected practice ideas are presented in Appendix B. Guided practice activities should occur immediately following the teaching of the vocabulary, but independent practice may occur later in the day when the teacher is not directly involved.

The vocabulary to be taught and practiced is chosen because of its importance to the selection to be read. In other words, these vocabulary words come from the selection and are important to the reading of the selection. The words chosen for teaching must relate to the story line, be key concept words, or be a part of the necessary basic sight vocabulary. Therefore, the application of the vocabulary will take place in the reading phase of the DRL. In order for the teacher to ascertain if the students can use the vocabulary that was taught in the actual reading, it is necessary for the teacher to ask the students one or more questions that would require the reading of the new vocabulary words in order to correctly answer the teacher's question. The question(s) asked by the teacher precede silent reading of part of the story where the answer can be found. If students are able to correctly answer the teacher's question(s), then there is some degree of certainty that the reader was able to apply the vocabulary to the real world of reading.

Reading and Discussing the Selection

How is reading the selection related to the Direct Instruction Model, and what is guided reading?

The actual reading of the selection is the body of the DRL. It is the part of the lesson that gives the reader an opportunity to apply or use the skill(s) or processes that were taught and practiced as well as the opportunity to use the vocabulary that was taught and practiced. The background was built in order to enable the reader to have a better understanding or to be better able to comprehend what is read. In a DRL, the reading of the selection should be guided by the teacher in some fashion. Selected techniques for guiding reading are presented in detail in Chapter 9. Almost without exception, the reading of the material should be silent. For this reason this part of a DRL is sometimes called Guided Silent Reading (GSR). Prior to the reading of any selection, the teacher should remind students what to apply while reading in order to help students develop their metacognitive processes.

Guided reading is having the purposes for reading set either by the teacher or by the teacher with assistance from the students, before the reading takes place. Often questions are posed to the reader as a means of giving the reader a purpose for reading. In other words, the reading is to take place in order for the reader to find out something. Purpose questions may be established for varying amounts of material. The less mature the reader, the more frequently the teacher needs to set purposes; conversely, the more mature the reader, the less frequently new purposes for reading must be set. Maturity in this sense refers to the reading ability, not the age of the students. For example, a beginning reader might need to have the teacher set a new purpose for reading almost every sentence, whereas a more mature reader might be able to sustain purpose for the reading of an entire selection. The purpose questions and the following discussion questions asked by the teacher should, at least in part, require the reader to use the skill(s) and vocabulary which have been taught. Some of the discussion questions should also require the students to extend their thinking about the selection. These questions would be both inferential and critical thinking questions.

Except for diagnostic purposes, students should read silently before they read orally. Therefore, during guided reading, the initial reading would be silent. Frequently very young children still read audibly even when asked to read silently. Teachers should not be overly concerned about this practice since the student usually thinks that the reading is silent—at least the reading is personal, and not for an audience. An overemphasis on inaudible silent reading at very low reading levels, or with very young children, may cause the student not to read at all but rather just to look at the page. Teachers should continue to suggest silent reading for students who read audibly and work toward this goal without undue stress. It is important that the teacher demonstrate and explain silent reading to the beginning reader.

In addition to purpose questions and discussion questions, the actual reading of a selection often contains some oral rereading of specific parts of the material. This oral rereading should be purposeful in nature rather than each student taking a turn reading a part of the material aloud while others in the group follow along. The teacher might ask a student to read the part of the selection that describes the sunset, or to read the part that tells how Mother felt when she found out about the accident, or to read the part that proves an answer correct, or for other specific purposes. When oral rereading occurs during the DRL, it is important for others to be listeners rather than attempting to follow along with the oral reading. If the oral reader has been given an opportunity to prepare the reading silently, there is a better chance for accuracy in the oral rereading. If others are expected to listen, they may not notice small errors and may not establish eye movements that coincide with those of the reader. Oral reading is a slower and more exact manner of reading and not a pattern of reading that should be developed by others through following along while another child reads orally. Oral reading should then be for an audience, after an opportunity for the reader to prepare through silent reading, and done to serve a specific stated purpose.

Figure 6-2 summarizes the process of GSR as discussed above. There are other ways of guiding reading that are discussed in Chapter 9 of this text.

What is the teacher's role during GSR?

During GSR, the teacher needs to be available to help students. At low reading levels when purposes are set for very short amounts of material, it is necessary for the teacher to be present to get answers to the questions, set new purposes, lead discussion, and help during silent reading; guided reading occupies the teacher's time. At higher reading levels, the teacher may not need to be present and assisting while the guided reading is occurring. If students are able to retain purposes for reading larger amounts of material, then they may read silently for the established purposes without the teacher's presence. They would reconvene at the end of the silent reading to answer purpose and discussion questions and for possible oral rereading.

FIGURE 6-2
A Model of GSR

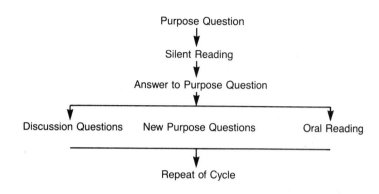

All of the guidance described in relationship to the reading of the selection is intended to lead to more and more independence on the part of the emerging mature reader. As a step in this process, it is important to help students begin to learn to take some of the responsibility for deciding purposes for reading. By middle elementary grades, students should begin to apply study systems in their reading. Teacher guidance would, at that stage, be directed toward helping students learn to survey the material and devise appropriate questions to be answered. As students begin to use their reading skills more in content or subject matter materials, and less in materials designed to teach the basic reading skills (basals), the guidance role of the teacher gives more emphasis to content reading. Sometimes study guides are used as a part of this step in development, where teachers and students work together to decide what questions should be asked and where and how they will be answered. Teachers need to be cautious not to attempt to move students to independence before they are able to read and answer teacher-devised questions with fairly high success.

Almost all basal reading manuals give some suggestions as to the kinds of questions that might be asked as students read. Sometimes there are too few questions suggested; sometimes there are too many. The number and type of questions that any teacher needs to ask during guided reading depends upon the skills and abilities of the students. Because of this, no teacher would be expected necessarily to ask all of the questions, and no others, that are suggested but teachers would be expected to be intelligent consumers of the ideas and suggestions presented in the manual.

Enrichment

What purpose does enrichment serve in a DRL?

The final phase of the DRL is known as the follow-up, appreciation, or enrichment phase of the lesson. It is designed to help build good attitudes toward reading and is an extension of the lesson. It may involve relating songs to what has been read, reading poems or other stories related to the topic of the lesson, or drawing a picture or making a model. This phase of the DRL should be a fun type of activity. It could be as simple as following up the discussion of the selection read or having the students illustrate their favorite part of the selection, or something as complex as a long-term project such as staging a show of some type.

In planning for the enrichment activities of a DRL, teachers should be careful to plan things that students will enjoy. This phase of the lesson should not be more practice work for the skills of reading that have been developed during the lesson but should extend to enrich students' desire to read. There need not always be a new follow-up activity for each DRL when several selections revolve around a central theme; one general or long-term project can be devised to serve as enrichment on a continuing basis for all of the selections. For example, several stories might be about different countries and their lifestyles. As a long-term follow-up for the stories, various students might make something to depict life in each country read about. This project might include a tasting party of foods from one country, dolls dressed to represent native costumes of various countries, or a collection of pictures showing the countryside of the countries. All students in the group would not necessarily work on the same part of the project. Some students might do additional research work in reference materials and bring the results of their findings to a following discussion. Any of the longer-term projects requires planning with the students and some division of the tasks to be completed.

SUMMARY OF DIRECTED READING LESSON

Summarize how the Direct Instruction Model fits into a DRL.

The Directed Reading Lesson and all of its phases are intended to describe all of the parts of a good reading lesson. It could be viewed somewhat as a basic recipe. When one is learning to make bread, it is important to know that most breads contain flour, shortening, and some liquid. After these basic ingredients are known, and something is known about how to combine them, then the cook can experiment with other additions to the basic mixture.

The DRL is somewhat like this: After the basic ingredients are known, and the methods of combining these ingredients are familiar, then variation is possible. Any of the steps for teaching a reading skill, such as sight words, decoding elements, or comprehension, may also be varied after the basic elements are familiar. But, just as with bread, if the basic elements are left out, the result may be something less than desirable.

Examine the chart summarizing the phases of the DRL, noting how the Direct Instruction Model fits into each phase. The DRL is simply a way of putting together all of the elements needed to teach skills and processes and integrate them into the total reading act.

Phase of DRL	Examples	Purposes
I. Skill development	A. Use any word recognition, comprehension, or study skill.	A. **Teach** Introduction, Instruction/Modeling, Guided Practice, Summary **Practice** Independent (**Apply** may also be included.)
II. Vocabulary and background	A. Use steps for teaching vocabulary in written context.	A. **Teach** new vocabulary. **Apply** word recognition skills to decode words.
	B. Play game with new words or do other activity using new words.	B. **Practice** new vocabulary independently.
	C. Present background on story—discuss, use pictures, relate to other events, etc.	C. Develop concepts, build oral language, motivate students.
III. Reading and discussing	A. Set a purpose for reading the story. Adjust to meet needs of individual; the less capable the group, the shorter the amount of material to be covered by each purpose-setting question.	A. Remind students to apply. Set purpose. Guide by sections if needed; discuss.
	B. Discuss after portions of the selection have been read silently and after the entire selection is read. Orally reread periodically during GSR or following it.	B. Check purposes. Check application. Extend understanding. Summarize skill and vocabulary use.
IV. Enrichment	A. Fun-type activities for building language or extending concepts developed in the story.	A. Build interests and develop creativity.
	B. Let students have a pleasant experience with their reading.	B. Extend concepts.

PRACTICE EXERCISE

Directions

This series of exercises is designed to help you practice and check your knowledge of the DRL. Complete each exercise; then check your answers with those in the Answer Key at the end of the text.

Part I

Match the activities listed in column A with parts of the DRL with which that activity would be most closely associated, listed in column B.

Column A

_____ 1. asking purpose questions

_____ 2. concepts for selection

_____ 3. teaching words

_____ 4. discussing the selection

_____ 5. reading a poem

_____ 6. outlining

_____ 7. oral rereading

_____ 8. teaching main ideas

_____ 9. short vowel bingo

_____ 10. making a table display

Column B

a. skill development
b. vocabulary/background
c. reading/discussion
d. enrichment

Part II

Match the activities listed in column A with the parts of the Direct Instruction Model listed in column B.

Column A

_____ 1. guided practice

_____ 2. using the skill or process

_____ 3. modeling

_____ 4. reading the selection

_____ 5. independent practice

_____ 6. introduction

_____ 7. worksheets

_____ 8. summary

_____ 9. games

_____ 10. answering questions about the selection

Column B

a. teach
b. practice
c. apply

Part III

Mark the following questions true (T) or false (F).

_____ 1. A DRL can be used with basal readers.

_____ 2. Modeling is an important part of teaching.

_____ 3. Games for skill practice are a part of enrichment.

_____ 4. The Direct Instruction Model is the same as a DRL.

_____ 5. The Direct Instruction Model takes place twice in a DRL.

_____ 6. Enrichment is designed to extend and broaden concepts of the selection as well as provide vocabulary.

_____ 7. Skills may be applied during the introduction of vocabulary.

_____ 8. Application of skills usually takes place during the skill development phase of DRL.

_____ 9. Good attitudes toward reading are enhanced during enrichment.

_____ 10. Reading and discussing the selection is the body of the DRL.

Part IV

Choose the best answer among the stated possibilities.

1. Guided practice takes place during
   a. teach
   b. practice
   c. apply

2. Students turning a selection that has been read into a play would be involved in which part of the DRL?
   a. skill development
   b. vocabulary and background
   c. reading and discussing the selection
   d. enrichment

3. Bringing a student's prior knowledge and experience into a discussion before reading is important because
   a. it improves comprehension
   b. it helps develop vocabulary
   c. it applies skills
   d. both a and b
   e. all of the above

4. Synonyms for teaching include
   a. showing
   b. telling
   c. demonstrating
   d. guiding
   e. all of the above

5. Practice can be
   a. drill, reinforcement
   b. continuing or terminal
   c. guided
   d. independent
   e. all of the above

7

Strategies for Prereading and Skill Teaching

What will you learn in this chapter?

Now that the Directed Reading Lesson (DRL) has been presented in Chapter 6, it is time to turn attention to the procedures for teaching the specific skills and processes of reading. Teaching the skills and processes of reading is *one* component of the DRL. Teachers need to be careful not to allow the teaching of these skills and processes to become the most important part of the reading lesson by teaching, testing, and evaluating them separately and apart from the overall reading act.

This chapter presents how to teach

1. The prereading skills using informal teaching and direct instruction.
2. Other reading skills and processes (see Chapters 3, 4, and 5) following the Directed Reading Lesson (DRL) model, using direct instruction.

THE DIRECT INSTRUCTION MODEL

What are the parts of direct instruction?

The specific direct teaching strategies included here are not all-inclusive in terms of methodology nor are they for every specific skill or process that can/should be taught. There are other ways to teach all of these areas; however, those strategies chosen for inclusion in this chapter are the ones that we have found to be the most versatile and useful to classroom teachers. No matter which aspect of reading is being developed by the teacher, the Direct Instruction Model, including the following steps, should be used.

Teach

1. Introduction—Explain to the students what they will learn, and the reason they will need to know it.
2. Instruction—Give example, explain, and model.
3. Guided practice—Have students try out what has been taught *with* teacher help and direction, giving corrective feedback.
4. Summary—Help students verbalize what was learned and why they will need to know it.

Practice

Provide an independent activity for students to complete on their own, focusing on what has been taught. This may be a game-type activity or a worksheet.

Apply

Use the skill or process in a real reading situation. Application of reading skills and processes should take place as students actually read the selection, using the skill or process that was learned during direct instruction.

TEACHING PREREADING SKILLS

Which prereading skills can be taught informally? How?

Prereading skills may be taught formally using direct instruction and informally. Informal lessons do not follow specific direct instructional steps; rather the teacher presents ideas and activities and discusses them with the students. Usually informal instruction includes some guided practice for the students that is directly related to the content of the informal lesson. The areas of auditory discrimination, visual discrimination, and directionality will usually be taught *formally*. Developing background of experience and oral language are most often taught *informally*. When informal instruction is used the teacher should still have a specific purpose in mind.

The following sample activities can be used to develop background of experience and oral language with students informally and can be generalized to a number of different situations.

Oral Language Development

In order to develop the oral language of students, it is necessary for them to both speak and listen. In a lesson designed to enhance the oral language development of students, the teacher might plan an informal lesson such as the following.

Sample Informal Oral Language Development Lesson

"Today we are going to learn about a group of foods that are good for us to eat." (Ask several questions such as those below, allowing time for several students to respond and comment. Remember that the purpose of this lesson is to develop oral language in the students.)

"What are your favorite foods?"

"What are some foods that your mother tells you that you should eat?"

"Our bodies are like a machine. They need several things to make them work correctly. One of the things our bodies need to work properly is a balanced diet—or the right foods to eat each day. Today we will talk and listen to each other as we learn about a group of these foods that is called fruits and vegetables. Be sure that you listen carefully to what each person says and try to think of something different that you can say as we talk about fruits and vegetables."

"Who can name a fruit?" Ask students to listen to each other's answers and add names of new fruits that they know. Show eight or ten pictures of fruits, putting them under a written label for that category—use a bulletin board or flannel board for display. Have students tell something about a fruit—how it tastes or what it looks like. Ask students to name some vegetables. Have students listen and add other known vegetables. Show pictures of vegetables and have students repeat the name of the vegetable and give other information about the vegetable such as whether they like it, how they like it prepared, when they like it, when they like to eat it, and/or how and where it grows. Add pictures of vegetables to the bulletin board or flannel board. Tell students that they need to eat at least one food from this group at every meal.

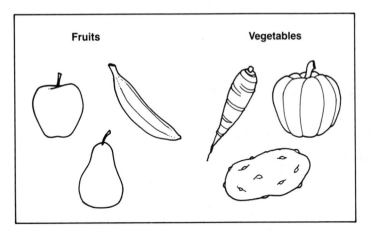

Show other pictures of fruits and vegetables and have students take turns coming before the group to tell what is pictured and one thing about it. Urge other students to listen and add anything they know about each fruit or vegetable as it is discussed. Repeat this process several times with different fruits and vegetables. Be sure to help students as necessary and to correct any mistakes.

Lead the group in a discussion of what they have learned and why they need to know which foods they need to eat each day. Be sure to let each of the students talk and urge others to listen.

Give each student a picture of a fruit or a vegetable and ask each in turn to come to the front of the group and tell something about the pictured food without telling the name of it. Other students try to guess what fruit or vegetable that student has

Sample Informal Oral Language Development Lesson *(continued)*

pictured. Have students paste the pictures on a large sheet of poster board. Display the completed poster on a bulletin board along with a written label, "Fruits and Vegetables That Are Good For Us."

The teacher would have designed this lesson so that the students benefit from learning new vocabulary—the names of the fruits and vegetables used in the lesson. The teacher would want the students' oral language to expand based on the listening and speaking of both the teacher and the other students in the class. The teacher attempts to accomplish this by asking students to respond and to listen to the responses of others in the group and by telling the students things they probably did not already know. Also, the teacher would probably want students to use the knowledge of this food group to improve their own nutrition.

The content of a lesson whose purpose is the development of oral language is not a key issue. Almost any topic could be used. The informal development of oral language might be centered around the reading of a book or story. If this were the case, the teacher would begin by talking to the students about what they know about the topic of the story and telling them to listen for some specific aspect of the story. Then the teacher would read the book or story, explaining unfamiliar words and concepts and showing pictures and discussing aspects of the story as it is read. Perhaps the teacher would ask students to predict what might happen next, remember what happened last, or react to how they might feel if the same thing happened to them. Several students might then be asked to summarize what was learned from the reading. Students might then be directed to complete an activity related to the book or story read. This might be one of many things, such as creative dramatics, an art activity, or a group writing activity. The important thing is for the teacher to have the development of oral language clearly in mind as the activity progresses, always reminding the students to listen carefully to what others say and encouraging each student to participate in the discussion.

There are many activities that can be used in the classroom to help children develop oral language. Many of these are incidental and informal; they do not follow the direct instruction model. Effective development of oral language requires many informal/incidental activities. Routine activities in the classroom that may be used as a lesson specifically designed to develop oral language might include the following:

• *Sharing Time.* Students bring something from home to show the group and are encouraged to tell something about the object they are sharing, like when they got it or where they got it. If students don't volunteer information, teachers should encourage classmates to ask questions or ask the student questions themselves.
• *Action Songs or Finger Plays.* Students participate in a song or rhyme with body movement to fit the words of the song or finger play. The teacher would introduce a song such as "Ten Little Indians" or a finger play such as "Where is Thumbkin?"

giving the students the words, tune, and/or actions, then leading them through the words and motions.

• *Following Oral Directions.* The teacher gives oral directions that one student or the entire group should follow. Games such as "Simon Says" or "May I?" could be used in this type of oral language development lesson. Other "made up" activities where the teacher asks students to listen carefully and do the three or four things in the order they were told might be used, such as: stand up, touch your nose, then turn around twice, and touch your toes. All students listen to the directions, then the teacher calls on one student to follow the directions with others watching to see if directions were followed correctly. If the directions said to put something under something, the word *under* might need to be explained and demonstrated; if directions said to bring the third book from the stack, the word *third* might need to be explained and demonstrated. These explanations would be designed by the teacher to improve the children's understanding of oral language.

Experiential Background

In order to develop students' experiential background, it is necessary to provide experiences for them in the classroom. In Chapter 2, it was pointed out that oral language development is often closely associated with broadening the experience backgrounds of students if sufficient discussion accompanies the experiences. For this reason it is possible for the same types of activities to be used to develop either of these aspects of prereading skills in students. In a lesson designed to broaden experience, the teacher might use essentially the same lesson cited earlier related to fruits and vegetables, emphasizing a different dimension as illustrated below.

Sample Lesson to Build Background Experience Informally

"Today we are going to learn about a kind of food that is good for you to eat at every meal. I expect that you already know about some of this type of food. The group of foods that we will learn about today is called fruits and vegetables. We should eat a fruit or a vegetable at each meal. As we learn about this group of foods, we will look at some of them and taste some of them. Try to remember the name of each one that we talk about during the lesson."

"Tell me the names of some fruits that you eat." (Allow students to respond.) "Today I have brought several fruits for us to look at, learn about, and taste." (Show first fruit.) "This fruit is called an avocado. It grows in very warm climates where there is no snow and no freezing temperatures." Show possible areas of growth on a map. Continue to explain by adding that it grows on a tree. Show a picture of avocado growing on a tree and discuss it. "There are several kinds of avocado and their size and the texture of their skin varies, depending upon where they are grown." Continue with other information that would interest the students about the avocado including how it is eaten or what it might be eaten with. Have the students feel the skin of more than one type of avocado if possible. Ultimately, peel the avocado with the students watching, cut it open and discuss the large seed, then let the students taste the fruit. This process can then be repeated with another fruit that the students are unlikely to

Sample Lesson to Build Background Experience Informally *(continued)*

know, then repeated with one or two vegetables. It may not be necessary to use unusual fruits and vegetables with young children. Many ordinary fruits and vegetables are unknown to them.

Next, the teacher might have students classify a group of pictures of foods into "fruits and vegetables" and "not fruits and vegetables." Taking turns, let one member of the group come to the front to complete the classification for one picture while others watch. Be sure to help children as necessary and reteach when errors occur.

Encourage the students to state that they need to eat one fruit or vegetable at each meal for good health. Review the names of the fruits and vegetables learned in this lesson and some other fruits and vegetables. Remember that the purpose of this lesson was to allow students to broaden their experiential knowledge of fruits and vegetables; therefore, the teacher would like for the students to know about some *new* fruits and vegetables as a result of this lesson.

The teacher might have the students draw a picture of the new fruit or vegetable that they liked best when they tasted it during this lesson. The teacher might move from student to student and write a sentence on each drawing stating the student's name and what they liked such as, "Angie liked the artichoke." These drawings might be used on a bulletin board or taken home.

There are many activities that can be used in the classroom to help children broaden their background of experience. These activities might be related to any content area in the curriculum. When teachers design lessons where students participate and get direct or indirect experience, the background of knowledge of the students grows. Informal activities that can be used to expand the experience background of students would include such lessons as:

• *Art.* Students could be taught what the primary colors are and then participate in an activity where they would mix primary color paints to form the secondary colors. For example, primary colors blue and yellow, when mixed, make the secondary color green. The primary colors of red and yellow, when mixed, make the secondary color orange. The primary colors of blue and red, when mixed, form the secondary color purple.

• *Science.* Students might be asked to bring in objects to form a classroom collection such as rocks or leaves. These objects could be examined under a magnifying glass, located in reference books, described, and labeled to give the students more knowledge concerning the collection that was assembled.

• *Social studies.* The teacher might plan for the students to know more about a particular community helper. For example, the mail comes to most schools every day; therefore, it would be easy for the teacher to have this community helper visit the classroom and talk to the students about the job. The teacher might plan in advance with the students concerning questions that they might ask. This broadens students' background knowledge.

Which prereading skills are taught formally? How?

The remaining areas of prereading skills can and should be taught formally using direct instruction. The following lesson in auditory discrimination is an example that can be followed in developing lessons in the areas of visual discrimination and directionality.

Auditory Discrimination

Students need to develop a keen ability to auditorily discriminate the sounds of our language in order to be successful in learning phonics. As part of prereading skill development, auditory discrimination lessons related to the sounds of the letters are important. This type of prereading lesson can and should be taught formally using direct instruction.

Sample Formal Auditory Discrimination Lesson

Teach
Introduction. "Look at this picture." Show a picture of a monkey. Ask the students to name the picture, then show some money and ask what it is. Continue to show pictures or objects that begin with the letter *m* for two or three more times. Then tell the students that they will be learning about the sound at the beginning of these things; this will help them learn how to pronounce words.

Instruction. Say the names of the pictures or objects one after another, such as *map, mud, man, moon, mustard, mop, money,* and *monkey.* Ask the students if they can hear the same sound at the beginning of each of them. Say that *man* and *monkey* both begin with the same sound. (Exaggerate and emphasize the /m/, but do not isolate it since it is easy to distort sounds of consonants in isolation.) Say that *mustard* and *money* begin with the same sound. Tell them that all of the words you have been saying begin with the same sound. Ask them to listen to other words that you will say to tell you if the new word begins like *monkey* and *money.* Show a picture of a *monkey* and *money* that students can refer to as they listen for the sounds in the new words. It is important that a key picture be displayed for each sound taught. Again, the initial sound should be exaggerated slightly, but not isolated. Proceed to say such words as *milk, map, kite, mop, marker, pop,* and so forth, always pointing to picture(s) and asking after each word if it begins like *monkey* and *money.* Be sure to tell the students the correct answer each time. Do this by saying something like "Yes, *milk* begins like *monkey* and *money,*" or "No, *kite* does not begin like *monkey* and *money,*" always emphasizing the targeted sound.

Guided Practice. Have each student respond individually to a new list of words as to whether or not it begins like *monkey* and *money* by touching their noses if it does begin the same way and touching their ears if it does not begin the same way as *monkey* and *money.* Say such words as *mail, mud, mush, sand, material, magic, marvel, me, chair, mug, more, meal,* and so forth. Match each student's response and give corrective feedback as needed. Reteach as necessary.

Summary. Guide the students to verbalize what was learned in the lesson and to give example words that begin with the same sound as *monkey* and *money.* Students should say something like "*Mop* and *milk* begin the same way, and that's what we learned today."

Practice
Give the students a worksheet filled with pictures, most of which begin with *m.* Have each picture named to assure correct identification of the pictures. Have the

Sample Formal Auditory Discrimination Lesson *(continued)*

students color all of the pictures that begin with the same sound as the one heard at the beginning of *monkey*. Reteach as necessary.

Apply
Full application of this skill comes as formal instruction in phonics is begun. Association of the letter name with its sound is the first step in this application process and should be begun when most students can correctly discriminate sounds of several letters.

TEACHING COMPREHENSION SKILLS AND PROCESSES

When teaching any of the comprehension skills and processes, direct instruction should be used. The steps are outlined in Figure 7-1.

FIGURE 7-1
Steps in Teaching Comprehension

Steps	Explanation
Teach	
Step 1: Introduction	Explain the skill or process in terms of concepts already known to the students. Teacher tells students what will be learned and relates it to prior experience.
Step 2: Instruction (Modeling)	
Concept	Tell students how and when to use the skill or process. Use concrete examples from their experience background.
Listening	Students are reminded to use the skill or process as they listen to the teacher read a short selection aloud.
Reading	Teacher models the use of the skill or process with a short selection. The teacher involves students in a second demonstration of the use of the skill or process.
Step 3: Guided Practice	Students are given a reading activity using the skill or process under the teacher's direct supervision. Corrective feedback and/or reteaching is provided as needed.
Step 4: Summary	Students are required to verbally summarize what has been learned and when to use it.
Practice	Students complete an independent activity using what has been learned.
Apply	Students read text and use what was taught.

EXPLANATION OF STEPS IN TEACHING COMPREHENSION

Teach

What are steps for teaching comprehension skills and processes?

Introduction.   Explain what is to be learned or reviewed and when it is needed. Relate what is to be learned to students' prior knowledge. It is not necessary for the skill to be named, but students should understand what they are to learn.

Instruction.   (Modeling). Develop the concept of the skill using students' prior knowledge and specific examples. Next, require the use of the skill at the listening level of comprehension where the teacher reads aloud and students listen to answer questions related to the use of the skill. The teacher tells the students what to listen for *before* reading to them. After the reading, students discuss with the teacher how they knew the answers to the questions when they were listening. Then model the skill employing reading by using printed material. It is important for the material used for modeling the comprehension skill or process to be reasonably easy for the students to read. In the modeling process, the teacher verbally points out where and how answers were found and what the thought processes were for locating the answer. It is the verbalization of the thought processes that is of major importance in the modeling process. After the teacher verbalizes the process, the students should try to do it also with another short passage.

Guided Practice.   With another easy-to-read piece of material, the teacher has student(s) talk through the use of the skill or process while the teacher questions and guides. Corrective feedback and reteaching are provided freely during this process.

Summary.   The teacher should not tell what was learned, but should elicit what was learned *from the students* by asking summarizing questions as necessary. This step is important in helping students internalize what they have learned and important to their metacognitive development.

Practice

Provide a worksheet or activity for students related to the use of the skill or process for them to complete independently. Reteach if results indicate the need.

Apply

Require the students to use the skill or process in reading a selection. Reteach as necessary.

Comprehension skills and processes should be systematically taught as a part of a reading program. The steps outlined above in direct instruction are designed to present a basic pattern for teaching comprehension. These basic steps can be generalized for use with any of the skills or processes of comprehension even though the example given below is for only one skill.

Sample Comprehension Lesson—Topic of Paragraph

Teach

Introduction. "Today we will learn to identify the topic of a paragraph. The topic of the paragraph is somewhat like a very brief summary of a paragraph; it tells, in a few words, what the entire paragraph is about. Do you remember the news clipping that we read this morning? The topic of that short article was what to do if a tornado is nearby."

Instruction (Modeling)

• *Concept.* "Who can tell me how dogs, cats, cows, and horses are all alike? Yes, they are all animals. What about apples, oranges, peaches, and pears? Good, they are all fruits. Name a group of vegetables please. We have been thinking about how things can be a part of a larger group of things. Today as we read, I want you to see how the bits of information can be put together to come up with an overall topic, just as we have been doing with fruits, vegetables, and animals." (Depending on the level of the students, higher level concepts should be used in this phase of direct instruction.)

• *Listening.* "Listen to this paragraph that I will read. Think about what one topic all of the bits of information fit under. I will ask you to tell me when I finish reading it."

Some people like to play baseball. Others like to go bowling. In winter, basketball is a favorite activity for some people. Skiing is also popular in winter. Many people enjoy swimming and jogging.

"First, let's think about the bits of information. This paragraph talks about what specific things?" (baseball, bowling, basketball, skiing, swimming, and jogging) "What topic would all of these fit under?" (Get response and correct by rereading, as necessary.)

• Reading. "Now let's look at a paragraph and see how to find the bits of information so that we can come up with the overall topic. Read this paragraph silently as I read it aloud."

Whenever I want a hamburger there are several places that I can go for one. Wendy's has hamburgers with lettuce and tomato. McDonald's has hamburgers with cheese. Burger King cooks its hamburgers on charcoal. Kettle Jo has hamburgers that taste homemade but are ready in a flash. No matter which place I choose, my hamburger is always delicious.

"First, let's locate the bits of information." Lead students and point to each of the bits of information—the names of the hamburger places and how the hamburgers are prepared. Underline the points. Talk about and explain how the topic is ascertained. Talk out loud as you do this. Then ask how all of the places are alike. Show them that in this example the overall topic is not stated. Be sure to make it clear to the students that sometimes the reader must come up with a topic that is not written in the paragraph, and sometimes the overall topic is written. Stress the thought processes used in coming up with the topic. Next, provide another paragraph where the teacher leads the students through the process with the students doing the modeling, pointing out, underlining, and explaining of their thought processes.

Guided Practice. Pair students and provide each pair with another simple paragraph where the topic is not stated. Go through the same process as described in instruction, only this time the pairs of students do the talking and pointing out, coming up with the overall topic. Listen carefully as partners share with the group. Correct as necessary. Provide a second paragraph for all of the students that offers choices for answers. Help them read the paragraph and choose the correct topic. Provide guidance and reteaching as needed.

Summary. Lead students to state what has been learned in this lesson and when

Sample Comprehension Lesson—Topic of Paragraph *(continued)*

to use it. Help them to state that they should look for the points of information in the paragraph, then think about how these points are related.

Practice

Develop a game or activity that requires the students to read short paragraphs and come up with the topic of the paragraph in order to move spaces on a game board or to gain points. Have the students work on the game or activity in small groups. For example:

Students are divided into teams. Each team is given a stack of fifteen 3″ × 5″ cards. Each card contains a paragraph and three choices of topic. The team is to choose the correct topic for the given paragraph. (Correct answers may be provided to the opposing team for checking.) If the answer is correct, the team scores points or moves ahead on a game board.

Worksheets may also be used as a part of a practice activity. Teachers should be careful not to assign too many worksheets and to be sure to provide corrective feedback following independent practice.

Apply

As students read their texts or basals following this lesson, be sure to require them to come up with topics for paragraphs, subsections, and the entire selection. They must use the skill in a real reading assignment. This normally occurs in the Reading and Discussion part of the DRL.

This same model for instruction should be used in the teaching and reteaching of any comprehension skill or process. Ideas for practice activities can often be located in the manuals of basal readers. Also, there are many books published that give teachers very specific ideas for use in practice activities. Many computer programs also exist that claim to provide students with practice in the area of comprehension. Several versatile ideas are presented in Appendix B of this text. It is important that the activities used match the skill or process that was taught.

Application has two levels—guided and independent. In most lessons taught in the elementary school, many students will need to have the application of a skill or process guided during the reading lesson. Independent application probably comes after readers mature and have left formal instruction in reading.

TEACHING DECODING SKILLS

How are decoding skills taught?

The two areas of word recognition that are sometimes referred to as the decoding skills are phonics and structural analysis. This section will focus on the steps of direct instruction when teaching new phonic or structural elements that a student will later use to analyze unknown words. Any phonic or structural element can be taught using the steps outlined here. In other words, when teaching beginning consonant sounds, blends, digraphs, short vowels, long vowels, compound words, affixes, or any other phonic or structural element, these are the steps that should be completed in the teaching phase of direct instruction. Figure 7-2 outlines the steps in teaching decoding.

FIGURE 7-2
Steps in Teaching Decoding

Steps	Explanation
Teach	
Step 1: Introduction	Explain what will be learned and how it will help them say unknown words.
Step 2: Instruction	
Auditory Identification	Present the element to be learned in several example words. Ask students to listen for something that is the same in each word and where it is heard.
Auditory Discrimination	Read pairs of words telling student when words contain the element and when they do not. Continue to read words asking students to tell when the words have the element and when they do not.
Sound/Symbol Association	Write words containing the element, underlining the written representation of the element.
Step 3: Guided Practice	Students put the element to use to pronounce new words with teacher guidance. The lesson element is substituted into known words to form new words.
Step 4: Summary	The teacher elicits from the students a summary of what has been learned and when to use it. Sometimes this is a generalization.
Practice	Students are given a game or worksheet activity to use independently that is directly related to what was taught.
Apply	Students are expected to use the newly learned skill to unlock unknown words.

EXPLANATION OF STEPS IN TEACHING DECODING

Teach

Introduction.   Explain to the students that in this lesson they will learn about a vowel sound, an affix, or whatever the element of the lesson will be. Emphasize that the students will need to use this skill to aid in the pronunciation of words they don't know.

Instruction.   Teach the skill using the following steps.

• *Auditory Identification.* In this step the element being taught is presented in several words. In phonics, this oral work should be with the element contained in words since many phonic sounds, especially consonants, are distorted in isolation. Students are asked to tell what element they hear that is the same in all of the words. Discuss where the element is heard (beginning, end, middle). Use these words as examples in later aspects of instruction.

• *Auditory Discrimination.* Read parts of words such as those listed below, telling students which words have the element and which ones do not contain the element. Then read a fairly long list of words, most of which contain the element, stopping to ask after each word if it contains the same element that the example words contained. If necessary to aid in the discrimination process, say an example word after each word on the list. Next, continue to develop auditory discrimination by saying pairs of words, asking if both of the words in the pair contain the element, or if just one of the words contains the element (if so, which word) or if neither of the words contains the element. The teacher can be more certain that the child does hear the element if the student can tell not only when the word has the element, but also when the word does not contain the element.

Phonics

Teacher says, "*ball-bat,*" then tells the students that the words begin the same.

Teacher says, "*ball-sun,*" then tells the students that the words do not begin the same.

Structure

Teacher says, "*rewind-reword,*" then tells the students that they have the same prefix.

Teacher says, "*Remake-unhappy,*" then tells the students that they do not have the same prefix.

• *Sound/Symbol Association.* In this step students learn to match the element being taught with the printed representation of that element. In phonics this is also referred to as phoneme-grapheme correspondence. In structural analysis, it would be necessary for the child to be able to match the prefix or suffix heard with the printed unit that represents the element heard. For compound words, the student would need to be able to see the two words that have been heard in Step 2, or in contractions, to be able to see the contracted form that has been heard. In the first two parts of the instruction, the students have learned to discriminate the sound or element from other sounds or elements; in this part students learn the symbol which stands for that sound or element.

Phonics

Teacher says, "*ball,*" and shows the word, pointing to the beginning letter, *b*, and says that this is what the sound you hear looks like in print.

Structure

Teacher says, "*remake,*" pointing to the *re* portion of the word (or underlining it) while saying that this is what *re* looks like. When you see *re* you will make the sound that you hear in *remake*.

Guided Practice.   In this step, the teacher carefully guides the students in using the newly developed skill to unlock the pronunciation of new words, receiving corrective feedback during the process. During guided practice, the teacher guides the students to look at a known word that does not contain the new element and put the new element in the place of an old element to form a new word, giving students help as needed. In this substitution process, the element which is being taught should always be substituted while previously known words are changed, using the new element to make new words or syllables. Substitution may take place in any part of a word or syllable: initial, medial, or final. Single consonants as well as blends or digraphs may be substituted. Students may need much practice with the substitution process. Assume the short *u* sound has been taught. Students already know the words *bat* and *cat*; now the teacher will guide them to take out the *a* and put in the *u* to make the new words *but* and *cut*. In structural analysis, substitution takes away a known element and adds the new element, or adds a new element to a base or root word. Usually the meaning of the new element, or the type of change in meaning that is brought about by the addition of the new element, would be discussed. In the following examples, the first word is a known word, the italicized part of the second word is the element that was taught in the lesson and is being substituted in this step.

Phonics

cat-*b*at; initial substitution, *b*.
cap-c*u*p; vowel substitution, *u*.
top-to*t*; final substitution, *t*.
brick-*sl*ick; blend substitution, *sl*.
that-*ch*at; digraph substitution, *ch*.

Structure

make-*re*make; addition of prefix, *re*.
premake-*un*make; substitution of prefix, *un*.
stops-stopp*ed*; substitution of suffix, *ed*.
into-*on*to; compound word substitution, *on*.

Summary.   In the summarizing step of teaching, the teacher wants the students to verbalize what the lesson was about and when to use the new knowledge. For some elements, after the above steps are completed, it is desirable to help students verbalize a generalization relative to what they have been taught. If the lesson had related to when to expect the soft sound of *c*, then the teacher would want the generalization brought out during the summary of the lesson that *c* is expected to have its soft sound when it is followed by the vowels *e, i,* or *y*. Most often a generalization is an appropriate summary at the conclusion of a decoding lesson dealing with phonics. When the decoding lesson has dealt with structural elements, the generalization may be less appropriate, but often will include discussion of the meaning of the structural element.

Practice

Following the teaching of any decoding skill, there should be independent practice activities provided for the students. This practice can take the form of games, learning centers, and/or worksheets.

Apply

It is necessary to give the students an opportunity to use what has been taught and practiced. Unfortunately, some students can do very well on a phonics test, but do not see any relationship between this knowledge and the unknown word on a printed page. It is important for teachers to remind or guide the students in the application of their decoding knowledge when new vocabulary is taught in the DRL and when they encounter new vocabulary in any reading.

In order to teach the decoding skill lesson for /ar/, a teacher might use direct instruction as follows.

Sample Decoding Skill Lesson—/ar/

Teach

Introduction. "Today we will study the sound of a vowel when it is followed by the letter *r*. You already know the short vowel sounds in usual patterns of words, but you will need to keep a keen eye out for the bossy *r* that we will begin to study today. When *r* follows a vowel, it controls, or changes, the sound that the vowel makes."

Instruction

• *Auditory Identification.* "Listen to these words: *car, barn, art, scarf.* Do you hear anything in these words that is the same sound?" (Students respond yes.) "Tell me where you hear the sound that is the same, is it at the beginning, middle, or end of *car*? Yes, at the end. Listen again, *barn*. Where is it in *barn*? Good, it is in the middle. Where is it in *art*? Super, you hear it at the beginning of *art*. Try *scarf*. Yes, it is in the middle of *scarf*. Try to remember this sound so that you can tell me if it is in the next words that I read."

• *Auditory Discrimination.* "Is the sound that you hear at the beginning of *art* and at the end of *car* in this word? *bark* (response), *farm* (response), *garden* (response), *bear* (response), *park* (response), *pet* (response), *charm* (response)" (continuing with such a list of words until most students respond correctly). Others will need to be retaught from this point on. "Now that you can hear the part of the word that we are learning about, let me show you how this part looks."

• *Sound/Symbol Association.* Write *art* and *car* on the board. Underline or point to the letters *ar*. Tell them that this sound is represented by two letters: the vowel *a* and the letter *r*. Show other words that were read in the previous step and have students come to the board and underline the letters that make the /ar/ sound.

Guided Practice. Write the word *cat* (already known) on the board and erase the *at* and substitute *ar*. Have the students pronounce the new word. Write the word *cat* again, erase the *a* and insert *ar*. Have the students pronounce the new word, helping as necessary. Continue by writing *bat*. Erase the *at*, insert *ar*, and help the students say the new word. Write *him*. Erase the *i* and insert *ar*. Help students pronounce the new word. Continue this process with many other words. The original word should always be a known word. Provide as much help as students need during guided practice. Each time a new word is made, it should be pronounced with attention drawn to the relationship between the sound produced by *ar* and the symbols representing that sound in the new words.

Summary. Get students to verbalize that when the vowel *a* is followed by the letter *r*, it makes a different sound and that sound is the one heard at the beginning of *art* and the end of *car*. Get them to say when they will need to use this knowledge.

Sample Decoding Skill Lesson—/ar/ (continued)

Practice
Students might be given a worksheet where they fill in the blank with words of the *ar* type such as the following:

The children went to the _____ to play. (cart, park)
It is _____ at night. (dark, harm)
It is not good to _____ on walls. (barn, mark)
At the store, we put food in a _____. (park, cart)
A fire might start from a _____ (spark, dark)

Another type of independent practice activity that students might be given would be a game containing *ar* words where they would roll dice and move the number of spaces indicated, saying the words on all the spaces as they moved. Each student would take a turn until the winner reaches the finish.

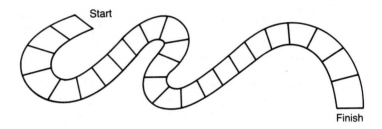

A third type of practice activity might provide some physical involvement as students practice the *ar* decoding skill. Here the teacher might make a floor game where students throw a beanbag on a word, then say it, or where students hop on a word and say it.

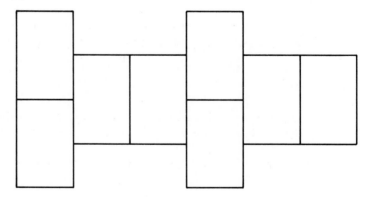

Apply
The application of the decoding skill work should come during the introduction of new vocabulary as a part of a DRL, during the reading and discussion of the selection part of the DRL, and during free reading. For example, if the selection to be read was the one that follows, students would be given an overall purpose for reading the entire selection such as: "Read this story to find out what Tom has and what he does."

Sample Decoding Skill Lesson—/ar/ *(continued)*

Tom is a farmhand. Tom has a farm cart.
A card is on the cart. The card says:

Tom's Eggs
12 for $.50

Tom puts eggs on the cart. Tom runs off to get a tart.
Cats get on the cart. The cats harm the eggs.
Tom runs back to the cart.

Following the reading of this selection, the teacher would ask the students what Tom has and what he does as well as other questions to bring out the students' knowledge of the *ar* words and for general comprehension of the selection. The responses of the students allow the teacher to know whether the students were able to read the *ar* words in the selection.

TEACHING STUDY SKILLS

How are study skills taught?

When study skills are taught, attempts are made to help students learn to organize information, locate information, interpret material, remember what was read, and apply their reading skills in the content areas. Some of the areas of study skills lend themselves to being taught using the same direct instruction steps as were used to teach comprehension skills and processes, namely organizing information, methods of study, and reading in the content areas. Other study skills, namely locating information, interpreting graphic and pictorial material, and adjustment of reading rate, should be taught using the direct instruction steps outlined in Figure 7-3.

EXPLANATION OF STEPS IN TEACHING STUDY SKILLS

Teach

Introduction.   Explain the use and purpose of the study skill being taught, such as the dictionary, a special reference, or how to use a map legend.

Instruction.   Explain *terms* that are related to the skill to be taught, such as guide words, cross reference, or representation. Teach the *skills* necessary for use of the tool, such as the use of guide words on a page of a dictionary, the use of cross references in an index, or the use of a legend on a map. *Model* the use of the specific skill being taught, using real content materials.

Guided Practice.   Guide the students to do exactly the same thing that has just been taught. The teacher should talk students through the use of guide words, cross

FIGURE 7-3
Steps in Teaching Study Skills

Steps	Explanation
Teach	
Step 1: Introduction	Explain to the students how the skill will help them learn.
Step 2: Instruction	
Terms	Explain terms that will be needed to learn the skill.
Skills	Teach the specific skills of using the study tool.
Model	Demonstrate the use of the skill, using appropriate materials.
Step 3: Guided Practice	Lead students through the use of the skill, using appropriate material. Provide corrective feedback and reteach as necessary.
Step 4: Summary	Have students explain what was learned and when to use it.
Practice	Students are given independent work related to the use of the skill.
Apply	Students are expected to use the skill with guidance or independently in completing assigned work.

references, or using the map legend, giving corrective feedback as necessary. Then students should repeat this process, saying what they are doing.

Summary. Have students verbalize what was learned and when they should use it.

Practice

Give students independent work that is directly related to what was taught. Students might record the dictionary page guide words for a list of entry words; think of several words that they might look under in an index to find information concerning five topics; or locate ten items on a map that were identified in the legend.

Apply

The teacher should be sure that students use the newly learned skill in real text reading or for real purposes in the world of learning.

In order to use direct instruction for the study skill of using a card catalog, the lesson might look something like the following.

Sample Study Skills Lesson

Teach

Introduction. "In libraries, there is a card catalog that lists all books contained in the library. On each card in the card catalog, there is information that helps a library user to find the book(s) that are needed. Today we will begin to learn to use this tool of

Sample Study Skills Lesson *(continued)*

locating information in books in the library. You would use this skill to help you find out what books the library has on the topic for which you need information, and where these books are located in the library."

Instruction. "There are several terms that you will need to understand as we talk about card catalogs. First, you may be thinking of a catalog as a book or magazine. As we talk about a card catalog, we will be talking about a cabinet with many small drawers in it. Each drawer is filled with 3″ × 5″ cards, and the outside of the drawer tells what part of the alphabet is contained in that drawer."

"There are three types of cards filed alphabetically in the drawers. One type of card is related to the subject of the book. These cards list the subject at the top of the card and are arranged alphabetically in the card catalog drawers. The second type of card lists the title of the book first on the card. These titles are arranged alphabetically in the card catalog drawers and are mixed in with the subject cards. The third type of card is called an author card. On these cards, the author of the book is listed first, and the cards are alphabetized by the author's last name. These cards are also put into alphabetical order with the title and subject cards. These three types of cards form the card catalog which is arranged alphabetically. On each card there are several bits of information" (show a card).

```
QT6173

.872            SMITH, WILLIAM A.

1981            Space Exploration.

                Merrill Publishing

                Columbus, Ohio  1981

An illustrated history of the exploration of space 1950–1980. pp. 210.
```

"Which type of card do you think this one represents? Yes, it is an author card. The author of this book is Smith. Now, let's look at other information on the card. In the upper left-hand corner you see some numbers. These are known as the call numbers of the book. They tell you where the book is shelved in the library. We will have another lesson another day about how to find the call number on the shelves, and another lesson about the meaning of each part of the call number. For today, we will just learn about what is on the card and how it is useful to a person looking for materials in the card catalog. Under the author's name is another piece of information. Here (point) you see the title of the book—Space Exploration. Following the title, you will see who published the book as well as where and when it was published. The last bit of information is a very brief description of what this book is about and how many pages are in the book. As you can see, the entry in the card catalog tells you many

Sample Study Skills Lesson *(continued)*

things that would help you know if this is a book that you would want to get from the shelves. You could decide if the book is current enough for your purposes, if it covers the period of time in space exploration that you are interested in, and if this is the book by William Smith that you need (he may have written others on different subjects)."

"Let's assume that you have been assigned to write a paper or give a report about the chronology of space exploration. You could have looked up space exploration as the title of the entry on the card catalog, or you could already know that William Smith has written several books on this topic, so you look up his name in the card catalog. In this case, you would have found valuable information. (Have students explain why.) Now you know that you need to find other information that continues this history after 1980." (Ask how this is known.) Proceed to review all parts of the card and why each bit of information is useful.

Guided Practice. Show card catalog cards (some title, some subject, some author) on an overhead projector or on a chart large enough for all to see. Ask a series of questions that they must answer by getting the information from the card, such as:

What is the call number of your book?

Who is the author of your book?

When was your book published?

What is the title of your book?

How many pages are in your book?

What is your book about?

This activity would be oral, with the teacher giving corrective feedback as necessary. A series of such cards could be used during guided practice.

Summary. Ask the students to verbalize what they have learned about the cards in a card catalog. Have them tell why each bit of information is useful and when it is useful to the person trying to find information.

Practice

Provide each student with three cards from a card catalog or have three cards reproduced on a worksheet. Ask a series of questions concerning information contained on the card, such as those used in guided practice:

Who is the author of the book titled _____?
What is the title of the book authored by _____?
When was _____ written?
Which is the most recent book?
What subject did _____ write about?

Another type of practice activity that might follow this lesson could be a similar series of questions on cards. When a student answers a question correctly, points could be awarded, with the student receiving the most points being announced the winner.

Apply

Take the students to the library and have them look up two or three topics in the real card catalog. Remind them to use this skill the next time they have a report to prepare.

CONCLUDING REMARKS

The specific teaching strategies for comprehension, decoding, and study skills described in this chapter are designed for use within the DRL. The Direct Instruction Model repeats twice within the DRL; once in the background and vocabulary section of the lesson and the second time in the skill development phase of the lesson. Normally, the application of reading skills and processes is carried out during the reading and discussion part of the DRL.

There is no one correct way of teaching reading skills. Basic steps, procedures, and elements for teaching reading effectively have been presented.

PRACTICE EXERCISE

Directions

The activities in this exercise are designed to give you an opportunity to check your understanding of the content of this chapter. After completing the exercise, check your answers with those in the Answer Key at the end of the text.

Part I

Identify the skill being developed in each of the following activities and indicate whether it would be a part of teach (T), practice (P), or apply (A). Be prepared to discuss your choices and ask questions to clarify concepts in this material.

1. The teacher writes the following sight words on the board and leads the group in dividing each one into syllables:

   basket
   pencil
   candy

   Skill? _____

   T, P, or A? _____

2. Students are being asked to substitute a word meaning the opposite for the italicized word in the following sentences:

   I will *start* here. _____
   That is a *big* dog. _____
   I *found* a pencil. _____

   Skill? _____

   T, P, or A? _____

3. The teacher introduces the following name on the board for the students to figure out before reading their story:

   Grace

   Skill? _____

   T, P, or A? _____

4. The student must complete the following sentence:

   The brown _____ ran through the woods.

               bare/bear

   Skill? _____

   T, P, or A? _____

5. The following sight words are written on the board. As the student pronounces each word, the teacher notes the silent letters and crosses them (it) out.

knob	dumb	wrong
knee	lamb	wrist
knife	limb	wreck

   Skill? _____

   T, P, or A? _____

6. The group plays a bingo game using synonyms. Each player draws words from a deck of word cards and covers a synonym on his card.

   Skill? _____

   T, P, or A? _____

7. The students are reading silently to answer the teacher's purpose question. In order to answer the question, the student must use a new vocabulary word.

   Skill? _____

   T, P, or A? _____

8. The teacher is guiding the students to understand the different meanings of the italicized word in the following sentences:

   The elephant has a *trunk*.
   The *trunk* of his car is full.
   Mary packed her *trunk*.

   Skill? _____

   T, P, or A? _____

9. The student is preparing an outline for an oral report she is to give in her science class.

   Skill? _____

   T, P, or A? _____

10. The student is in the library gathering material about a topic in which he became interested while watching a TV show.

    Skill? _____

    T, P, or A? _____

11. The teacher writes the following sight words on the board and helps the group make different words by substituting the beginning blend of a word for one of the blends given below:

    stuck   sleep   dream
    st   str   tr

    Skill? _____

    T, P, or A? _____

12. Each child reads sentences like the following and selects the correct word to complete the sentence:

    Bill rolled over and over when he slipped on the _____ football field.

    happy   muddy   automobile

    Skill? _____

    T, P, or A? _____

13. The teacher reads a paragraph from the board after asking the students three factual questions from the selection. As she reads, she underlines the answers to the questions.

    Skill? _____

    T, P, or A? _____

14. The teacher gives the group the following story to read silently. The students are instructed to find out what animal the story is about and which way he faced.

    The Yeast Beast
    The yeast beast ate the least food. As he ate, he faced east.

    Skill? _____

    T, P, or A? _____

Part II

Match items in column A with those in column B. Answers in column B may be used more than once, and column A items may match more than one column B item. Be prepared to discuss your choices.

Column A

_____ 1. substitution

_____ 2. visual discrimination

_____ 3. listening

_____ 4. oral language development

_____ 5. modeling

_____ 6. experience background

_____ 7. introduction

_____ 8. teaching terminology

_____ 9. auditory discrimination

_____ 10. sound/symbol association

Column B

a. formal prereading instruction
b. informal prereading instruction
c. teaching comprehension
d. teaching decoding
e. teaching study skills

Part III

Look at the teaching steps listed below. Decide when the teaching steps would be used and if all steps are included. If steps are not in the correct order, make the appropriate corrections. The first item is completed for you as an example.

1. Auditory identification, auditory discrimination, guided practice, sound/symbol association.

   steps used to teach _____*decoding*_____

   all correct _____*no*_____; errors _____*guided practice*_____

   correction: _____*sound/symbol should come before*_____
   _____*guided practice*_____

2. Introduction, instruction, guided practice, summary.

   steps used in_____

   all correct _____; error _____

   correction: _____

   _____

3. Listening, modeling, concept.

   steps used to teach _____

   all correct _____; error _____

   correction: _____

   _____

4. Terms, skills, guided practice.

   steps used in _____

   all correct _____; error _____

   correction: _____

   _____

5. Teach, practice.

   components of _____

   all correct _____; error _____

   correction: _____

   _____

8

Background and Vocabulary Development

What is this chapter about?

This chapter presents a discussion of what a teacher can do to make certain that the reader is prepared for reading particular materials or selections. The focus is directed to the background and vocabulary development phase of the Directed Reading Lesson (DRL).

This chapter discusses:

1. The importance of background of experiences in a DRL.
2. The teacher's role in developing the reader's background of experiences.
3. Activities that promote the development of background of experiences.
4. Strategies for preteaching vocabulary.
5. Strategies for expanding and enriching vocabulary.
6. The place preteaching vocabulary has in the Direct Instruction Model.

How can one experience a lack of readiness for reading?

When people decide to read a novel for pleasure they probably get the book, sit down, and begin reading. They usually don't wonder if they have the necessary background to read the book nor do they study some of the words used in the novel before reading. Most people assume they are ready to read. If, however, after a few pages of reading, the author's message is unclear, many people would put the novel aside. In this case a lack of readiness for reading the novel has occurred. In other words, the reader may not have the background and vocabulary needed to read the novel.

Students in a classroom usually are not able to put aside an assigned reading because they do not have the appropriate readiness. They are expected to read and understand what they have read. It becomes the teacher's responsibility to assure that students are ready to read the assigned material by attending to the readiness factors that will help students get ready to read. These factors are called background of experiences and vocabulary development.

BACKGROUND OF EXPERIENCES

How does schema relate to reading, and how can background knowledge be developed?

For years classroom teachers have found that unless a reader has some prereading knowledge or understanding of a specific concept(s) presented in a reading selection, the reader's comprehension of that selection will be hampered (Burns, Roe, & Ross, 1984). Researchers have supported this position recently through the development of the schema theory which holds that when comprehending, a reader relates what is read to the preexisting knowledge structure or schemata that reader has (Pearson et al., 1979). Readers of this text may have experienced how a "hole" in their schemata had an adverse effect on comprehension when they read the krashanky story in Chapter 1.

A reader's experience can be a hindrance to that reader's comprehension of a specific selection. Imagine how confused a reader would become whose schema for *period* involved only the dot placed at the end of a sentence and the material to be read was:

> The town grew tremendously in size during the period of 1905–10. This period was followed by one of almost no movement.

Unless the reader's background of experience is expanded to add to the schema of *period*, comprehension will be hindered, if not prevented.

Subject-area teachers encounter this dilemma frequently when dealing with vocabulary having general meanings that differ significantly from the concepts being used in the specific subject area. Classroom teachers are met with lack of comprehension when students are required to read either informational or literary selections encompassing concepts foreign to, or different from, the schemata held. Requiring a third-grade student from a rural area to read about a city tenement district without expansion or building of background could be dooming the reader to failure.

Research has determined that by presenting background information related to a topic to be learned before requiring a reader to read a selection, the reader is helped to comprehend or learn from the selection (Hayes & Tierney, 1982). It is unfortunate, however, that this same research does not provide specific guidelines on how to employ this background development. It therefore becomes the teacher's responsibility to become aware of students' schemata and to devise efficient ways of developing the background the readers need to comprehend the text or reading selection (Burns, Roe, & Ross, 1984).

There is no single technique or activity for developing the appropriate background of experience a reader may need to comprehend a selection. The background to be developed should relate to the key concepts or story line of the specific material to be read. The techniques or activities should be chosen in accordance with the reader's schemata and the nature of the concepts presented in the material to be read. The techniques may be either direct or vicarious in nature and could include any of the following:

1. *Exploring objects related to the concept.* Example: Examine the apparatus for measuring blood pressure (sphygmomanometer).

2. *Examining and discussing pictures that reveal information about the concept(s).* Example: Show pictures of colonists.

3. *Field trips.* Example: Visit a local fire station.

4. *Witnessing demonstrations.* Example: Demonstrate the need for oxygen to maintain fire.

5. *Reviewing movies, slide shows, or other visual media.* Example: Show a movie or slides of animals usually found in a zoo.

6. *Sharing knowledge and experiences through discussion.* Example: Share personal experiences from a trip.

7. *Experiencing analogies.* Example: Blindfold students to develop an awareness of what it is like to be blind.

VOCABULARY DEVELOPMENT

Why is vocabulary development necessary, and how may vocabulary be pretaught? List steps.

It has been a convention for years in the educational community to recommend that students be taught important and relevant words before encountering those words in a reading selection. The correlation between knowledge of vocabulary and reading comprehension is high and has certainly been established (Anderson & Freebody, 1981).

The responsibility a teacher must assume concerning vocabulary development of students involves two areas: preteaching needed vocabulary before a selection is read and expanding and enriching students' vocabularies.

Preteaching Vocabulary

Preteaching vocabulary refers to introducing students to the words they need to know before they can comprehend the selection to be read. Students should recognize and know the meanings of the words as soon as they see them.

Some help in deciding which words to preteach is provided by the material itself. For instance, the manuals accompanying basal readers list those words deemed to be necessary for preteaching; subject-area manuals often list, italicize, or in some way indicate the words the authors consider important for understanding the content. Teachers should be aware, however, that the words denoted by manuals or texts may not be the discrete list of words needed to be pretaught for a particular group of students. Students may already know some of the words suggested for preteaching and/or may not know other words in the selection to be read. An understanding of students' schemata and background of experiences will guide the competent teacher in making appropriate additions or deletions in the list of vocabulary suggested by the manual or text. Four strategies for preteaching vocabulary are discussed next.

Whole Word Strategy.   The following five-step strategy for teaching vocabulary relates to the teaching phase of the instructional model. It is a sequence which would be used to teach words when *no phonic* or *structural analysis* is to be used in the teaching process. It should be used with irregular words, with words for which the rules have not yet been learned, or with students who find phonic or structural analysis difficult.

1. *Show the word to the students in the context of a phrase or sentence.* Point out the word to be taught. Ask if students can read the sentence. If the new word is already known by all students, the meaning used in the reading selection should be discussed and the remaining steps needed not be completed.

2. *Tell the students the word.* Then have a student(s) read the sentence or phrase.

3. *Discuss various meanings of the word with the students.* Include the meaning of the word as it will be used in the reading as well as other common meanings. Structure words in our language such as *of, if, when* and *then* are difficult to define. When this type of word is being taught, have the students use the word correctly in a sentence.

4. *Ask the students to use the word in a sentence orally.* Note if a student essentially parrots the sentence in Step 1; guide the student to make a *new* sentence.

5. *Present the word again in a written context.* A new context is desirable and even more than one may be beneficial. The sentence given in Step 4 may be used.

Figure 8-1 summarizes the steps just given.

FIGURE 8-1
Whole Word Strategy

Step	Example
1. Show word in phrase or sentence. Point out new word.	1. On a 4″ × 6″ card have a phrase written such as: The table was *set*. Underscore or write the word in a different color. Do not read the sentence.
2. Tell word.	2. Pronounce the word and have the sentence read.
3. Discuss meanings.	3. Ask what *set* means. Elicit several meanings of the word: to put or place; a group of subjects; six tennis games. Discuss all meanings needed for the selection and some additional meanings.
4. Use in sentence orally.	4. Have several students orally use the word in a sentence with any meaning. Record the sentences.
5. Read word in a new sentence. Point out new word.	5. Present another sentence using the word; one prepared by the teacher in advance, or one students made and teacher recorded from Step 4. Have the sentence read and the new word pointed out.

Word Analysis Strategy. The following five-step strategy for teaching vocabulary is a sequence that would be used to teach words when *phonic* or *structural analysis is to be used.* The kind of analysis used in Step 2 will depend upon the prior knowledge of the students relative to the skills needed to do the analysis. This sequence should be used whenever possible to assist the students in applying the phonic or structural knowledge at their disposal in attacking a new word.

1. *Present the word to the student in a phrase or sentence.* Do not read the phrase or sentence. The phrase or sentence may be on a card or the chalkboard with the word underscored in a different color or framed by the teacher's hands. Ask if the word is known. If it is already known by all of the students, there is no need for analysis; if it is unknown, proceed with the analysis. Write the word in isolation for analysis.

2. *Use phonics or structure to analyze the word.* Phonics means that individual sounds will be dealt with and *blended* together, not isolated, to form the new word. Analysis might include consonant substitution where the student is reminded of known words that contain most of the needed sounds or reminded of words that rhyme with the new word. If phonic or structural analysis is being used for attacking the new words, the students should *already have been taught* the needed skill. They are now applying that knowledge of phonic or structural elements to attack a new word. This step ends with the pronunciation of the new word.

3. *Direct the students to read the original phrase or sentence.* Discuss the various meanings of the word with the students, including the meaning of the word as used in the reading material and other common meanings of the word. Meanings cannot easily be discussed for the structure words in our language; therefore, discussion of meaning would be replaced with usage of the word in sentences.

4. *Ask the students to use the word in a sentence orally.* Note if the sentences essentially parrot the sentence in Step 1; guide students to make new sentences.

5. *Present the word again in written context.* This may be a new phrase or sentence prepared by the teacher or a student's sentence from Step 4. Underline the word and have the students pronounce it before the new sentence is read. The steps in the word analysis strategy are summarized in Figure 8-2.

Within any given lesson some words might be taught by either the whole word or word analysis strategy. In any case, a given sequence is used with each word individually until all new words have been presented. Each of these sequences is intended to illustrate basic steps for teaching vocabulary.

Dictionary/Glossary Strategy. The strategy for using the dictionary or glossary to teach vocabulary involves the six steps given below. It can be used at all instructional levels when the teacher does not demand specific dictionary skills which the students have not developed, for example, use of diacritical markings.

1. *Show the word in written context.* Mark the word to be taught.

2. *Have the students locate the word in the dictionary.* Phonetic respelling and/or the pronunciation key should be used by the students to pronounce the word. If students do not have the skills necessary to pronounce the word, the teacher should pronounce it.

FIGURE 8-2
Word Analysis Strategy

Step	Example
1. Present word in a phrase or sentence.	1. Put one phrase on card or chalkboard. Point out new word. Rewrite word in isolation for purposes of analysis. Do not read sentence. The sun will *shine*. shine
2. Analyze word.	2. Underscore the *sh*. Remind students that this is the sound heard at the beginning of words like *ship* and *shore*. Then ask who remembers what the final *e* does to the preceding vowel. Mark the *i* long and the *e* silent: *sh īné* Have students pronounce the new word.
3. Read Step 1 sentence and discuss meanings.	3. Point to the original sentence and have it read (probably by different students from the one who pronounced the word). Discuss meanings of *shine* such as to be outstanding and to reflect light.
4. Use word in a sentence orally.	4. Ask students to use the word in other sentences.
5. Read new word in a sentence.	5. Present a new sentence to be read that contains the word. This sentence might be on a card before the lesson begins or written as students make a sentence. Have new word pointed out.

3. *Have the students orally read the sentence or phrase presented in Step 1.*
4. *Have the students read all the meanings given for the word in the dictionary and decide which meaning is the same as the meaning used in the sentence from Step 1.* Discuss how the decision was made.
5. *Ask the students to use the word orally in a sentence, using the meaning indicated in the original sentence.* Students may then use the word in sentences employing the various meanings presented in the dictionary.
6. *Present the word in new sentences and have students read them orally and discuss the appropriate meaning of the new word in each sentence.* The steps in the dictionary/glossary strategy are summarized in Figure 8-3.

Picture Clue Strategy.   A picture is not always worth a thousand words; however, there are instances in which the use of a picture may aid a reader in learning new vocabulary words. Use of picture clues as a strategy for unlocking vocabulary is one of the earliest strategies used by readers. When the only picture on a page is a *ball* and a word is printed beneath it, the reader naturally assumes the word is *ball*. In this case the picture is used to associate the written word to its oral language and meaning counterpart. It is obvious that the best use of the picture clue strategy is in situations when words represent concrete concepts or when the picture cannot be interpreted in different ways.

FIGURE 8-3
Dictionary/Glossary Strategy

Step	Example
1. Present the word in a phrase or sentence.	1. Put the phrase or sentence on the chalkboard or large chart tablet. Example: The *period* was two hours. Point out the new word.
2. Find word in the dictionary.	2. Locate the word and pronounce it.
3. Read the sentence from Step 1.	3. Students read the sentence orally from Step 1.
4. Read all meanings and choose appropriate one.	4. Students read all meanings and choose the one used in the sentence given in Step 1. Discuss reasons for choice.
5. Oral sentences.	5. Students use the word in a sentence employing same meaning as in Step 1. Students then give oral sentences using other meanings of the new word.
6. Read new sentences.	6. Present new sentences with word using the various meanings. Students read sentences orally and discuss the meanings of the new word.

Expanding and Enriching Vocabulary

How can teachers expand and enrich students' vocabularies? List steps.

Competent teachers at all grade levels strive continuously to expand and enrich students' vocabularies. Techniques may focus on the development of new meanings for known words, the relationship of pronounceable units and meanings among words, and word clues provided by titles and graphics in reading selections. The following strategies demonstrate how this can be accomplished.

Adjusting to Context Clues.   This strategy permits the teacher to determine the schemata students have for particular words. The schemata are then expanded to include new and different meanings.

1. *The teacher selects the words to be used.* Words are listed on the chalkboard, overhead projector, or on a pupil handout.
2. *The students and teacher pronounce the words.* Student mispronunciations are corrected. Students give *general* definitions of the words.
3. *The teacher asks a student to pair any two words in the list in an oral sentence.* The sentence is written by the teacher on the chalkboard or overhead projector, verbatim without comment.
4. *Other students pair any two words in the list and give an oral sentence.* Words may be repeated. The procedure continues until all the words have been used in a sentence, until a specified amount of time has passed, or until students produce no more sentences.
5. *The students silently read the selection containing the words.* They are instructed to: (a) underline the vocabulary words, (b) try to determine the contextual meanings of

FIGURE 8-4
Adjusting to Context Clues

Step	Example
1. List important words from reading selection.	1. expiration sentences license validation permit issue clerk period
2. Pronounce words and give general meanings.	2. Teacher and students pronounce words together. Correct mispronunciations. Students give *general* meanings of words.
3. Students pair words to make sentences.	3. Students choose any two words on the list to use in an oral sentence, continuing until all words have been used.
4. Sentences are recorded.	4. Without comment, teacher records the student sentences so students can see them: *Sentences* may end with a *period*. Older students may write their own sentences and share them orally.
5. Silent reading.	5. Students read the selection silently, underline the vocabulary words, and check the meanings of the words in their sentences with the meanings in context: The *clerk's* responsibility was to *issue* certificates which gave *license* to seek a building *permit*. The certificate uses ten *sentences* to explain the *period* of its *validation*. Before his *expiration* the clerk issued 300 permission certificates.
6. Evaluation and modification of sentences.	6. Students note problem sentences and suggest changes. New sentences are made: The license has a one-year *validation period*.
7. Construction of new sentences.	7. Students compose additional sentences such as: *Expiration* can mean death.
8. Record final sentences.	8. Students choose and record the best sentences, using all words in at least one sentence.

the words, and (c) check the accuracy of the words as used in the recorded sentences from Steps 3 and 4.

6. *The teacher has students read selected portions of the selection orally while guiding an evaluation of their recorded sentences from Steps 3 and 4.* The students modify their sentences to match the meaning the vocabulary words have in the reading selection.

7. *The teacher provides the opportunity for new sentences to be composed, recorded, and evaluated.*

8. *Each student records the final accepted sentences.*

The steps in the adjusting to context clues strategy are summarized in Figure 8-4.

Vocabulary Prediction. This strategy enables the teacher to make judgments concerning students' schemata related to the concept(s) in a reading selection and helps the teacher know the appropriate background that needs to be developed. It is often used when the vocabulary words can be suggested by the title and/or such visual aids as pictures, maps, and graphs found in the reading selection.

1. *Students review the title, pictures, and other graphics in the selection they will read.*
2. *Through teacher encouragement, students suggest words they would expect to encounter in the reading.* Record words on the chalkboard.
3. *Students read the selection silently and note whether the words on the predicted list appear.*
4. *Discuss the inclusion and exclusion of words from the predicted list.* Misconceptions concerning concepts are clarified.
5. *Some selections may be read orally by students to confirm the inclusion of words from their predicted list.*

Compare and Contrast.   This strategy focuses on the structure or syllables of words and how they are like parts of other words. To use it students need not be aware of syllabication generalizations but must be able to discriminate among the sounds of beginning, middle, and final syllables of words.

The procedure in using the compare and contrast strategy involves the identification of a vocabulary word by deciding which parts of clue words are joined to form the vocabulary word. The parts of the clue words must be spelled and must sound the same as the parts in the vocabulary word. Thus the italicized letters in the clue words bi*ops*y, *my*self, and tra*gic* can be used to form the vocabulary word *myopic*. The letters of the unknown vocabulary word are represented by blank lines that are filled as students identify the appropriate letters of the clue words.

1. *The teacher selects the vocabulary words and the clue words.*
2. *Students are divided into two teams and game rules are explained.*
   a. The team members take turns asking questions about the vocabulary word; the teacher answers yes or no.
   b. Appropriate questions are:
   Does the word begin like ___(clue word)___ ?
   Does the word have a middle like ___(clue word)___ ?
   Does the word have an ending like ___(clue word)___ ?
   Does the word begin like ___(clue word)___ ends?
   Does the word end like ___(clue word)___ begins?
   c. A "yes" answer enables the team member to try to guess the word.
   d. A "no" answer shifts the turn to a member of the opposing team.
   e. Points for guessing the vocabulary word begin at 10 and decrease by one point for each "no" response from the teacher.
3. *The teacher draws lines on the chalkboard to represent the number of letters in the mystery word.* Clue words are written beneath the vocabulary word. The best clue words would have some relationship to the mystery word.

Example: _ _ _ _ _ _ (myopic)
     biopsy
     myself
     tragic

4. *Students and teacher pronounce the clue words.* Meanings of the clue words may be discussed.

5. *The teams take turns asking appropriate questions* (see Step 2) *about the vocabulary word.*

6. *The teacher records the portion of the vocabulary word* when a player receives a "yes" response to the question asked:

"Does the word begin like 'myself'?" "Yes."

<u>m</u> <u>y</u> _ _ _ _

Steps 5 and 6 are continued until the vocabulary word is pronounced by a team member. Appropriate points are awarded to the team whose member says the vocabulary word.

7. *The winning team garners the highest number of points from all words.*

Variation of this strategy can be made by adding a time element, assigning words to specific students to select the clue words for a game, or supplying the teams with a written part of the word. The strategy can be used with young students by using clue words that have a beginning letter and sound, middle letter and sound, and terminal letter and sound as a three- or four-letter vocabulary word. An example would be:

_ _ _ (dip)
b*i*t
to*p*
*d*ot

DIRECT INSTRUCTION AND VOCABULARY

How is direct instruction used when dealing with vocabulary?

The four vocabulary strategies for preteaching vocabulary presented in this chapter fit into the teach phase of the Direct Instruction Model presented in Chapter 6. Good teaching strategies alone will not ensure that readers have added the new vocabulary to their store of knowledge. Regardless of the choice of teaching strategy or vocabulary, it is important to follow the teaching phase with drill or practice. The amount of practice needed before reading the selection depends on how quickly students retain the words. Some students remember words easily, while others need much repetition. Review is crucial, and words taught one day may well need to be reviewed several times. Practice activities may be game-like, a workbook page, or one of many suggestions offered in the manuals for basal readers.

Following practice, students should be given the opportunity to apply the vocabulary they have learned. Some students can do the practice activities well but do not know the same words when encountered in a reading selection. The application of vocabulary should take place in the reading phase of the DRL. In this phase, the teacher poses questions whose answers require that the students have read the vocabulary taught.

The plan for teaching vocabulary and developing background given in Figure 8-5 is designed for the novice and demonstrates using one of the vocabulary strategies discussed in this chapter. Other strategies could be employed by using the appropriate teach steps along with the practice and application activities.

FIGURE 8-5
Sample Plan: Teaching Vocabulary and Building Background

Steps	Example
Teach	
Step 1: Introduction	Teacher tells students they will learn words that are new in their story for the day.
Step 2: Instruction	1. Show sentence on a card: "I can *catch* a butterfly." Ask if the word is known.
	2. If not, tell word, and have students read the sentence and point out the new word.
	3. Talk about the meanings of *catch* such as to confine, the hook on a dress, and so forth.
	4. Students use *catch* in sentences.
	5. Show students new sentence with *catch*. "You can catch a cold if you are wet." Have the new word pointed out and sentence read.
	6. Repeat procedures 1-5 for new word *net* beginning with the sentence, "The fish is in the *net*."
Step 3: Guided Practice	1. Students match words *net* and *catch* printed on the cards with the same words in sentences used in instruction.
	2. Meanings of the words are discussed as matching occurs.
Practice	Include new words from this lesson along with other known words on a checkerboard. Regular rules of checkers apply for moves except the word must be correctly read before a checker may be placed on a square. New words will be on the checkerboard many times.
Background	Pictures and mounted butterflies are examined and discussed. Students are encouraged to share their knowledge about experience with butterflies.
Reading the Selection	
Apply	Students will read the following story silently to answer the purpose questions: "What did the children have, and what did they do with it?" "The boys and girls like to catch butterflies when the weather is nice. They found a net to help them catch the butterflies. They will make a display of different kinds of butterflies. They will try to find names for each kind."

In most classroom reading lessons, more than two new words would be presented in each lesson. Usually after all words are *taught individually*, all are *practiced together*. The material used for application should also include all the words that were new for the lesson. This would normally be in the reading phase of the DRL.

PRACTICE EXERCISE

Directions
The activities in this exercise are designed to give you an opportunity to check your understanding of the content of this chapter. After completing the exercise, check your answers with those in the Answer Key at the end of the text.

Part I
Match items in column B with those in column A. Column B letters can be used more than once.

Column A	Column B
_____ 1. whole word	a. preteaching vocabulary
_____ 2. compare/contrast	b. expansion/enrichment
_____ 3. vocabulary prediction	c. phonic/structural analysis
_____ 4. word analysis	d. students guess word from the clues
_____ 5. dictionary/glossary	e. teacher records students' sentences
_____ 6. picture clues	f. students select appropriate meaning
_____ 7. adjusting to context clues	g. title, visual aids
_____ 8. building background	h. words introduced in context
	i. words paired in sentences
	j. field trips, demonstrations

Part II
Look at the steps of each strategy below. Name the strategy and then put the steps in the correct order. (Not all steps in each strategy may be presented.)

1. a. Find entry word.
   b. Students create oral sentences for multiple meanings of word.
   c. Teacher presents word in context.
   d. Students choose appropriate meaning of word.

   Strategy _____

   Correct order of steps _____

2. a. Students pair words in sentences.
   b. Teachers/students pronounce words.
   c. Silent reading of selection.
   d. Teacher selects words.
   e. Students modify incorrect sentences.

   Strategy _____

   Correct order of steps _____

3. a. Students use new word in oral sentence.
   b. Teacher shows word in context.
   c. Word meanings are discussed.
   d. Teacher pronounces word.
   e. Students read additional sentences containing new word.

   Strategy _____

   Correct order of steps _____

4. a. Teams are formed and rules are explained.
   b. Teacher selects vocabulary and designs format.
   c. Students ask questions using clue words.

   Strategy _____

   Correct order of steps _____

5. a. Word is presented in context.
   b. Students use word in oral sentence.
   c. Phonic or structural analysis is applied.
   d. Word meanings are discussed.

   Strategy _____

   Correct order of steps _____

6. a. Students read selection silently.
   b. Title and visual aids are reviewed.
   c. Students discuss inclusion/exclusion of words from list in the selection.
   d. Students compile list of words.

   Strategy _____

   Correct order of steps _____

7. a. Students review pictures.
   b. New word is pronounced.

   Strategy _____

   Correct order of steps _____

Part III
Choose the one item in each group that does not belong and state the reason.

1. a. Dictionary
   b. Word analysis
   c. Whole word
   d. Compare and contrast

   _____

2. a. Exploring objects
   b. Reviewing movies, slides and other visual aids
   c. Word presented in context
   d. Experiencing analogies

   _____

3. a. Whole word
   b. Vocabulary prediction
   c. Adjusting to context clues
   d. Compare and contrast

   _____

4. a. Teach steps
   b. Application
   c. Practice activities
   d. Skill building

   _____

Part IV
Circle the *best* answer from the choices given. Be able to defend your choice.

1. A prerequisite skill students must have before a teacher can use the dictionary/ glossary strategy is?
   a. ability to use pronunciation key
   b. knowledge of alphabetizing
   c. ability to read phonetic respellings
   d. all of the above

2. Both preteaching of vocabulary and vocabulary expansion strategies
   a. occur before the Reading Component of the DRL
   b. are used only at intermediate grade levels
   c. are best used with primary grade levels
   d. deal with word meaning

3. Picture clues
   a. should not be overemphasized
   b. are probably best for primary levels
   c. should be emphasized at all grade levels
   d. are one of the best vocabulary strategies

CHAPTER **9**

Reading and Discussing the Selection

What will you learn in this chapter?

The first two phases of the DRL prepare the reader to be successful in reading the selection. Throughout skill development and vocabulary and background building, the teacher is using the first two parts of direct instruction: teaching and practicing.

The third part of direct instruction, applying, takes place during reading and discussing the selection. Application can take place during skill development but usually takes place during the reading of the selection. This chapter presents:

1. The importance of reading and discussing the selection.
2. How to carry out reading and discussing the selection.
3. How to teach students to monitor their comprehension.

IMPORTANCE OF READING AND DISCUSSING THE SELECTION

What are the major purposes for reading and discussing the selection?

Reading and discussing the selection is the keystone of the DRL and of direct instruction because it is here that the teacher provides students an opportunity to apply the processes, skills, vocabulary, and background which they have been developing. Reading and discussing the selection provides students a place to use the processes and skills they have been learning in the reading of *real* or *natural* text. Research and

163

professional opinions in reading instruction clearly document the importance of having students apply what they had been taught in the reading of "real text" (Anderson et al., 1985; Baumann, 1984). Therefore, one of the major reasons for having students read and discuss selections is to provide them with opportunities to apply what they have been taught.

Reading and discussing selections is also important because it helps readers develop their comprehension and provides teachers a place in the lesson to check the readers' abilities to comprehend. The questions teachers ask during this section of the DRL guide the readers' comprehension; the answers students give let the teacher know whether or not they have understood the selection. At the same time, the teacher's questions, if asked appropriately, can help students develop a better understanding of what they are reading (Beck, 1984). The asking of questions is not actually teaching the skills and processes of comprehension. The questions may lead the reader to a better understanding of the specific selection being read and will allow the teacher to check the students' comprehension (Durkin, 1978).

Reading and discussing the selection is also important because it helps readers develop and extend their thinking processes. Reading comprehension and thinking are processes that operate together. Students must learn to read and think critically in order to become effective readers. The development of critical reading/thinking (higher order thinking skills) is important in the process of teaching reading and preparing students to operate within society (Chaffee, 1985). Therefore, during the discussion of a selection, students must be asked some questions that extend their thinking and require them to think critically and creatively.

Developing students' positive attitudes and expanding their interests are important goals of effective reading instruction. Therefore, exposure to high quality literature and exciting content helps achieve this goal. During reading and discussing the selection, students encounter much exciting reading material while further developing their processes and skills of reading. An exciting, lively discussion of a selection can serve as the motivating force to encourage students to read other selections and books on the same or related topics. It should always be remembered that the goal of effective reading instruction is to get students to read beyond their basal reader or other instruction materials. The remainder of this chapter will discuss how to carry out this portion of the DRL.

PREPARATION FOR READING A SELECTION

What three things must the teacher know to prepare for reading the selection?

In preparation for having students read a selection, there are several things a teacher needs to know. First, what skill or process must students apply? During any reading situation, a reader is using many skills and processes simultaneously. However, for the purposes of teaching and using direct instruction, the teacher is usually concerned about checking the application of one skill or process at a time. The skill or process to be checked for application is the one that was taught in the skill development portion of the lesson. It is possible and desirable to have some selections read where students are expected to apply several skills and processes that they have been learning; this is known as cumulative application. Next, the teacher must recall the vocabulary that was taught so that the application can be checked as students read. Finally, the teacher must know whether the selection students are going to read is narrative or expository.

If the selection is narrative, teachers must know the story line and be aware of the setting, characters, problem, action, and resolution. It is very helpful to prepare a map of the story to help clarify these points and see how they are related.

If the selection students are to read is expository, teachers will need to list the main ideas of the selection. The selection should have been read by the teacher before developing vocabulary and background. At this point, the teacher is ready to think about and prepare for reading and discussing the selection.

PATTERNS FOR READING AND DISCUSSING THE SELECTION

What are steps in the first of the two patterns for reading and discussing the selection?

There are two basic patterns for reading and discussing the selection (Cooper, 1986). The first pattern is called *section-by-section* or *page-by-page guided reading*. The second pattern is *whole selection reading*. The pattern that should be used with students will depend on their reading levels and abilities.

Section-by-Section Guided Reading

In section-by-section or page-by-page guided reading, the teacher begins by reminding students of the reading skill or process to apply. This is followed by the teacher giving or developing an overall purpose with students for reading the entire selection. Next, the teacher gives students purposes for reading the first section of the selection. When students have completed their reading, the teacher checks the purpose with the students and directs a discussion of what was read. The teacher then gives another purpose to direct students' reading; after the reading is completed, the teacher checks the purpose and discusses the section. As a part of this discussion, the teacher may have students read orally to prove their answers to questions. This pattern continues until the entire selection is read. At the conclusion of reading the entire selection, the teacher discusses the selection with the students, first checking the overall purpose set. Questions are asked that will help students develop an understanding of the entire selection and to see how the ideas brought out in the section-by-section reading are related to the overall understanding of the selection.

Reminding Students of Skill to Apply.   Reminding students of the skill or process to apply helps to develop students' metacognitive abilities by letting them know what skill or process they will need to use in successfully completing the reading task; having this knowledge is an important part of metacognitive development (Baker & Brown, 1984b). This act of reminding students serves as a bridge between what has been taught and practiced and what is to be applied. For example:

Decoding Reminder

"Yesterday we learned about words that begin like *brick* and *bring* (write words on the board). As you read your selection today remember to use what you know about *br* to help you figure out some of the words in your selection."

Comprehension Reminder

"You have been learning how to use the author's clues and your own experiences to figure out things that are not stated in a selection. As you read this selection today, remember to do this."

Study Skills Reminder

"You have learned how to read a map. As you read this selection, use your map skills to figure out where the old king went on his long journey."

Setting the Overall Purpose.   As students read selections, they need an overall purpose to direct their reading (Pearson, 1982). This purpose should require students to focus their attention on the entire selection and should require them to use inference as much as possible (Pearson, 1984). The purpose that students are given for reading may take the form of a question or may be a statement that guides them to look for something as they read. Following are examples of two different purposes for reading a make-believe story about the adventures of two bears on a camping trip:

Purpose Question

"How do you think the bears felt after they won the prize that the other animals wanted? Why?"

Purpose Statement

"Read the story to tell how you think the bears felt after they won the prize that the other animals wanted."

Notice that the difference in the two examples is simply the form in which the purpose is presented. Both require students to use inference and relate the story to their own experiences. Both require students to focus on the entire selection; they are not purposes that can be achieved by reading only one page.

The setting of the overall purpose for reading the selection should be a natural outgrowth of the vocabulary and background building; one section of the lesson should flow directly into the next. For example, if students read the story about the bears mentioned above, the background development might include a discussion of what it is like to win something that is really important to someone else. As students relate their own experiences to this topic, pull the discussion together by saying:

"In the story you are going to read today, the bears have an adventure like we have been discussing. Read the story to tell how you think the bears felt after winning the prize that the other animals wanted so badly."

At the beginning levels and with less able readers, the teacher must provide students with the overall purpose for reading the selection. However, students should become responsible for setting their own purposes to guide their reading. Therefore, the teacher and students together should begin to set the purpose for reading the selection as soon as possible. This is done by having the students help to formulate a purpose for reading the selection as an extension of the background development. Teaching students to use such strategies as SQ3R will help students learn to set their own purposes for reading.

The overall purpose set to guide students' reading of the selection should be checked in the discussion immediately following the reading. Research evidence indicates that this must be done if the purpose is to be of value in helping readers improve their comprehension of selections (White, 1981).

Questions for Guiding Reading by Sections.   Breaking a selection into sections for reading should be done in locations where the break is natural and makes sense. The length of each section should also be determined by the students' abilities to read and the difficulty of the content. In this pattern of guided reading, the teacher will set a purpose or pose a question for each section, have students read it, and discuss it with students; this pattern is followed until the entire selection is completed.

The guide questions and the discussion questions that teachers should use depend upon the type of selection. If the selection is narrative, the questions used should bring out the story line, including the story's setting, characters, problem, action, and resolution of the problem. If the selection is expository, the main ideas and important supporting details should be brought out by the questions and discussion over the sections read. In both narrative and expository texts, the teacher's questions used in guiding section-by-section reading should follow the order of the story line or main ideas in the selection.

The questions that are used for guiding reading and discussion can also check the application of reading processes and skills. The following examples illustrate how questions might be used to check application of different aspects of reading. Assume that students are reading the following text:

Snowshoe rabbits live where it is very cold. In the winter snows, they change color. Their fur turns white. In the spring and summer they are brown. This helps to save them from many wild animals.

Application Check of Vocabulary

(Assume that the word *change* was pretaught.)
Question: "What happens to the fur of the snowshoe rabbit in winter and summer?" The focus in this question is on the meaning of *change*. Students are applying what they learned about this word.

Application Check of Decoding

(Assume that students have been taught the consonant blend *br.*)
Question: "What color are snowshoe rabbits in spring and summer?" Students use their knowledge of *br* to help decode *brown*.

Application of Comprehension

(Assume that students have been taught to infer.)
Question: "What could happen to snowshoe rabbits if they didn't change colors each season?" Students must apply what they know about making inferences to answer this question.

Why is it important to help students pull the selection together?

Discussion of the Overall Selection.   The discussion following the section-by-section reading should help the teacher and students accomplish five goals:

1. Pull together the ideas presented in the selection.
2. Check the overall purpose that was set for reading.
3. Extend the students' thinking beyond the selection.
4. Check application of the reading skills and processes.
5. Provide for meaningful, natural oral reading.

These purposes should all be achieved through a natural discussion where there is interaction between the students and the teacher.

Since students have been reading the selection in sections, they must be directed in pulling together the big ideas of the selection and seeing how they are related. This can be done very naturally by returning immediately after the reading has been completed to the overall purpose that was set to guide reading of the entire selection. The discussion of this purpose helps the students develop an overall schema of the selection.

The questions that are used in the discussion after silent reading help students extend their thinking about the selection. These questions should require students to infer and think critically and creatively.

Imbedded in the follow-up discussion should be questions that further check application of the reading skills and processes. These questions should be a natural part of the discussion and should show the teacher whether the students are applying reading skills and processes.

The discussion following the guided silent reading is also a natural place to build in meaningful oral reading. Students can be asked to read parts that prove or support their answers to questions or points brought up during discussion.

Throughout guided reading and discussion, it should always be remembered that a major purpose for teaching reading is to help students develop a positive, enthusiastic attitude toward reading. Therefore, this part of the directed reading lesson should not become an interrogation of the student after reading has been completed. The teacher's warmth, enthusiasm, and relaxed manner in directing reading and discussion naturally will help achieve a positive attitude. Carrying out guided reading and discussion in the manner described in this text is a much more effective teaching procedure than using "round-robin" reading where students simply read orally one after another.

When should section-by-section guided reading be used?

When to Use Section-by-Section Guided Reading.   Section-by-section guided reading is the pattern that should be used at the beginning reading levels and with students who are having difficulty learning to read. This systematic type of guidance helps students develop an overall understanding of selections and guides them to building their comprehension skills and processes. It is often necessary to wean students away from this type of guided reading by gradually increasing the length of the sections required for reading. The goal should be to get students to read entire selections as soon as possible but *this should not be rushed.*

Many times, students in the intermediate grades or higher would profit from

FIGURE 9-1

Old Red
Takes a Ride

"I've seen a lot of foxes, Tim. But I've never seen one like Old Red," said Uncle John. "He sure is clever. But just wait. I'll catch him!"

For months Old Red had been taking chickens from the farm. Uncle John set traps. But Old Red never got caught.

"Next time," said Uncle John, "I'll get out the dogs. Those hounds will pick up his scent. And then we will get him."

The next morning Uncle John ran into the house. "Let's go," he said. "Old Red was just here. I'll get my gun. You get the

108

hounds. We have to move fast."

I met Uncle John at the chicken house. The two hounds followed me. Soon they picked up the scent. And they were off!

Across the fields they ran, barking all the way. Uncle John and I couldn't keep up. But the barking told us the way to go. "They're in the woods," I said. "They're heading for the railroad tracks."

109

"And listen," said Uncle John. "Here comes a train."

We ran to the top of a hill. Below us was the train. And there was Old Red.

"He can't get across the tracks!" cried Uncle John. "We have him this time."

Then Old Red showed us just how clever he was. He jumped to a big rock near the tracks. A railroad car piled high with logs was going by. Old Red jumped again. This

110

time he landed right on top of the logs. And away he rode!

We just stood there. Then all at once Uncle John started to laugh. "I guess it's right for that old fox to get away," he said. "He's a clever one, for sure!"

"How long do you think he'll stay on the train, Uncle John?" I asked.

"I don't know," he answered. "But I hope he crosses half the country. I've had enough of that foxy old fox!"

111

Source: From ''Old Red Takes a Ride'' by Archibald Rutledge, *Reader's Digest, New Reading Skill Builders*, Level 2, Part 4 (pp. 108–111). Reprinted with permission from *Reader's Digest, New Reading Skill Builders*, © 1969 by The Reader's Digest Assn., Inc.

section-by-section guided reading and discussion. This is especially true when students are reading expository text with many difficult concepts. Therefore, this procedure should be one that is learned by all teachers, not just those who plan to teach at the primary levels; it should be used in reading instruction as well as when students are reading content texts.

Sample Section-by-Section Guided Reading. Figure 9-1 illustrates section-by-section guided reading using a narrative selection, "Old Red Takes a Ride," that is approximately second-grade reading level. Following the selection is a story map to help you see why the guide questions were asked, the background and vocabulary that would have been developed, and the questions used for guided reading and discussion. As you study this material, notice how the:

1. Students are reminded to apply the reading skills.
2. Overall purpose is set.
3. Guide questions bring out the story line as identified in the story map and check application.
4. Discussion questions check the purpose, pull together the selection, extend thinking, and check application.

Story Map for "Old Red Takes a Ride"

Characters: Tim, Old Red, Uncle John, dogs (hounds)
Setting: Uncle John's Farm
Problem: Uncle John is trying to catch Old Red.
Action: 1. Old Red returns to the chicken house.
2. Uncle John, Tim, and the hounds follow Old Red's scent from the chicken house.
Resolution: Old Red jumps on a train loaded with logs and gets away.
Theme: A fox can outsmart people.

Background and Vocabulary
The following background and vocabulary would have been developed before students read this selection:
Background. Students need to know that foxes are supposed to be very clever and that they often kill and eat chickens and other small animals on farms. If students have no experience with trains and the hauling of logs, this, too, would need to be discussed.
Vocabulary. The following key words would be pretaught as a part of background development for the selection—*hounds, caught, clever, scent,* and *landed.*

Skills to Be Applied
Assume that the comprehension skill of inference has been taught and is to be applied in this selection.

Dialogue for Guided Reading and Discussion
Conclusion of background and vocabulary

Say: "We have been talking about foxes and how sneaky and clever they are. We have learned some words that would help you read about foxes. In today's story, we are going to read about one clever fox, Old Red."

Story Map for "Old Red Takes a Ride" *(continued)*

Reminder to apply skills	*Say:*	"We have learned how to use the clues in our story to figure out what the author means when he doesn't really tell us. As you read your story today, try to use the author's clues to do this."
Lead in to overall purpose for reading	*Say:*	"Open your books to pages 108 and 109. I want someone to read the title." (Student responds.) "Look at the picture. What do you think is happening?" (Students respond.)
Overall purpose	*Say:*	"As you read this story, find out if our prediction was correct and the dogs do catch the fox." (If students don't make this prediction, just give them this as the purpose.)
Begin section-by-section reading	*Say:*	"Now let's read our story. Read the first three paragraphs on page 108 to yourself to find out who is in our story." After students have completed their reading, use the following questions for discussion.

Bringing out characters
Bringing out setting
Bringing out problems
Application of inference

1. Who are the characters in our story today?
2. Where is the story taking place?
3. What is Uncle John trying to do?
4. How do you think Uncle John is going to try to catch Old Red?

These four questions bring out the first three parts of the story map and check application of inference.

Say: "Read to the end of page 109 to find out what happens." After students complete their reading, use the following questions for discussion.

Bringing out the action
Bringing out the action
Checking application of vocabulary
Application of inference

1. What happened?
2. Where did the dogs go?
3. How did the dogs know where to go?

4. What do you think the fox is going to do? Why? These questions are bringing out more of the story line and checking application.

Say: "Read the next two pages to see which of your predictions were correct." After students complete their reading, use the following questions for discussion.

Checking purpose for these two pages
Bringing out resolution

1. Which of your predictions were correct?

2. How did the fox finally get away? The guided reading has brought out the story line and checked application of inference. Now students should discuss the entire selection and extend their thinking.

Checking overall purpose and pulling story together

Say: "When we started to read this story, you predicted that the dogs were going to catch the fox. Were you right? What really happened?" The questions that follow should be used to extend students' thinking about the selection, further check application, and incorporate oral reading.

Story Map for "Old Red Takes a Ride" *(continued)*

Extend thinking and check application of inference	1. Why do you think Uncle John was so concerned about catching the fox?
Extend thinking, check application of inference, oral reading	2. How do you think Uncle John felt when the fox jumped on the train? Read aloud places to prove your answer.
Check application of inference	3. Do you think people are right when they say foxes are clever? Why?
Extend thinking	4. How would you have handled this situation if you had been in Uncle John's place? Why?

Whole Selection Reading

How is whole selection reading different from section-by-section reading, and how is it done?

The second pattern for reading and discussing the selection is whole selection reading. This pattern encompasses many of the features of section-by-section reading but differs primarily in that students read the entire selection without having it broken into parts. In this type of reading the teacher reminds students of the skill or process to apply, guides them in setting an overall purpose for reading, and then has students read the entire selection. It is very important that the purpose focus on the entire selection and require students to infer as much as possible. By having a purpose that is inferential in nature, readers are required to activate and relate more of their experience to the text they are reading.

The discussion after reading helps students bring out the story line or main ideas and extend their thinking. These questions should be asked in an order which brings out the story line or main ideas in the order in which they occur in the selection. This helps the reader in constructing meaning for the selection. The discussion should then focus on extending the students' thinking about the selection by requiring them to infer and think critically and creatively.

Throughout the discussion, questions that check new vocabulary and application of the reading skill or process taught should be asked. These questions can be asked at any point during the discussion as long as they fit naturally into the flow of the discussion. Oral reading can also be incorporated naturally into the discussion by having students read parts from the selection that support their answers.

When should whole selection reading be used?

When to Use Whole Selection Reading. Whole selection reading is usually used in the intermediate grades or with students who are very capable readers. As was noted earlier in this chapter, the goal of reading instruction should be to get students to read the whole selection as soon as possible. Even primary students who are developing their reading ability successfully should occasionally be given opportunities to read the whole selection at one time.

Sample Whole Selection Reading. Figure 9-2 illustrates whole selection reading using an expository selection, "The Builders of the Bridge," that is approximately

FIGURE 9-2

THE BUILDERS OF THE BRIDGE

Edwin Muller   Based upon the book by D. B. Steinman

In 1883 the Brooklyn Bridge was a marvel of engineering. It still is.

WHEN the Brooklyn Bridge was finished in 1883, it was the longest single span ever built. It was the tallest and strongest and the first to use steel cables. Today there are bigger bridges. But they never could have been built had not Brooklyn Bridge showed the way. Its story is still the greatest bridgebuilding story of all.

The best time to see the Bridge is at dawn. From the mists hanging low on the water rise two mighty towers. The four big cables sweep down from the towers in great curves to meet the roadway. The delicate spiderweb of the wire supports holds all together. Although built for strength, the Bridge also is very beautiful.

This great span is the magnificent monument of two men. John A. Roebling dreamed of the bridge and then put his dream into practical plans. Washington Roebling, his son, built it. It is a monument such as few men in all history have had, but it cost them much suffering.

As a young engineering student, John Roebling saw the first suspension bridge built in his native Germany. He was fascinated by the suspension method. He wrote his college graduation paper about this method.

In 1831, at the age of 25, Roebling came from Germany to western Pennsylvania. After

36

37

Portraits from Brown Brothers

John A. Roebling

Washington A. Roebling

Workmen attaching suspenders to the cables, to support the roadway

Culver Service

FIGURE 9-2 *(continued)*

clearing a farm, he worked at building houses and as a surveyor. But in the evening he studied the building of suspension bridges.

One day John Roebling watched some men using heavy hemp rope, three inches in diameter, to haul heavy loads. Suddenly one of the ropes broke. The heavily loaded car crashed down the slope and killed two men.

In a flash, an idea came to John Roebling. If a rope could be made of iron wire that would bend, it would be stronger than a hemp rope four times its diameter. On his farm in Pennsylvania, he made the first wire rope by hand power. This wire rope completely changed bridgebuilding.

Before building Brooklyn Bridge, Mr. Roebling was successful in building other bridges. He built the first railroad suspension bridge in the world over the Gorge at Niagara Falls. He became famous as the nation's greatest bridge-builder.

In 1860, the only way to get from Brooklyn to New York was by ferry. The slow trip often took two hours when there was fog or ice. It seemed impossible to build a bridge across the East River. Such a bridge would have to cross the river in a 1600-foot leap 130 feet above water level. The height was needed so that river shipping could pass underneath.

Mr. Roebling believed that he could build such a bridge. In 1857, he wrote a letter to a New York newspaper suggesting that it was possible. The letter was read and talked about by many people.

Roebling worked on the idea for ten years. At last the government of New York State agreed to it. A private company was to build the bridge. Mr. Roebling was made Chief Engineer.   38

He sent his son Washington Roebling to Europe to study

Culver Service

The Brooklyn Bridge in 1883

FIGURE 9-2 *(continued)*

how men could work under water. Washington learned that they worked under water in big wooden boxes called caissons (KAY-*suns*). The caissons were filled with compressed air (as in auto tires).

On July 6, 1869, John Roebling was at work planning where to place the Brooklyn end of the Bridge—the tower that was to hold the cables. He was so interested in his work that he didn't notice the approaching ferry. The boat bumped into the dock on which Roebling was standing. His foot was badly crushed.

Everything that doctors could do was done to help Mr. Roebling. But the injury was so serious that he soon died. Before his death, he begged the men who were paying for the Bridge to let his son Washington become Chief Engineer. They agreed.

To get a strong foundation for the Bridge, it was necessary to dig 75 feet through soft mud to reach the bottom of the river. Men had to work in caissons. They were deafened by the noise of hammer and drill. The pressure of the compressed air grew greater as the caisson went down inch by inch to reach the hard bottom. It takes hardy men, called "sand hogs," to work in caissons.

Today doctors know about a sickness called "the bends." But when the Bridge was built no one knew the cause of this mysterious illness. It is caused by working under air pressure and then being brought up to the surface too quickly. Two workmen died of the strange sickness. Then young Roebling himself was taken sick with the same painful illness. He did not die, but he never was completely well again.

Knowing that he was very ill, he explained his ideas for the Bridge to his wife, Emily. She learned to give the other engineers his instructions.

Roebling lived near the Bridge and, through field glasses, watched it go up. On August 14, 1876, he saw the first strand of steel wire hung in its graceful curve from tower to tower. There were finally four cables—each having 19 strands of wire. On October 5, 1878, the last wire was run across.

Early on the morning of May 24, 1883, Roebling saw through his field glasses the opening of the Bridge. President Arthur and Governor Cleveland were there. Naval vessels boomed a salute. The men paraded through Brooklyn's streets to the Roebling house. Emily was at her husband's side when they congratulated him.

Roebling never grew strong and well again. But he lived to see his Bridge carry all the traffic of the automobile age. He built well. The Bridge is carrying safely several times the load it was built to carry.

Brooklyn Bridge is more than a bridge of steel and stone. It is a victory of the human spirit.

39

40.

Source: From THE BUILDERS OF THE BRIDGE by D. B. Steinman, copyright 1945 by Harcourt Brace Jovanovich, Inc.; renewed 1973 by Irene Steinman. Reprinted by permission of the publisher. Adaptation from *Reader's Digest, Skill Builders,* Level 5, Part 1 (pp. 36–40), 1959, Pleasantville, N.Y.: The Reader's Digest Assn. Reprinted with permission from Reader's Digest, Skill Builders.

fifth-grade reading level. Following the selection the main ideas are presented and then the same pattern used for "Old Red Takes a Ride" is followed. As you study this material, notice how the:

1. Students are reminded to apply the reading skills.
2. Purpose is set.
3. Discussion after reading focuses on the main ideas.
4. Questions check purpose application and extend thinking.

Main Ideas for "The Builders of the Bridge"

1. The building of the Brooklyn Bridge is the story of a strong and beautiful bridge.
2. John Roebling became interested in suspension bridges as a college student.
3. John Roebling came to the United States and became known as a great bridge builder.
4. John Roebling was hired to build the Brooklyn Bridge.
5. There were many problems building the Brooklyn Bridge:
   —John Roebling died and his son took over.
   —There were problems working under water.
   —Washington Roebling became ill from underwater work.
6. The bridge was finally completed; it still stands as a victory of human spirit.

Background and Vocabulary

The following background and vocabulary would have been developed before students read the selection.

Background. Students need to understand why the building of a suspension bridge was so difficult during the time when the Brooklyn Bridge was built and why accomplishing this was such a feat. The building of this type of bridge could be compared to similar events related to space exploration in today's world.

Vocabulary. The following key words would be pretaught as a part of background development—*suspension, compressed air, the bends.*

Skills to Be Applied

Assume that the following skills have been taught and will be applied in this selection:

Decoding	Using phonetic respellings to determine pronunciation
Comprehension	Using context to determine word meaning
	Identifying the main idea

Dialogue for Guided Reading and Discussion

Conclusion of background and vocabulary	*Say:*	"We have been talking about the building of suspension bridges. Open your books to page 36 and look at the pictures on these pages showing the Brooklyn Bridge which is a suspension bridge. How is the roadway held up?" Students respond.
Reminder to apply skills	*Say:*	"As you read this article today, remember to use what you have learned about phonetic respelling and context to figure out words. Also, use what you have been learning about determining main ideas."

Main Ideas for "The Builders of the Bridge" (continued)

Setting purpose to read entire selection	*Say:* "Open your books to page 40. Read the last paragraph to yourself." Students read silently. "What do you think this means?" Discuss briefly. "Read this selection to find out why the author said the building of the Brooklyn Bridge was a victory of the human spirit." Students read the entire selection. The purpose was set by the students and the teacher together; it requires students to infer, think critically, and focus on the entire selection.
Checking purpose and pulling together the selection	1. Why did the author say that the building of the Brooklyn Bridge was a victory of the human spirit?
	2. How does the author of this article describe the Brooklyn Bridge in terms of appearance and use?
Bringing out the main ideas of the selection and checking application of main idea	3. When and how did John Roebling become interested in suspension bridges?
	4. What is meant by a suspension bridge?
	5. What happened to John Roebling because of his interest in bridges?
Checking application of phonetic respelling and context	6. What problems occurred during the building of the Brooklyn Bridge?
Checking vocabulary	7. What were *the bends*?
	8. How were the men able to work under water?
Checking application of phonetic respelling and context	9. How did people feel about the opening of the Brooklyn Bridge? Read the place that proves your answer.
Extending thinking	10. How do you think the opening of the Brooklyn Bridge changed people's lives? Why?
Checking application of main ideas of paragraphs	11. Reread the first full paragraph in the second column on page 38. What happened to John Roebling?
Checking application of main ideas of paragraphs	12. Reread the last paragraph at the bottom of column one on page 39. What important idea is the author stressing in this paragraph?
Extending thinking	13. How do you suppose people using the Brooklyn Bridge for the first time might have felt? Why?

GUIDED READING VERSUS INDEPENDENT READING

What is the difference between guided reading and independent reading, and how can more independent reading be fostered?

The guided reading that takes place during reading the selection should not be confused with the independent reading that students must also do as a part of their reading program. Reading the selection is the part of the directed reading lesson where the teacher is checking application of reading skills and processes taught. This is where *guided application* is provided.

The reading program, however, must also provide sufficient opportunities for students to have *independent* application that takes place in materials that students have selected themselves; this reading is oriented to fun and enjoyment. There is considerable support for being certain that time for independent reading be provided as a part of all reading programs at all levels. It has been recommended that at least two hours per week be allotted for this purpose by the time students reach third grade (Anderson et al., 1985). The amount of time for independent reading below third grade would be somewhat less.

An interesting and exciting way to incorporate independent reading into the reading program is through uninterrupted silent reading. Under this plan, everyone in the classroom or school reads something for a designated amount of time. Everyone reads—teacher, students, principal, custodian, etc. This builds good reading habits and provides students with adult models who read.

For uninterrupted silent reading to be effective, students must have an opportunity to talk about their reading with someone. This *doesn't* mean making a book report. Simply take a few minutes at the conclusion of the reading time to let students talk to a partner or the entire class about what they read. The effective reading program must have a balance of instructional time and independent reading time.

TEACHING STUDENTS TO MONITOR THEIR READING

What are the steps involved in monitoring?

Good readers must learn to monitor their reading and know whether what they are reading makes sense; this is known as *comprehension monitoring* and was discussed in Chapter 3. Readers can be taught how to monitor their reading by using a very systematic approach that teaches them to use four simple processes as they read: summarizing, clarifying, questioning, and predicting (Palincsar & Brown, 1984a, 1984b).

What is recipro-cal teaching, and how is it done?

The use of these four steps for monitoring can be taught using a strategy known as *reciprocal teaching* which has been the focus of several research studies (Manzo, 1968; Palincsar & Brown, 1984a, 1984b). Reciprocal teaching is a simple technique where the teacher and students read together silently and take turns playing the role of the teacher in leading the discussion. The teacher is modeling the use of the process of monitoring for students. Students then apply the process immediately under the teacher's direction. This is a form of direct instruction where modeling and application are closely woven together. Teaching the process of monitoring should not replace the use of the directed reading lesson; it should be done in addition to the DRL. The following steps can be used to teach students the process of monitoring using reciprocal teaching.

1. *Select stories or articles that are at the student's instructional reading level.* These can be taken from the basal reader but should not be material that will be needed for instruction.
2. *Present the four steps of the process to students, showing them how to use each step while they are reading* (Cooper, 1986).
Summarize—What did I read? (Tell it.)
Clarify—Was it clear to me? (Reread or discuss parts that are unclear.)

Question—What question could a teacher or test ask over this material? (Pose the question.)

Predict—What is likely to happen next (or later) in this text? (Make predictions.)

Put each step on a chart or bulletin board with the questions. Refer to them when the process is used.

3. *Identify a time for reciprocal reading.* Carry out the procedure for fifteen to thirty minutes per session (Cooper, 1986). At the primary levels, use the process once a week; at the intermediate levels use it twice a week (Cooper, 1986).

4. *Use the procedure in the following manner:*

Say: "Today we are going to do our reading together and take turns being the teacher. First I will be the teacher and then you will be the teacher. We are going to use the four steps we have been learning—Summarize, Clarify, Question, Predict." Refer to the chart and questions. Develop any background or vocabulary for the selection that would be needed. "Now, read the first paragraph to yourself, and I will be the teacher first." The reading can be broken into one or more paragraphs as is appropriate for the students' level. *After everyone (teacher and students) has completed the reading, proceed as follows.*

Say: "This paragraph was about _____." (Summarize the main idea of the paragraph.) "But I didn't understand the first sentence (or anything you wish to point out)." The teacher should point out something because this is a part of the modeling. "Let's reread that sentence. Who can explain it for me?" Students and teacher participate in the discussion. "I think a good question to be asked over this paragraph would be _____." Teacher poses question. "From what we have read, I think the next selection will _____." Teacher predicts what is to come next or later.

Say: "Let's read the next paragraph (or section) and I will select one of you to be the teacher." The pattern continues in this manner:

—All read silently the designated section.

—*Teacher* plays *teacher.*

—All read silently.

—*Student* plays *teacher.*

—All read silently.

—*Teacher* plays *teacher.*

—All read silently.

—*Student* plays *teacher,* etc.

Teaching students to use this strategy will help them think about their reading while they are reading. It will make it possible for students to know whether their reading is making sense while they read.

CONCLUDING REMARKS

This chapter has discussed how to carry out the portion of the DRL that involves reading and discussing the selection. It also presented a strategy to teach students to monitor their reading. The importance of having students read independently was stressed. It takes all of these procedures to make an effective reading program.

PRACTICE EXERCISE

Directions
This series of exercises is designed to help you practice and check your knowledge of the procedures you learned in this chapter. Complete each exercise; then check your answers with the Answer Key at the end of the text.

Part I
Select the best answer for each question.

1. The reading and discussing the selection portion of the DRL is where
   a. students apply skills and processes which have been learned
   b. students learn a new skill
   c. students extend their thinking about what they have read
   d. a and c

2. In order to carry out the reading and discussing portion of the DRL, the teacher must know
   a. the story line or main ideas and the skills to be applied
   b. only the story line
   c. the process of reciprocal teaching
   d. every detail of the selection

3. The type of guided reading where the teacher has students read the entire selection at once for a single purpose is known as
   a. section-by-section reading
   b. independent reading
   c. whole section reading
   d. reciprocal reading

4. When carrying out section-by-section guided reading, the teacher's questions used for guiding each section should first
   a. extend thinking
   b. require oral reading
   c. check application
   d. bring out the story line

5. Knowing the story line or having a story map in mind is important for the teacher when having students read
   a. narrative text
   b. expository text
   c. longer text
   d. factual text

6. The purpose that students are given to guide their reading of an entire selection should
   a. be inferential if possible
   b. focus on the entire selection
   c. be checked immediately after reading
   d. all of the above

7. Guided reading by sections means that the teacher
   a. has students read the whole selection at once
   b. has students read portions of the selection one at a time and discuss them
   c. gives students a written exercise after reading individual sections of a story
   d. has students take turns being teacher

8. Guided reading by sections is usually used for
   a. primary grades and advanced readers
   b. intermediate grades and less able readers
   c. primary grades and less able readers
   d. intermediate grades and advanced readers

9. Teaching students to think about their reading as they read is known as
   a. reciprocal teaching
   b. monitoring
   c. application
   d. guided reading

10. In order for students to know what skills to apply when reading a selection, the teacher should
   a. teach phonic lessons first
   b. remind students of the skill to apply
   c. ask inference questions
   d. use the workbook

Part II

Use the paragraph on page 167 and write questions that would accomplish the following:

1. Be a good purpose to guide reading of the whole passage.

2. Check application of the digraph *wh*.

3. Check application of details.

4. Extend students' thinking about the paragraph.

5. Check application of sequence.

6. Check application of vocabulary.

Part III

1. Use "Old Red Takes a Ride" (Figure 9-1) and write down the questions and procedures you would use to carry out whole selection reading. Label all parts.
2. Use "The Builders of the Bridge" (Figure 9-2) and write down the questions and procedures you would use to carry out section-by-section guided reading. Label all parts.

CHAPTER 10

Enrichment

**What types of
activities are
acceptable for
enrichment?**

Most children enter school with a strong desire to learn to read. They anticipate great pleasure from learning to read. Somehow, this desire and excitement over reading is lost in the first years of reading instruction for too many students. The enrichment phase of the DRL should serve to sustain and/or increase the pleasures of learning to read. In this chapter, types of activities that are appropriate for enriching and extending the reading experience are presented. The suggestions, which are by no means intended to be all-inclusive, will be centered around the following types of activities: reading, audiovisual materials, direct experience, creative art, drama. and writing.

There is some difference of opinion concerning appropriate activities for this phase of the DRL. There are those who believe that the enrichment or extension phase of the lesson may be used for continued independent skill practice. Others, including the authors of this text, believe that the enrichment portion of the lesson should be used literally to enrich the learner by providing experiences related to the content of the selection. Keep in mind that the process of learning to read is not always a fun-filled experience for some students, even though the practice activities may be gamelike and the contents of the selections may be pleasurable. This final phase of the lesson should provide both success and pleasure for the learner. Because of this, a variety of activities need to be used by the teacher to assure meeting the needs of individual students.

All activities used for enrichment should require some degree of active student participation. The amount of participation depends on the type of activity, but the reader should never be totally passive. Enrichment activities should correlate with the contents of the selection read during the prior parts of the lesson or with an entire unit of selections. Therefore, some enrichment activities are completed quickly at the conclusion of the lesson; others extend over a period of time.

READING

Reading aloud to students is a very valuable enrichment activity because it broadens and extends background knowledge of students. This is especially true when discussion, which allows for student participation, accompanies the oral reading. The reading may be done by the teacher in person or may have been tape recorded earlier for students to listen to independently while the teacher works with other students. Commercially prepared tapes to accompany books can also be used. It is important for the teacher to reconvene the group to discuss what was heard after the students have listened to a tape.

There are many kinds of appropriate literature available for reading to students. The choice of material depends upon the age and background of the students. The most obvious type of material to be read is a story. Young children, especially, enjoy hearing a story. Special types of stories such as myths, legends, mysteries, or adventures may be more appropriate for older students. Young children enjoy finger plays and nursery rhymes where they may participate first with actions and later by saying the words along with the teacher. Poems of various types also make a good choice for reading aloud to students.

Older students may participate in choral readings in much the same way as younger children participated in finger plays and nursery rhymes. Choral readings are often poems or rhymes where students read specific parts aloud. For example:

Boys read:	Peter Piper pick'd a peck of pickled peppers.
Girls read:	Did Peter Piper pick a peck of pickled peppers?
All read:	If Peter Piper pick'd a peck of pickled peppers, where's the peck of pickled peppers Peter Piper pick'd?

All read:	Pease porridge hot,
	Pease porridge cold,
	Pease porridge in the pot,
	Nine days old.
Group 1:	Some like it hot
Group 2:	Some like it cold
All read:	Some like it in the pot
	Nine days old.

Choral readings can be created by groups of students based on material from the selection that has been read, or they may be taken directly from printed materials. Sometimes students enjoy memorizing choral readings and performing them for other students.

Factual information provides another source for obtaining material to be read during the enrichment phase of the DRL. Factual information may be obtained from such sources as books, magazines, or newspapers and often will enhance concepts for students. It is not always necessary for the materials to be "words." Photographs and illustrations may be shared and discussed as part of enrichment. Maps and globes provide yet another source of materials to be "read" while extending student knowledge. Travel posters and pamphlets may also be appropriate sources of enriching information. Having students read related stories, articles, books, or poems is also appropriate in enrichment. Reading activities as part of enrichment should stress the need to get students to use their reading in "real" sources, since that's the purpose of teaching reading. The choice of appropriate materials to be read to or with students depends on the topic of the unit or lesson and the age, interests, and backgrounds of the students. There are many appropriate sources that teachers might use to locate related readings such as the library, the teacher's guide of basal readers, anthologies, or fellow teachers.

AUDIOVISUAL MATERIALS

Audiovisual aids often provide good vicarious experiences for students. It has been said that a picture is worth a thousand words. When the pictures also have accompanying sound, they provide an even greater advantage of broadening the experiences of the learner. Filmstrips can often be located that relate to topics of selections that have been read by the students. Many times the students can view a filmstrip independently, while the teacher works with another group of students. Then the group can reconvene for discussion of the contents of the filmstrip. Video recordings and 16-mm film may also provide appropriate follow-up and enrichment information and may be shown to the group independently of the teacher.

Audio tapes and records may be valuable additions to enrichment activities under some circumstances. Tapes might be first-person, factual, and/or historic in nature. For example, tapes might provide students an opportunity to hear an important person present a speech, an opportunity to hear poets read their own poetry, or a firsthand tape of the launching of a space shuttle. Records might include the music of a particular country, music associated with a circus, or songs that the students might sing.

DIRECT EXPERIENCE

Real experiences may also be provided for students as a part of enrichment. The most obvious real experience might be for the students to take a trip as a part of following up a unit of reading. For example, students might visit the post office after reading selections concerning communication or a zoo after reading selections about wild animals. Field trips, though excellent enrichment, are not likely to happen very often because of the expense of both time and money.

Perhaps more realistic direct experiences as part of enrichment might include such activities as having a food tasting party, dressing in costumes of a country after reading about clothing and customs of children around the world, or bringing in dolls dressed as those children might dress. Models of animals might be introduced to students instead of a trip to the zoo, or models of the digestive system might be used after reading about nutrition. Real farm implements from olden days and their modern equivalents might be viewed and discussed after reading about agriculture.

Whenever possible direct experience with real things provides good enrichment and extension of concepts for students. However, as worthwhile as direct experience is, it loses much of its value unless there is conversation or discussion concerning the experience that both explains it in terms that the students understand as well as relates it to the topic of the selection that has been read.

CREATIVE ART ACTIVITIES

Art activities often are fun for students as an enriching activity to follow the reading lesson. Sometimes art activities can be completed immediately after the lesson, and sometimes they are of longer duration. For example, students might draw a picture of their favorite part of a selection after reading about a trip to the World's Fair or make a pinwheel after reading about wind resistance. They might fill balloons with helium, attaching their names and addresses along with a note asking for a response, after reading about this kind of activity.

Creative art activities of longer duration might include making a tabletop display of an Indian fort after reading a unit concerning Indians or developing a bulletin board depicting various tribes of Indians and their customs, depending on the actual topics of the selections. Individual or group dioramas might be constructed to illustrate the holidays around the world, or model satellites might be constructed after a unit related to space. Long-term creative art activities can be completed by students under the guidance of the teacher without direct supervision; therefore, it is nice to have an activity of this type periodically during the school year, freeing the teacher to work with other groups and/or individuals while some students work on an enrichment project.

DRAMA

Another type of creative enrichment activity is creative dramatics. This type of enrichment normally takes several days to complete. Here, students would perhaps stage a reenactment of what has been read with or without props and costumes. They might also prepare a creative play that is a takeoff on the style and/or contents of what has been read, rather than a mere reenactment.

Students often need some type of physical involvement incorporated into reading lessons. Creative dance might be one such involvement. Students might attempt to put to music the feelings of one of the characters about whom they have read. They might also develop marching formations after reading about school bands.

Puppets have great appeal to many students. Creative dramatics can easily include the making of one of many kinds or types of puppets or marionettes that could then be used in a dramatic presentation to other members of the class or students in another class. One of the simplest types of puppets can be made by stuffing a paper bag with newspaper, tying it on a stick with a string, then making features on the head with construction paper. Students are usually very good at using their imagination to complete this type of puppet. Another easy-to-make type of puppet is one made from a sock. The sock is pulled over the hand, allowing the bottom of the foot of the sock to become the mouth of the puppet by putting the fingers in the toe of the sock and thumb into the heel of the sock. Next, the part of the sock that is on the back of the hand can be given eyes, ears, and other features with such things as yarn, buttons, beads, sequins, or construction paper. Finger puppets, where characters or props of the drama are made from cardboard with holes so that fingers can be inserted for legs, are yet another easy way to include puppets in enrichment activities.

Pantomime with or without puppets is another form of creative dramatics enjoyed by students of all ages. Some types of creative drama may take place quickly at the conclusion of the lesson, while other dramatic activities may be ongoing.

WRITING

Writing is a natural ally of reading as well as creative drama and can often be used in conjunction with reading as a part of enrichment. Much creative writing and rewriting may need to take place before the actual drama can begin. Writing to be used in creative drama gives students a real purpose for writing, which is desirable. When the writing is directly related to the reading, often students can use either the style and/or the exact words of the selection author, thereby giving students an excellent model for writing. When writing is directly related to reading for the purpose of creative drama, the writer has no need to develop topics independently but can logically follow the story line of the original author. This is not to say that all students' writing must always be modeled directly from what has been read, rather that modeling is an excellent first step in the process of relating reading and writing.

Creative writing may also be an outgrowth of the reading experience when students are asked to write about their own experiences that relate to the topic of the selection. Making this connection between reading and writing enhances the reader's comprehension of the selection. For example, if students have read a selection concerning a vacation trip, and then write about their own vacation as an enrichment activity, they may well understand the content of the selection read better than before they completed their own writing. If students have read a myth or legend, attempting to write a myth or legend of their own will enhance their understanding of this type of selection. In all cases of the reading/writing connection, it is necessary for the teacher to encourage students to consider ways that authors use language to convey meaning. In other words, some attention is given to such things as looking at the selection read as a model of writing style, components of a story, conventions of writing such as sentence and paragraphs, spelling, and knowledge of word connotations.

Other advantages of the writing/reading connection are that student writers need to use phonic and structural analysis generalizations that were taught in reading in order to spell the words for their writing. The conventions of writing such as capitalization and punctuation that were used by the selection writer can be imitated by the student writer. Students might also be encouraged to write a summary of the selection or to prepare a written outline of the selection if they have been taught to do these things. Rewriting portions of the selection using synonyms, antonyms, or figures of speech for the author's words sometimes produces fun results to be shared with classmates, especially when students can see that the original meaning of the author has been distorted by their changes. This helps students understand the need for precision in choice of words for writing as well as precision in reading exactly what the author said.

Language experience stories, as discussed in Chapter 11 of this text, may be a natural outgrowth of the reading experience. For example, if students have read several mysteries, they might try to write their own mystery. These writings might then be shared with other groups of students in the same classroom or with students in another classroom.

Vocabulary enrichment activities will improve both reading and writing. Activities designed to expand vocabulary attempt to get students to think about and use words in their environment and in their life. Definitions of vocabulary words alone are not sufficient to improve comprehension (McKeown, Beck, Manson, Pople, 1985). Rather, if students can be motivated to use expanding vocabulary in their daily lives both orally and in writing, comprehension is improved. Students might also be encouraged to build vocabulary webs and maps as a way of creating better understanding of word meanings.

Why should enrichment be included in a DRL?

There are many exciting and educational activities that can and should be a part of the enrichment phase of a DRL. Most basal reader manuals offer many suggestions for enriching and extending student knowledge at the conclusion of each lesson. Usually, there are more suggestions than a teacher could possibly use. It is important, therefore, for the teacher to use discretion in the selection of appropriate activities for the specific group of students. Unfortunately, even though there are many suggested activities, this is the phase of the reading lesson that is most often slighted by classroom teachers. The reason? Many teachers feel the pressure of time and a feeling that they must complete a book by some designated time. Therefore, in the name of expediency, they move on to the next lesson without engaging in enrichment activities, thinking that they are much less important than the other parts of the lesson. The authors of this text do not agree with educators who would omit or diminish this phase of reading instruction. Instead, *we believe that enrichment from one lesson provides the basis for broadened oral language development and experiential background that lays the foundation for future lessons.* Language and experience form the foundation of reading instruction; therefore, it is critical for their development not to be slighted in favor of more skill work and drill. As surely as skill development, vocabulary and background, and reading and discussing the selection are important parts of a reading lesson, so is enrichment!

PRACTICE EXERCISE

Directions

This series of exercises is designed to help you practice and check your knowledge of enrichment activities. Complete each exercise; then check your answers with those in the Answer Key at the end of the text.

Part I

Mark the following statements true (T) or false (F).

_____ 1. Another word for enrichment is extension.

_____ 2. Playing a vocabulary game is a good enrichment activity.

_____ 3. Choral readings could be effectively used for enrichment.

_____ 4. The writing/reading connection enhances comprehension.

_____ 5. Field trips are the best and most practical type of direct experience enrichment.

_____ 6. Real rather than vicarious experiences should always be provided during enrichment.

_____ 7. If there is not time for everything in a DRL, the first thing to "go" should be enrichment.

_____ 8. Enrichment experiences can always be completed on the same day that the lesson is finished.

_____ 9. Picture books and records may be used as part of enrichment.

_____ 10. Enrichment activities should require some active participation on the part of students.

Part II

Think of an appropriate enrichment activity for the following selection topics. Record your ideas.

1. A unit on farms:

2. A story about the Wright brothers:

3. A selection about tropical fish:

4. A "how to" selection on drying flowers:

5. A story about a birthday party:

6. A unit on the Civil War:

7. A biography of George Washington:

8. The history of the World Series:

9. A unit on fantasy:

10. Constellations:

11
Effective Approaches to Teaching Reading

Thus far this text has presented discussions of what reading is, prereading, comprehension, word recognition, study skills, the Directed Reading Lesson (DRL), strategies for teaching reading, and strategies for enrichment. This chapter will present
systems or approaches for teaching reading in the classroom that aid students in
developing reading ability with increasing progression. Research concerning systems
or approaches for teaching reading has shown that no single approach is successful
with all readers (Durrell, 1958). It, therefore, seems logical that the competent
teacher must know a variety of approaches and materials in order to meet the various
learning needs of students.

Over the years many approaches for the teaching of reading have been developed
and used by educators at all levels. This chapter will discuss only those approaches
for teaching reading that are widely accepted and have been proven to be successful.
It will present the philosophy, materials, procedures, strengths, and weaknesses of
the (1) basal reader approach, (2) linguistic approach, (3) individualized reading
approach, and (4) language experience approach. In addition, computer assisted
instruction as an approach for teaching reading will be discussed briefly, since it is
being used more widely each day and appears to have promise for the future.

Approaches to teaching reading are not mutually exclusive and, in fact, can be and often are used by teachers simultaneously. An eclectic approach employs the best of several approaches to meet the various learning needs of the individual students.

Every approach for the teaching of reading is based on a philosophy about what occurs during the reading process and how readers learn to read. These postulates help the teacher determine which approaches or combination of approaches have the potential of being successful for the particular student(s). It is the teacher who must decide which approach or approaches to use. The teacher, then, is the key variable in the success students have in learning to read.

THE BASAL READER APPROACH

What is the basal reader approach? What materials are included?

For many years, basal readers have been the primary instructional materials used in the elementary grades. The format of the Directed Reading Lesson (DRL) presented in Chapter 6 is based on the basal reader approach.

Design and Content

Basal readers are a series of books that form the basis of instruction in reading. Basal readers provide for the systematic introduction of reading skills through the use of a series of books of increasing difficulty that lead the reader from a nonreading status to a high degree of reading proficiency. The books are commonly referred to as a basal series. Each book in the series represents a level of reading that is a prerequisite for the following levels. There is a systematic plan for the sequential introduction of skills level by level. This plan is commonly referred to as a scope and sequence. In this way, basals provide a curriculum plan for reading instruction for various grades. Newer basal reader series range from prereading through eighth grade; some older series have a narrower range of kindergarten through sixth grade.

Materials

Since basal series operate on the assumption that students learn to read best through the use of a variety of materials, all basal programs consist of a number of materials that vary from series to series but may include:

1. A student reader(s) for the selected grade level range. These may include one or more prereading (readiness) books or workbooks.
2. A teacher's edition of the reader for each level that includes lesson plans for the use by the teacher.
3. Various supplements for the practice of skills such as workbooks or activity books that correspond to the students' readers.
4. Teacher editions of students' workbooks and activity books.
5. A management system that may include pre- and posttests for each level, placement tests, an informal reading inventory, and record-keeping devices.
6. Additional supplementary materials such as vocabulary flashcards, records, tapes, computer programs, etc.

Most teachers are expected to use basal readers. A discussion of the various levels of basal readers and materials along with their place and use in a basal reader approach will aid in understanding this widely used approach.

Readiness Books

Basal series usually begin with one or more books or workbooks that address the prereading skills and factors that need to be developed before a formal program of reading is begun. Although these materials are designed to be used before the students begin to learn to read, they are not commonly called prereading materials; instead, most publishers label these materials readiness.

The readiness books or workbooks are usually softbound and do not contain words to be read in story form for meaning although some may present some character names and high-frequency words students will encounter in first-grade books. The activities are designed to develop visual discrimination, auditory discrimination, language, and directionality.

First-Grade Readers

There are usually many materials available at the first-grade level. This is due in part to the fact that first grade is composed of three reading levels: preprimer, primer, and first reader. Basal series contain several preprimer books that are sequential in vocabulary development and degree of difficulty. The typical number of preprimers is three although some series have two to four.

The *preprimer* is a softbound book of about twenty pages with large, colorful pictures and simple sentences that may contain one or more words. Large print is employed in the book for the benefit of young readers.

Preprimers emphasize the development of word recognition skills and vocabulary; however, some preprimers contain lessons in comprehension development. In most, however, comprehension receives attention through questions and discussion in the reading and discussion component of the DRL.

Preprimers are accompanied by a teacher's manual and a workbook(s). The workbooks provide additional practice of vocabulary, comprehension, and word recognition skills. Some series have only one workbook for all the preprimer readers while others have a workbook for each reader.

Following completion of the preprimers, the student reads the first hardbound book, the *primer*. The primer is longer than any of the preprimers (50-100 pages) and is also accompanied by a teacher's manual and a workbook. Sentences and the reading selections themselves are longer in the primer than in the preprimer. Vocabulary development is emphasized, and more attention is given to word recognition skills and comprehension development.

The *first reader* level follows the primer level. It is longer than the primer, has a workbook and a teacher's manual, and is similar in appearance to the remaining books in the series.

Second- and Third-Grade Readers

At these grade levels, most basal series have two readers for each grade level. The workbooks and manuals at the second and third grade emphasize numerous reading skills according to the sequence cited in the scope and sequence for the series. By the end of the third grade, most word recognition skills have been introduced.

Fourth-, Fifth-, and Sixth-Grade Readers

At these intermediate grade levels, most series have only one basal reader with an accompanying teacher's manual and student's workbook. Reading instruction now shifts to a reinforcement and expansion of reading skills, an emphasis on comprehension, and a concern with the development of study skills such as library usage. Students at these levels are expected to read to learn.

Seventh- and Eighth-Grade Readers

The single basal reader per grade level is used in schools in which reading is taught to all students as a course or as part of language arts or English classes in middle school or junior high. The readers are an extension of those used at the intermediate levels. They are accompanied by a teacher's manual and a student's workbook as are the intermediate grade readers.

Coding of Basal Readers

The reading levels of basal readers are expressed by a code. The code for the levels may be letters, numbers, or symbols. When letters or numbers are used, they are chronological or sequential in order and do not necessarily denote a grade level. For instance, a book labeled 4 may actually be a preprimer in a particular series. In another series, the label 4 may indicate a primer.

Teachers' Editions

How should teachers' editions and workbooks be used?

Most basal series include a number of materials for both students and teachers. This abundance of materials can be overwhelming and does not in itself guarantee a successful program. As mentioned earlier in this chapter, the teacher is the key to the success of any reading program. It is important that the teacher be familiar with the design and use of the most common materials.

Teachers' editions may be one of the greatest advantages in using a basal series. These manuals are designed to help the teacher develop the reading skills and abilities the students need to progress through a total reading program. Teachers' editions contain detailed lesson plans that can be incorporated into a Directed Reading Lesson, suggestions for specific techniques, and suggested resources for teacher and student use. Proper use of teachers' editions is not following them verbatim; rather, a competent teacher is both knowledgeable and flexible in using these editions to satisfy the students' learning needs. In other words, the teachers' edition suggestions should be followed when they meet students' learning needs and modified, adapted, or supplemented when they do not.

Use of Workbooks

Workbooks are probably the most frequently used supplementary material for a basal series. When properly used, workbooks can have much educational value for students. The workbooks' effectiveness or ineffectiveness is dictated by the manner in which they are used. Using the workbooks for "busy work" designed to free the teacher for other activities is not effective use of workbooks. Workbooks can be effective and provide significant educational value when used to:

1. Provide meaningful practice under teacher guidance for mastering essential reading skills.
2. Identify students who need additional instruction for specific skills.
3. Aid the teacher in diagnosing the effectiveness of instruction.

Not all students need to complete every page of every workbook, and some may need more practice than the workbook provides. The workbooks, like teachers' editions, should be used to satisfy the learning needs of students.

Advantages of Basal Readers

What are the advantages and criticisms of basal readers?

Although not all basal series are the same, there are some major strengths of the basal reader program in general that need to be recognized.

1. The books are carefully graded to provide systematic instruction and review from the prereading level through more advanced levels.
2. If properly used, continuity of instruction is provided that attends to all phases of a reading program. This comprehensive coverage includes both cognitive (knowledge) and affective (attitude) aspects.
3. Use of materials and suggestions saves the teacher much valuable planning time.
4. The controlled vocabulary of most series helps prevent frustration for the beginning reader.
5. Most materials have appealing illustrations and artwork.
6. The graded materials enhance the teacher's flexibility in providing individualized instruction.

Criticisms of Basal Readers

Basal series have been the object of much criticism throughout the years. The most frequently cited and prominent of these weaknesses include those given below.

1. The controlled vocabulary creates dull stories that do not match readers' spoken language.
2. The content is not interesting and presents stereotyped white middle-class situations.

3. The manual is regarded as a verbatim guide that must be used in toto for all students.

4. More attention is given to skill practice and assessment than to direct, explicit instruction.

5. Students are expected to move through the series in a lockstep manner by reading every page in every reader and completing every page in every workbook.

6. The basal reader becomes the sole source for teaching reading.

7. The materials do not provide for differing learning styles or teaching styles.

8. Little attention is given to recreational reading.

There is no doubt that some of these criticisms are justified; however, review the criticisms above and determine which are actual criticisms of basal series themselves and which are really criticisms of the way in which the basal series are used.

LINGUISTIC APPROACH

What is a linguistic approach, and how does it work?

Linguistics, a scientific study of language, has had an influence on the teaching of reading. Although there is no one linguistic approach for teaching reading, some linguistic principles have been applied to the development of some materials for the teaching of reading. These materials are in the form of a series and are basal in that they are graded and provide for continuity of skill development. These series differ from the traditional basal series in that they are based on the linguistic principle of using minimal variation within words as the basis for instructing beginning readers. The following example of what might be found on a page from a beginning book in a linguistic series illustrates the principle of minimal variation within words:

> Dan can fan.
> Dan can fan Van.
> Van can fan Dan.
> Dan, fan Nan.

The variation (difference) between the words is only one (minimal) sound and one letter. Beginning students learn to read by learning to pronounce a phonogram such as *an* or *at* and the words constructed by adding one letter and one sound to the phonogram. New phonograms are added as the student masters a particular phonogram and the variations produced by adding a sound or sounds to it.

In linguistic readers the following procedures are generally applied:

1. Beginning readers learn one sound for a letter or phonogram. Other sounds for the letter or phonogram are introduced only after the first has been learned. In other words, all phonograms that contain the short vowel sounds for the letter *a* are learned before the long vowel sound or other sounds for *a* are introduced.

2. In the beginning stages only regularly spelled words are taught, for example, *can, fan, Dan, Van.* Irregularly spelled words are avoided, for example, *laugh, have.*

3. In the beginning levels, sentence structure is dictated by minimal variation and may not reflect natural speech patterns, for example, *Dan can fan Van.* In more advanced levels, the sentence structure becomes more reflective of natural speech patterns.

4. In some series high-frequency words such as *the* and *a* are taught to help the sentences sound more like normal speech.

5. Emphasis is placed on oral reading following the position that reading is changing writing into speech.

6. Sounds are not pronounced in isolation; that is, /b/ is not pronounced as "buh."

In some series pictures are excluded since they are viewed as an undesirable crutch. In addition, mastery of recognition of regular spelling patterns (*an, at, ap,* etc.) is required before students are permitted to move on to new patterns.

Linguistic readers are like the traditional basal series in that teachers' editions and workbooks are a usual accompaniment. An exception to this is the first linguistic series, *Let's Read*, published in 1961 (Bloomfield & Barnhart, 1961). Since that date, however, new editions of that series as well as those published by other companies have included materials common to many traditional basal series.

THE INDIVIDUALIZED READING APPROACH

What is the value of the individualized reading approach?

A competent teacher of reading provides daily individualized instruction that promotes the student's progress in reading through teacher attention to individual needs and strengths. The individualized reading approach is the ultimate in individualized instruction in which the student establishes an independent pace and sequence for reading instruction and selects the material to be used for the instruction. The teacher provides assistance and instruction when the need becomes apparent (Veatch, 1978).

Description of the Individualized Reading Approach

The purposes of the individualized approach for teaching reading are basically threefold:

1. To focus reading instruction on the reading needs of the individual.

2. To help teachers guide students toward assuming the responsibility for their own growth in reading.

3. To permit students to select the material they will read.

During the operation of this approach for teaching reading the students select something to read—a library book, a basal reader, and so forth. Following the silent, independent reading of the book, students meet individually with the teacher in a conference period. During the conference period the teacher notes each student's individual reading needs as each student engages in oral reading and discussion of the book. A record of the book(s) read and each student's strengths and reading needs are recorded. During the individual conference the teacher may provide instruction and/or may group those students for instruction when similar needs are determined.

To implement this approach it is imperative that the teacher be familiar with the reading process, various organizational skills, a scope and sequence for skill development, a variety of reading materials, record-keeping and management techniques, and evaluation and assessment techniques.

Components of the Individualized
Approach for Teaching Reading

How does the individualized reading approach work?

The philosophy of this approach for teaching reading rejects the lockstep approach often associated with the use of basal readers. Since the degree of success of the approach relies heavily upon each individual teacher, the approach itself is somewhat difficult to define. However, several ingredients or components of the approach have evolved through the years. If followed, these components will aid in establishing an individualized approach for teaching reading in the classroom.

Self-selection

Self-selection and self-pacing are probably the most basic ingredients in the individualized reading philosophy. Students are permitted to choose the materials they will read based on the criteria of "I like it" and "I can read it." Each student in the class may select a different book. Teacher suggestions or help are given only if requested by the students. However, when students seem to be unable to select material, the teacher could aid by praising a book or offering some guidance. General guidelines can be followed by students to expedite book selection:

1. Read one or two pages to see if the book has appeal.
2. If there are more than five unfamiliar words per page, the book may be too difficult.
3. If there are no unfamiliar words per page, the students may be able to read a more difficult book on the same topic.
4. Look for books in a particular interest area and related areas.

Essential to this self-selection ingredient is an ample and appropriate supply of reading material. Books on various reading levels and on a variety of topics are needed to satisfy the students of any particular classroom. Veatch (1978) suggests that the teacher supply at least three to five titles per student in the class. The teacher may supply books from the school library, public libraries, bookmobiles, book clubs, and old sets of basal readers. Magazines, newspapers, and other periodicals may also be used as reading materials.

Self-pacing

Each student reads the selected material at a pace selected by the student. Thus, less capable students are not rushed, and more capable students are not held back. Class time is designated for the silent reading time. It is during this time that the teacher and students engage in the next component, student-teacher conferences.

Student-Teacher Conferences

The student-teacher conference is central to this approach. It is during this time that the student receives individual direction from the teacher. The conference is a brief session during which the teacher devotes time to the individual student to:

1. Assess the student's mechanical ability with reading. This is accomplished by having the student read segments orally for the teacher.
2. Assess the student's comprehension. The teacher must be familiar enough with the material to ask a variety of types of comprehension questions.
3. Provide individual instruction in skills or areas of need for the particular student. If more than one student needs aid in a particular area or with a specific skill, the teacher would group these students to provide instruction.
4. Formulate plans for a sharing time. The sharing activities can vary from dramatic presentations to a simple reflection on the book's contents.

Record Keeping

In order to manage an effective individual reading approach, an adequate and appropriate record-keeping system for each student is of paramount importance. Vital information would include:

1. Students' independent, instructional, and frustration reading levels. These are discussed in Chapter 12.
2. Students' reading strengths.
3. Students' reading needs.
4. Conference dates and reading help planned for each student.
5. Instruction provided for each student and the result.
6. Books read.

Advantages and Disadvantages

The main advantages of the individualized approach for teaching reading are as follows:

1. The stigma attached to being in a particular reading group or at a specific level is eliminated since most of the materials are not marked by a coding system. Students are constantly regrouped for specific instruction.
2. Each student is permitted to learn to read at his or her own rate.
3. Students are motivated to read since they choose their own reading material.
4. Each student has the advantage of one-to-one contact with the teacher.

Problems in using the individualized approach are experienced primarily because

1. Much accurate record keeping is required.
2. The time for scheduling individual conferences is limited in a school day.
3. The teacher must be keenly aware of a usable sequence for teaching skills without aid from a teacher's guide.

4. The teacher must be able to plan meaningful activities for students to free the teacher for individual conferences.

5. The large supply of reading materials must be continually replaced.

6. The teacher must be very familiar with the content of a large number of books and other reading materials.

7. The scheduling and planning for diagnosis requires much preplanning.

The manner in which these problems are handled determines the degree of success of the individualized reading approach.

THE LANGUAGE EXPERIENCE APPROACH

What is LEA, and how does it work?

Although some components of the language experience approach (LEA) were used in the 1920s, LEA has only been widely used for about twenty years. The approach uses the already existing language and background of experiences of the reader to develop reading, writing, and listening skills. In this way, LEA is a total language arts approach.

Since the average child entering school has a very adequate and well-developed language facility, the use of this language combined with the child's background of experiences ensures a familiarity with the content and vocabulary used in the reading activities. In this way, LEA actually facilitates the bridge between the learner and print. One of its greatest values is that LEA emphasizes the relationships among thought, oral language, and reading. Roach Van Allen (1976), a well-known advocate of LEA, discusses the premises upon which LEA is built in this way:

What I can say, I can write.

What I can write, I can read.

I can read what I write and what other people can write for me to read.

Using LEA

The teacher must provide some type of common experience that will motivate the students to express their thoughts. Such experiences might include a field trip, the necessity to prepare for a class party, the observation of a teacher-demonstrated science experiment, or an accounting of a class project such as planting and subsequent growing of seeds. Oftentimes a mere mention of something such as activities planned for an approaching holiday stimulates the students to express their personal thoughts and experiences. The responsibility of motivation is a task the teacher should not take lightly. Simply asking a group to tell a story the teacher will record is usually *not* stimulation for soliciting students' oral expressions.

After the group has experienced a common activity or has been properly stimulated to express thoughts, the group is ready to compose a story—an experience story. Students are permitted to add comments to the story that the teacher records for all to see. The recording may be on the chalkboard, a large chart tablet, or on an overhead projector transparency. As each student offers a thought for the story, the teacher usually denotes whose contribution it is by including such phrases as, "Dorothy said . . ." The teacher must record *exactly* what the student contributes without correcting grammar; however, the spelling should be correct and not written in the student's dialect. For example, the teacher would write "get" when the student says, "git," and "poor" when the student says "po." An example of a language experience story is shown in Figure 11-1.

FIGURE 11-1
A Language Experience Story

"We planted seeds in egg cartons," said Drew. Joni said, "We watered them every day." "Then we watched them grow," Brian said. "We took them home Mother's Day," said Bob.

After the teacher records each student's contribution, the teacher reads it orally. After all contributions have been recorded, the teacher orally reads the entire story. In order to emphasize correct directionality, the oral reading of the story should include the teacher's hand moving in a sweeping left-to-right motion under each line. Then as the teacher's hand again sweeps in a left-to-right motion under each line, the students join the teacher in an oral rereading of the story. The teacher may solicit a story title from the group that is also recorded. At this point, the reading session may end.

At the next reading session and for each following session, the teacher begins by rereading the story to the group. The group then reads the story orally with the teacher. Volunteers may be requested to read all or part of the story with the teacher. Students generally enjoy reading their own specific contributions to the story. Each student should be given the opportunity to read parts of the story while the teacher fills in words the student may not be able to read.

After each student has read a part or all of the story, the teacher will ask students to locate particular words in the story. Words that have a special meaning to the students because of their background such as "McDonald's", the name of a pet, and so forth are the ones most likely to be identified by the students. The teacher may also show students sentence strips (prepared ahead of time) and have students match these with lines in the story. Students may even reconstruct the entire story from the sentence strips. The sentence strips may be used later as an independent activity for the students. The teacher may provide a copy of the story for each student, where words the student knows (recognizes) can be marked and then placed on word cards to become part of a word bank.

When the students have compiled an adequate word bank, the words may be used to create new stories, for visual and auditory discrimination practice, for the development of a picture dictionary, for learning alphabetizing skills, and for comprehension development. In the latter case, students may use their word cards to respond to comprehension questions posed by the teacher. The word bank, then, is a rich source for use in teaching reading.

Students may illustrate the language experience story or may make it into individual booklets or a large class book. These stories also become the basis for developing comprehension and for studying punctuation, capitalization, and so on.

As time passes, the students may write experience stories by themselves by referring to their word banks for assistance. The students should learn how to edit their stories so others can read them. This is an excellent way to relate reading with the teaching of the writing process. All these activities will require much teacher guidance at first; later, many students should be able to work independently.

Soon students should be able to read what others have written. At first, this is the writing of classmates; ultimately, it is the writing of authors in published books. In this process, students should be encouraged to find and read words they know in any printed material such as signs, magazines, newspapers, and books.

Advantages and Disadvantages of LEA

What are the values of and problems in using LEA?

Perhaps the most valuable feature of LEA is that it incorporates an integration of all the language arts—reading, writing, speaking, and listening. As a result, students learn the relationship among all the language arts.

Since LEA incorporates all modes of learning, students with a preference for the auditory, visual, or kinesthetic mode are satisfied through the dictation and reading aloud of stories, the silent reading of stories, and the writing of stories. The teacher may emphasize the activity that best serves the students' preferred learning mode.

Use of LEA helps promote the students' positive self-concept. This is accomplished when students realize that what they have to say is important enough to be written and that others are interested in reading it. LEA also promotes a positive, close relationship between the teacher and students.

Finally, LEA is valuable as an approach for older students who are just beginning or have failed to develop adequate reading ability. Use of the approach provides high-interest material for these students rather than the lower interest commercial materials available for low-level older readers.

The disadvantages of LEA revolve primarily around a misuse of the approach or the teacher's lack of understanding of the reading process and the sequential development of skills. A good teacher can plan an LEA program that provides sequence in skill development.

Critics of LEA fault it for the amount of time it requires both for implementation and for teacher planning. In addition, some educators regard the rereading of the stories as a boring activity that, in turn, prevents students from learning how to read.

The language experience approach is probably best used as the total reading program for a limited time. It seems to be best used in combination with other approaches such as the basal approach. Remedial teachers and teachers of beginning older readers may find that LEA is a valuable approach in helping students begin to develop reading ability. Then, as the reading ability grows, other approaches may be successfully employed.

COMPUTER ASSISTED INSTRUCTION

What is CAI, and how does it work in reading?

Although Computer Assisted Instruction (CAI) cannot be currently viewed as a widely used approach for teaching reading, it has the promise of increasing popularity as the number of computers in our schools increases. The proponents of CAI as an approach for teaching reading laud its value as that of providing:

1. Interesting individualized instruction.
2. Pacing set according to the needs of the learner.
3. Immediate response to the learner's work or action.

Assuming the computer (hardware) is available, the heart of CAI is the program (software) that actually provides the instruction. Software can take the form of printed pages with symbols and language that must be entered into the computer's memory via the keyboard, prerecorded cassette tapes, or prerecorded disks.

What happens when a student uses a computer into which reading instruction has been entered?

1. The program is presented to the student by appearing on the computer's screen.
2. The student responds to directions, information, or requests shown on the screen by typing on the keyboard or by manipulating a special pen, stylus, or mouse.
3. Some computer programs may give directions, present material, or ask questions via an auditory component.
4. The student receives immediate feedback once the response has been entered into the computer. The feedback may appear as language or symbols on the screen and/or an auditory signal.
5. Student responses or work can be recorded (saved) for future reference or inspection.

In addition to knowing how to operate the computer, another crucial responsibility of the teacher in using CAI is the ability to write desirable computer programs and/or the ability to evaluate existing available commercial programs. Since the quality of available software (programs) varies significantly, the teacher is wise to preview any software before purchasing or using it. Three major guidelines are useful for judging the quality of software:

1. Is the program instructionally sound? Often computer programmers are not knowledgeable about the reading process and/or reading skills.
2. Are directions clearly and explicitly given in the software itself? Are the directions written at the students' level?
3. Is the material, work, or activity on the software appropriate for the students' needs?

At this point in the development of CAI for reading instruction, the use of the approach as the sole approach for teaching reading does not seem plausible. The lack of appropriate software that actually instructs rather than just providing drill and practice is the chief obstacle.

CAI Advantages and Disadvantages

A definite value of CAI lies in its ability to provide much needed skill practice for students. It is also infinitely patient. The use of CAI for practice frees the teacher for other tasks while it provides the students with immediate feedback concerning performance.

Another value of CAI is its use as a vehicle for management through the computer's record-keeping capacity. Students can be tested individually, scores recorded, and weaknesses and strengths noted. This provides readily available records and information for the teacher who uses individualized instruction.

A disadvantage of CAI is that students may not use it properly and thus not learn—they may simply become a "puncher of the keyboard." Another is that not all available software is educationally sound. It is more difficult to omit sections or small portions not deemed appropriate on software than it is to eliminate a page in a workbook.

Finally, learning how to write programs for the computer so that appropriate activities are available for a class or individual student requires much teacher time. Most teachers would prefer to buy commercially prepared software even if it does not adequately satisfy student needs.

There is little reason to believe that CAI will not increase in popularity in schools. No teacher can afford not to be familiar with the approach or with the workings of computers.

A competent teacher is one who is knowledgeable about different approaches for teaching reading so that the needs of various groups of students can be adequately met. The teacher who is able to employ only one approach, even though very well, is certain to create a situation in which some students are unable to grow maximally in reading ability.

Many teachers find it beneficial to use a combination of methods or to select the most desirable aspects of a number of different methods to teach reading. Choices should be based upon the school's program and philosophy of teaching reading as well as the reading needs of the students. For example, a teacher may supplement a basal reader approach with language experience, individualized reading, or CAI. The approaches chosen to be supplementary may be employed for one or two days a week with the primary approach being used three or four days a week. Another pattern may be the use of an approach as supplementary for a limited period of time such as six or nine weeks. The limitations of selection and pattern of use of approaches are limited only by a teacher's creativity and, in some cases, by the schools' resources.

PRACTICE EXERCISE

Directions

This series of exercises is designed to help you practice and check your knowledge of approaches for teaching reading. Complete each exercise; then check your answers with those in the Answer Key at the end of the text.

Part I
Match the items in column B with those in column A. Items in column B may be used more than once.

Column A

_____ 1. employs reader's own language

_____ 2. graded books

_____ 3. no special materials

_____ 4. manuals, workbooks, supplementary materials

_____ 5. minimal variation in words

_____ 6. software—floppy disks

_____ 7. record keeping is essential

_____ 8. student/teacher conferences

_____ 9. complete language arts program

_____ 10. library books, basals, periodicals

Column B

a. basal reader approach
b. linguistic
c. LEA
d. individualized
e. CAI

Part II
Choose the best answer for each item.

1. Which set of factors describes the basal reader approach?
   a. systematic, sequential, scope and sequence
   b. dictated stories, no text, oral language expression
   c. phonograms, minimal variation, regular spelling
   d. none of the above

2. Which level(s) of basal readers are considered first grade materials?
   a. first reader
   b. preprimer, primer
   c. 1^1, 1^2, 2
   d. a and b

3. Which approach does the following sentence suggest? A cat sat pat.
   a. CAI
   b. LEA
   c. linguistic
   d. individualized

4. The factors of self-selection and self-pacing are vital to which approach?
   a. CAI
   b. LEA
   c. linguistic
   d. individualized

5. Computers are necessary for using the _____ approach.
   a. basal reader
   b. LEA
   c. individualized
   d. CAI

6. The most widely used approach for teaching reading is the _____ approach.
   a. individualized
   b. linguistic
   c. basal reader
   d. language experience

Part III

Mark the items true (T) or false (F). Explain each false (F) response.

_____ 1. Basal readers usually range from prereading to the fifth grade.

   Comment _____

_____ 2. Group teaching should occur in LEA and the individualized approaches.

   Comment _____

_____ 3. In LEA, students choose what they will read.

   Comment _____

_____ 4. Teachers' manuals are an important component of the individualized approach.

   Comment _____

_____ 5. Students should learn regular spelling patterns before irregular spelling patterns when using the linguistic approach.

   Comment _____

_____ 6. It is not wise to combine different approaches for teaching reading.

   Comment _____

_____ 7. The approach is the key in the success students have in reading.

   Comment _____

_____ 8. The DRL is based on CAI.

   Comment _____

_____ 9. Materials labeled ''readiness'' are usually prereading materials.

   Comment _____

12
Informal Classroom Assessment

What will be learned about assessment?

In this chapter the necessary processes and procedures to aid teachers in obtaining information about a classroom of students will be discussed. Determining exactly where students are in the process of learning to read is indispensable to effective teaching and should be an integral, continuous part of the instructional program in reading. This process is referred to as a diagnostic process, assessment, and/or an evaluation process. This chapter will present information about informal measures for the following areas: (1) interests and attitudes, (2) functional levels, and (3) specific reading skills.

Assessment is a process of finding out about the student's strengths and weaknesses in reading. It is a tool the diagnostic teacher uses to determine what the students need to be taught, and which reading levels and type of materials are best used for teaching reading.

Assessment makes the organization and management of the classroom more effective and efficient. The assessment process makes it possible for the teacher to plan instruction directly related to the needs, strengths, and interests of a particular group of students. Another advantage of the assessment process is that the diagnostic processes will help the teacher determine the specific skill needs of the members of the group so that they may be grouped according to their own needs.

Every teacher needs to assess student strengths and weaknesses at the beginning of each year. Some students change in their reading ability following a summer vacation.

New students from other schools also need to be assessed when they enter the school because the instructional programs of the two schools may be somewhat different. Assessment, however, is not a one-time procedure. Effective assessment is a continuous process that permits the teacher to adjust teaching to the needs of the students. The competent teacher wants to be aware of students' changing reading needs.

GENERAL ASSESSMENT PROCEDURES

In the process of assessment, teachers should take on a different role. Many teachers are so accustomed to helping students with any task with which they have difficulty that it is hard for them to switch over to being a diagnostician. However, during the assessment process, it is important not to teach; rather, the teacher is attempting to find out what the students know.

During this process, teachers should be supportive of students, giving as much praise as can be justified. In addition to verbal praise, it is helpful to smile occasionally and to make the students feel comfortable. It is probably also good to explain the purposes of the assessment measures to the students.

Often all assessment measures should not be given in one sitting; probably thirty to forty-five minutes is long enough. Normally two or three such sessions would yield sufficient diagnostic information for the teacher to have a good base of knowledge of the students' abilities.

The remaining sections of this chapter will deal with some specific, but informal, procedures that might be used to assess reading levels and skills. The type of activities outlined herein might be completed several times during a given year.

INTERESTS AND ATTITUDES

What are some methods for assessing interests and attitudes, and how do they differ?

Most teachers are aware that students work more effectively and efficiently on any given task if they are interested in that task. If during assessment the students' interests are determined, then this knowledge can be used to make the classroom activities coincide, in part, with the students' interests.

One useful technique for determining students' interests is to have them make a *collage* about themselves and what they like to do or want to be. This can be done as an independent activity by the entire class with a brief oral sharing time following the activity.

Another useful technique for determining students' interests and attitudes is *teacher observation*. During free-choice activity times, teachers can make anecdotal records of the individual student choices of activities as well as the students' attitudes toward these activities.

A third means of determining students' interests and attitudes is through the use of an *interest inventory*. Many of these inventories are designed to be given to an entire classroom of students at one time. Examples of various types of interest inventories follow.

Individually Administered Interest Inventory

Excellent information concerning interests may be obtained when the classroom teacher sits with the individual students for a few minutes and talks about what things they like to do. This is a particularly good activity at the beginning of a school year when it is important for the teacher to get to know the students. An individual inventory may also be used by having each student read and respond independently to inventory items. This may not be effective for all students if the actual reading and writing processes are difficult for the students. Figure 12-1 presents an example of an individually administered attitude and interest inventory.

FIGURE 12-1
Individual Attitude and Interest Inventory

Name _____ Age _____ Birth Date _____

Grade _____ Classroom Teacher _____

Directions: This inventory should be administered informally. It may be administered orally in a conversational manner or with a student writing responses.

1. What things do you like to do:

   After school? _____

   On the weekend? _____

   During the summer? _____

2. How do you feel about reading? _____

   What do you read? _____

3. What do you like most/least about school?

   Most _____

   Least _____

4. Tell me about something you do with your family/friends.

   Family _____

   Friends _____

5. What do the people in your family read? _____

   When do they read? _____

6. Do you ever take special trips to visit someone, for a vacation, or to see something special? Tell me about some of these. _____

   _____

7. What clubs, special lessons, or hobbies do you enjoy?

   _____

8. Are there any other special things about you that it would be fun for you to tell me about? _____

   _____

Group Interest Inventory

Any interest inventory can be adapted for group use if multiple-choice questions with answers or checklists are used rather than open-ended questions requiring lengthy written responses from the students. The adverse effects of the students' reading problems are eliminated by the group inventory since the *teacher reads all the questions and answer choices* to the students. The students simply mark the answers of their choice.

Figure 12-2 presents two questions from the previous individual inventory that have been adapted for group use. More complete group interest and attitude inventories can be found in such sources as *Group Assessment in Reading* (Warncke & Shipman, 1984).

FIGURE 12-2
Group Attitude and Interest Inventory

Name _____ Age _____ Birth Date _____

Grade _____ Teacher _____

Directions: Listen to your teacher read the questions and answers. Circle your answers.

1. Circle all the things you like to do after school.
play with friends	study
watch TV	nothing
read	work
rest	listen to music
sleep	something not listed

2. Circle all the things you like to do over the weekend.
visit relatives	watch TV
visit friends	go to the library
travel out of town	go to the museum
play sports	read
go to movies	study

Interest Inventories for Nonreaders

Interest inventories for use with nonreading students can be constructed by using such devices as happy, noncommittal, and sad faces as answer choices. Students mark their responses to questions on the form as they are read orally by the teacher. Figure 12-3 is a sample of this type of inventory.

FIGURE 12-3
Interest Inventory for Nonreaders

Items Read by Teacher

1. I like to read.
2. Going to the library is fun.
3. I want to read better.
4. I want to read as well as my friends.
5. Sometimes, I like to cook.
6. I like to read about animals.

Students' Response Form

Name _____

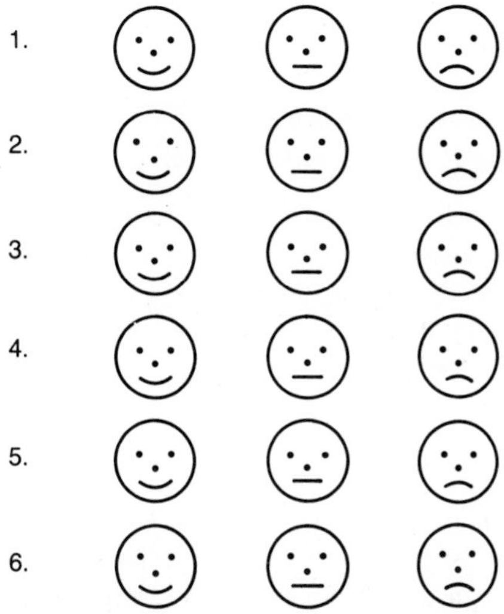

FUNCTIONAL LEVELS

What are functional reading levels for students, and what is the potential level?

Each student usually has three functional reading levels—independent, instructional, and frustration levels. In assessing these levels, teachers determine at what level the student can work alone, can work with help, and cannot work, respectively. Each level is determined on the basis of criteria in the reading skill areas of word recognition and comprehension. Percentages of accuracy in word recognition and comprehension are used to determine each of the three levels. The percentages used are not absolute; they serve as rough guidelines for the teacher.

Independent Reading Level

The independent reading level of a student is the level at which that student is able to read alone without the teacher's assistance. This is the level at which one would expect most of the students' recreational or free reading to be and the level at which most of the work assigned by the teacher to be completed independently by the student should be. The criteria for determining this level are *99 percent accuracy in word recognition* and *90 percent accuracy in comprehension.*

Instructional Reading Level

The instructional reading level of a student is the level at which that student will be able to read the material satisfactorily after being taught the necessary word recognition and comprehension skills. It is possible that a student might have a range of reading levels that are instructional. That is, it is possible for a student to be teachable at more than one level of reading material. The criteria for determining this level are *95 percent accuracy in word recognition* and *75 percent accuracy in comprehension.*

Frustration Reading Level

The frustration reading level of students is the level at which they can no longer function effectively, even with instruction from the teacher. At the frustration level the student has too many problems with word recognition and/or comprehension. The criteria for determining this level are *less than 95 percent accuracy in word recognition* and *less than 75 percent accuracy in comprehension.*

Potential Level

Some measure of a student's capacity for learning to read is also needed in a total assessment of a student's functional levels. In light of what is known concerning language development and reading, listening comprehension appears to be one of the most valid measures of reading capacity or potential. It must be remembered that capacity is a theoretical construct that is not absolutely proven and that capacity may grow as the experience background is broadened for the student. The highest level at which a student can listen to material being read orally and *comprehend 75 percent* of that material is defined as the potential level. Figure 12-4 summarizes the criteria for determining these functional levels.

GROUP READING INVENTORY (GRI)

What is a GRI, and how does it work?

The GRI is a series of graded reading selections that are relatively short and designed to be administered to groups in order to determine students' functional reading levels and their comprehension and study skills strengths and weaknesses. Each reading selection is accompanied by multiple-choice comprehension questions that test the

FIGURE 12-4
Functional Levels

Functional Levels	Word Recognition Ability	Comprehension Ability
Independent Reading—reads with ease without teacher assistance	99 percent accuracy	90 percent accuracy
Instructional Reading—is successful with teacher assistance	95 percent accuracy	75 percent accuracy
Frustration Reading—student's reading skills break down. Material is too hard even with teacher assistance	below 95 percent accuracy	below 75 percent accuracy
Potential—student's listening level	not assessed	highest level at which a student answers 75 percent of the questions over material that has been read to him

students' abilities to understand what was read. The comprehension questions range from meaning vocabulary to those requiring the students to make evaluative judgments. When using the GRI to determine reading levels, use only the criteria listed under comprehension ability in Figure 12-4, since no oral reading occurs.

Constructing a GRI

Teachers can construct a GRI by following these steps:

1. *Locate a series of graded reading selections.* The levels chosen should provide a range that will include all students in the class.

2. *Choose a portion of each of these to use in the GRI.* The portions should be one or two paragraphs long and should range in number of words from approximately 75 to 100 at the preprimer level to approximately 350 to 400 at the twelfth-grade level. Figure 12-5 presents a sample of a GRI selection.

3. *Construct multiple-choice questions for each reading selection.* Eight to ten questions per selection are sufficient. Include a variety of comprehension questions. Some study skill questions can be included for the levels beyond third grade. Figure 12-6 presents an example of some GRI questions with a code indicating the type of comprehension or study skill involved.

4. *Develop a scoring scale for each reading selection to determine the number of questions needed to be answered correctly for each of the reading levels.* For example, if there are ten questions, the scale would be:

independent level (90%): 9 correct answers
instructional level (75% or higher): 7½ correct answers
frustration level (below 75%): 7 or fewer correct answers

5. *Duplicate the reading selections and questions with answer choices for each student.*

FIGURE 12-5
Sample GRI Selection: Grade 4 Level

More than anything Jami wanted to be a pitcher on the Little League baseball team. This wasn't going to be easy because, you see, Jami is a girl, and the pitcher for the Golden Eagles had always been a boy.

The day for team tryouts came, and Jami prepared to display her pitching talents. She was the last of ten to try out. All of the others were boys. All of them had been a pitcher on a team before, and they were good. Finally, it was Jami's turn. As she stood on the pitching mound, she had a lump in her throat. She looked straight ahead and pitched with all her strength. The batter attempted to hit the ball. He couldn't. He tried two more times and missed both times. Four more batters tried to hit Jami's pitches, but they couldn't either! Jami was nervous as the coach walked up to her. "Well," he said, "welcome to our team, pitcher."

Administering a GRI

How can a GRI yield reading levels?

A GRI is administered to an entire class or group of students in a classroom. It may be administered at the beginning of the school year and repeated during the year when students have completed materials from a particular reading level and appear to be ready to change reading levels.

Most basal readers have accompanying tests to be administered to students upon the completion of material at a specific level. These tests usually measure the students' abilities to use skills in isolation and *not* their ability to read at a specific reading level. The attainment or lack of attainment of a satisfactory score on these skill tests cannot tell the teacher whether the students are ready to go on to the next higher level or should read additional material at their current level.

Determining Reading Levels

Directions for administering the GRI to determine functional reading levels are as follows:

1. *Begin the assessment by using the stories and questions that represent a range that extends from two levels below to two levels above the assigned grade level.* For example, fourth-grade students would read stories from second-grade level to sixth-grade level.

2. *Assign one story at a time for the students to read silently.*

FIGURE 12-6
Sample GRI Questions

D (detail)

1. How many people were trying out for the team's pitcher?

   a. _____one   d. _____five

   b. _____two   e. _____ten

   c. _____four

Seq (sequence)

2. How many batters tried to hit Jami's pitches after the first batter?

   a. _____four   d. _____three

   b. _____none   e. _____two

   c. _____one

MI (main idea)

3. This story tells about

   a. _____hitting the ball

   b. _____a coach

   c. _____getting on a baseball team

   d. _____boys on a baseball team

C/E (cause/effect)

4. Why would it be hard for Jami to be the team's pitcher?

   a. _____She was too little.

   b. _____The pitchers were always boys.

   c. _____She couldn't pitch well.

   d. _____She was frightened.

   e. _____No one liked her.

Inf (inference)

5. How many batters tried to hit Jami's pitches?

   a. _____one   d. _____three

   b. _____two   e. _____five

   c. _____four

V (vocabulary)

6. What did the word *tryouts* mean in this story?

   a. _____a test

   b. _____practice

   c. _____a league

   d. _____batting

Dict (dictionary)

7. Where would you look in a dictionary to find the word *talent*?

   a. _____in the middle

   b. _____toward the beginning

   c. _____toward the end

Source: Adapted from *Group Assessment in Reading: Classroom Teacher's Handbook* pp. 34–37 by E. W. Warncke and D. A. Shipman, 1984, Englewood Cliffs, N.J.: Prentice-Hall.

3. *After each story is read by the students, read the questions orally to the class as they follow silently and then read each alternative answer choice.* Instruct the students to mark the answer of their choice. Read the questions and answers twice if necessary.

4. *Continue the reading of selections, questions, and answer choices until all selections within the range are completed.*

5. *Score each student's answers for the selection read.* Use a scoring guide to determine the reading level each story represents for each student. Figure 12-7 indicates how this may look for a student.

6. *If further assessment is needed to determine the three reading levels for some students, regroup those students at another time and have the appropriate stories read until the levels can be determined.* The assessment is not considered complete until a student has reached the frustration level on two consecutive selections and has scored at the independent level on one selection. The latter may not be possible for students with little reading ability—they may not have yet developed an independent reading level.

To determine the students' potential levels for learning to read, follow the same procedures as when administering the GRI to determine the three reading levels *except* read each story orally to the students before reading the accompanying questions and multiple-choice answers. Do not use the same selections used for the reading assessment. Score by counting the number of questions answered correctly for each story. Assessment is considered complete only after students have scored *below* 75 percent on two consecutive selections.

FIGURE 12-7
GRI Record Form

Name _____ Drew _____ Date _____ Sept. 12 _____

Story Level	Number Right	Reading Level
2	9	Independent
3	9	Independent
4	8	Instructional
5	8	Instructional
6	5	Frustration
7	3	Frustration

Scoring Guide

Number right:		Reading levels:	
9–10		Independent	3
8		Instructional	4–5
7 or less		Frustration	6

Analyzing and Interpreting GRI Scores

Use the GRI results to determine the three reading levels by following these guidelines:

1. When more than one selection is scored as independent, select the highest level as the correct independent level. In Figure 12-7, Drew's independent level is grade 3.
2. When the instructional level extends over several grade levels, teacher judgment should be used in deciding which of the levels is best used for instruction. It is usually more appropriate to begin instruction at a lower level and then move the student to a higher level later. Fourth-grade level would be an appropriate instructional level for Drew (see Figure 12-7).
3. Two consecutive scores at the frustration level are an indication of *real* frustration. The lower of those two levels would appropriately be designated as the frustration level. In Figure 12-7, Drew's frustration level would be sixth grade.
4. If a student's scores move directly from an independent level to two consecutive frustration levels, the highest independent level should be selected as the instructional level.

The student's potential level for reading, determined by using the scores that the student made on the questions answered for selections as the teacher read orally, is the highest level at which the student scored at 75 percent or more. A potential score very near that of the instructional score indicates that the student may need help in further developing language skills. A potential level significantly higher than the instructional level indicates the student is capable of doing better in reading and should profit from instruction in reading.

Determining Comprehension and Study Skills Ability

How can GRI results be analyzed?

Once the students' functional levels have been determined, an examination of the type of comprehension and study skills questions each student answered correctly gives an indication of the students' strengths in those areas. Any area of comprehension and any area of study skills in which the student answered all questions correctly *at and below* the instructional level indicate strength in those areas. The areas in which the student missed questions at or below the designated instructional level may be indications of areas of weakness.

Brian's errors in answering questions on a GRI are recorded below. His instructional level is first reader, and he has missed or answered correctly the following types of comprehension questions in the preprimer through first-reader level:

	Missed	*Answered Correctly*
Preprimer:	sequence	detail
	main idea	inference
		vocabulary
Primer:	main idea	inference
	cause/effect	detail
	sequence	
First Reader:	cause/effect	synonyms
	main idea	vocabulary
		detail

Brian seems to have strength in detail, inference, synonyms, and vocabulary. His weaknesses appear to be in main idea, sequence, and cause and effect. Brian's comprehension strengths are those developed up to and including first grade. As his instructional level increases, those skills should be taught, retaught, or reviewed at the higher levels.

Analyzing Reading Mannerisms

As the students read the GRI silently, make note of reading mannerisms that particular students may exhibit. These could include lip movement, vocalization, finger pointing, and head movement. Other mannerisms should also be recorded such as fidgeting, grasping the material tightly, lack of attention, and so forth. A student's mannerisms may be indicative of faulty habits that slow the pace of reading and/or hinder comprehension, signs of frustration, or indications of a visual problem.

INFORMAL READING INVENTORY

What is an IRI, and how does it differ from a GRI?

Like a GRI, the Informal Reading Inventory (IRI) is a series of graded paragraphs designed to assist a teacher in determining students' functional levels. IRI paragraphs normally begin with a preprimer level paragraph and continue with a primer level, a first-grade level, and so on. Each paragraph contains a series of comprehension questions related to the content of that material. These questions are asked orally after the material has been read. The IRI differs from the GRI in that the former is designed to be administered to individuals rather than to groups. The purposes of the IRI are the same as the GRI.

Choosing an IRI

IRIs accompany most basal series. These IRIs are designed to have a direct relationship to books in that particular series and to aid classroom teachers in the placement of students at the proper instructional level in the series. Choosing this type of IRI has some merit when instruction will center mainly around the use of these books.

There are also several published IRIs. Three such inventories authored by Burns and Roe (1985), Woods and Moe (1985), and Silvaroli (1986) are listed in the References. These IRIs are designed to assist the teacher in determining general functional levels as they might relate to published materials from a variety of sources as opposed to a particular basal series.

Teachers may choose to construct an IRI. The following steps are those needed to do so:

1. *Select a short passage from the first third of each book in a series that represents the range of levels the IRI will include.* At the preprimer (PP) level, the selection might be an entire story since stories are short at this level. At higher levels, selections increase from approximately 100 to 300 words in length as they move from first-grade to sixth-grade level.

2. *Make a copy of the selection to use for recording a student's errors as the passage is read orally.*

3. *Write comprehension questions to accompany each passage.* Take care to ask several types of comprehension questions. Usually, there are from five to ten questions per passage.

Determining Reading Levels

How can the IRI be used for assessing students' reading ability?

Two or three forms of graded paragraphs should be included in an IRI. One of these series of graded paragraphs should be administered orally, the second silently, and the third may be used as a measure of potential. Normally, an IRI is administered first orally. When the three functional reading levels have been established orally, then determine these levels with silent readings of another form of the IRI. It is the combination of the results from both the oral and silent IRIs that is used to finalize the reading levels.

Oral Administration.   Two copies of the IRI are needed for the oral administration of an IRI. One copy is for the student to read, and the other is for the teacher to mark the oral reading errors and comprehension responses. The following steps are used to administer an oral IRI:

1. *Determine the student's starting point in the IRI.* Most published IRIs contain a graded word list as the first part of the inventory. This listing of words is designed to assist the teacher in determining a starting point for the oral administration of the paragraphs. Specific directions would be included in the directions for the particular IRI. When a word list is used to determine the starting point for an IRI, the student reads the list aloud. The teacher marks the student's errors on a record sheet. Usually the student would continue reading each graded word list until more than 25 percent in one list is missed. The starting point for the oral IRI would be the highest level at which the student scored 100 percent of the words correct in the word list. The student whose scores from reading the word lists appear in Figure 12-8 would begin the oral IRI at second-grade level. This starting point should be the student's independent reading level.

FIGURE 12-8
IRI Word List

Word List Level	Percentage Correct
PP	100%
P	100%
1	100%
2	100%
3	80%
4	70%

FIGURE 12-9
A Marked IRI Passage

Today it is/snowing. The wind is ~~blowing,~~ too. *snowing* C

The wind and the snow ~~make~~ big ~~drifts.~~ It is not (very) *makes a drift*

cold so the snow is (very) wet and heavy. ~~Nobody~~ *uk / no one*

wants to go/~~outside~~ today. Maybe/tomorrow it will be *doors*

fun to play in the snow and/build a snowman. *uk   uk*

1. What is it doing today? (detail)
2. What one word might describe what the passage was about? (main idea)
3. What does the word *heavy* mean in this passage? (meaning vocabulary)
4. What made the snow wet and heavy? (cause and effect)
5. Why wouldn't anyone want to go outside? (inference)
6. Would you be willing to go out on a day like the one described? Why? (critical)

Scoring Guide

	Errors	
	WR	**CS**
Independent	1	1
Instructional	2–3	2
Frustration	4 or more	3 or more

If a word list is not used, and the teacher has no prior knowledge of the student's reading levels, the IRI should be started at the PP level. If an estimated instructional level is available, begin administering the IRI at *two levels below* the estimated instructional level. If this selection does not prove to be at the student's independent level, the next easier or lower level paragraphs should be administered until the independent level has been determined.

2. *The student reads orally.* The student should begin reading the selections orally. Some IRIs instruct the teacher to read a motivation to the student before the oral reading of each selection. There is some debate among diagnosticians as to the advisability of reading this verbal motivation as well as to including pictures and titles with the selections to be read (Burns & Roe, 1985; Cooper et al., 1979). Some believe that any or all of these give the student undue assistance or clues to comprehension. Others believe that these inclusions in an IRI serve to capture the student's attention and will produce more realistic results.

When the IRI is administered orally, the teacher should carefully record, on a separate copy of the IRI, each word recognition error made, as shown in Figure 12-9. There are seven types of word recognition errors that are usually marked:

    a. word(s) unknown by the student.

    b. word(s) omitted from the text by the student.

    c. word(s) mispronounced in the text in any way.

    d. word(s) inserted or added to the text by the student.

    e. word-by-word or hesitant reading by the student.

    f. repetitions of words or phrases in the text.

    g. the self-correction of a previously made error by the student after reading on in the selection.

Each of these word recognition errors is usually marked with a system of short-hand shown in Figure 12-10. The first three of the errors are almost always counted in determining the overall percentage of accuracy for the word recognition aspect of the criteria for determining reading levels. The last four types of errors are more often considered judgmental. Some diagnosticians advise teachers to pronounce words the student does not know (Silvaroli, 1986). This action can create the same condition that reading motivation and using pictures create in giving students clues to comprehension. The authors of this text suggest that these words be marked as unknown (UK).

FIGURE 12-10
Marking Oral Reading Errors

	Type of Error	Marking
Errors Which Are Counted to Meet Criteria	1. Unknown	The country air was cold. *(UK)*
	2. Omissions	. . . dog was at home. (Circle word omitted.)
	3. Mispronunciations	The big tall . . . (Cross out and write in.) *bag*
Judgmental Errors—Not Counted to Meet Criteria	4. Insertions	The big tall . . . (Use caret and write in word.) *and*
	5. Hesitations	The/big tall . . . (Mark between words.)
	6. Repetitions	The big tall . . . (Underline.)
	7. Self-Corrections	The big tall . . . (C) *bag C*

3. *Student answers the comprehension questions.* Following the oral reading of each selection, the story is either covered or removed from the student's view. Then the student is asked the comprehension questions. The student's responses are recorded.

    If the first story the student reads orally does not produce scores at the independent level in both word recognition and comprehension, the next story read should be the level just below (easier) where the oral reading began. This procedure of reading successively easier stories should be continued until independent scores in both word recognition and comprehension are obtained. Some students may read the lowest level story and not score at the independent level in word recognition and comprehension. This student probably has not yet developed an independent reading level.

4. *The student continues to read and answers questions at successively higher levels until frustration scores are reached in both word recognition and comprehension.* This can be determined by using a scoring guide such as the one shown in the record sheet presented in Figure 12-11.

5. *Check marking and scoring. Summarize results on the record summary sheet.* Figure 12-11 is a sample of such a record sheet.

FIGURE 12-11
Sample IRI Record Form

Name _____ Joni _____   Date __ Sept. 7 _____

Level	Oral IRI Word Recognition	Comprehension	Silent IRI Comprehension
PP	Independent (100%)	Independent (100%)	Independent (100%)
P	Independent (99%)	Instructional (80%)	Instructional (80%)
1	Independent (99%)	Instructional (80%)	Instructional (80%)
2	Instructional (95%)	Instructional (80%)	Frustration (70%)
3	Frustration (90%)	Frustration (70%)	Frustration (50%)

Scoring Guide	Errors	
	WR	**CS**
Independent	1 (99%)	1 (90%)
Instructional	2–3 (95–98%)	2 (80%)
Frustration	4 or more (90% or less)	3 or more (70% or less)

Silent Administration.   After the oral administration of the IRI, but perhaps at a different time, the student's silent reading levels are determined. This IRI administration is based on the results of the oral administration and involves the use of a *different form* of the IRI. The following steps are used to administer a silent IRI: ·

1. *The student begins silent reading at the independent level reached on the oral IRI.* If the oral IRI did not produce an independent level, the student begins silent reading at the lowest IRI level.

The student should be told to read the selection silently and that comprehension questions will be asked following the reading. As the student reads silently, record the observable mannerisms as discussed in relationship to the GRI.

Following the silent reading of the passage, ask comprehension questions. The comprehension questions are asked orally, and student's responses to the questions are recorded for later analysis.

2. *The student continues to read successively higher levels and answer questions until the frustration level is reached on two consecutive levels.*

Determining Potential for Reading

The IRI may also be used to determine a student's potential reading level by using a third form of graded selections. In this case, the teacher would read to the student and determine the potential level on the basis of accuracy of comprehension. Begin the reading at the student's instructional level as determined by the oral and silent administrations of the IRI. After reading each passage, comprehension questions are asked and accuracy is determined. Continue to read to the student and to ask questions until the student can no longer respond with at least 75 percent accuracy on two consecutive levels.

Analyzing and Interpreting the IRI

What can an analysis of an IRI yield, and what judgments should the teacher use?

The administration of an IRI should produce an independent, instructional, and frustration level for oral and silent reading. Although specific criteria have been cited for the establishment of these levels, it is important for the teacher to use some judgment in applying these criteria. The lines between these levels are not always quite as precise as these percentage criteria might lead one to believe. Several factors should be taken into consideration as the criteria are applied.

The first of these factors to be considered is the student's use of *context clues*. Sometimes as a student makes a mistake in reading, the mistake still makes good sense as the material is read. This type of mistake is not as significant as a mistake in which the sense of the material is lost. If the mistakes retain the original meaning, a few more word recognition mistakes would be acceptable in the establishment of the reading level using a percentage criterion. Often context leads the student to insert a word(s) that does not change the meaning. In this case, the insertion should not be counted in determining reading levels. The insertion should be counted if it changes the meaning.

A second factor related to teacher judgment in assessment relates to student *omission of punctuation* and/or slow *word-by-word reading* of the material. When the reader pauses after nearly every word read, even when pronouncing the words correctly, and does not show appreciable variation in these pauses at the ends of sentences or other punctuation, there is reason to believe that understanding may not occur. This may indicate that even when word recognition criteria have been met that the material is difficult for the student.

A third factor to be considered in the judgmental aspects of determining reading levels is the *repetition of the same mistake*. If the student does not know how to pronounce two proper nouns contained in the material, these words may be mispronounced every time they are encountered. This may *not* be a significant error. If, however, the student is unable to pronounce several key concept words in the material, and these errors are repeated throughout the material, it will affect the understanding of the material if these words are unknown. These errors are much more significant in determining reading levels.

A fourth factor to be considered in determining reading levels is the *general behavior* of the student during oral and silent reading. A profusion of reading mannerisms may indicate that the student feels uncomfortable, insecure, or frustrated by the reading. They may also indicate faulty reading habits or a visual problem.

A final factor to be considered is that of *repetitions of words or phrases* during the reading of the material. This may indicate that the student is using context clues effectively but is having difficulty with word recognition at this level. It may also be indicative of a careless reader. If there is a continuing pattern of repetitions, it may mean that this material is difficult for the student.

Estimating Functional Levels

In the establishment of overall reading levels, consider the results of both the oral and silent administrations of the IRI. After noting differences in silent and oral results, consider a composite of these scores to determine overall reading levels for each student.

Sometimes when an IRI is administered silently, the results are higher in the area of comprehension than they were when it was administered orally. Several factors might account for this fact:

1. Silent reading often has a more continuous flow.
2. There is less chance of overconcentration on word pronunciation and more chance of concentration on understanding what has been read.
3. There is no embarrassment over missed words and hesitations or repetitions, which may aid in understanding.

Sometimes when a student is asked to read silently, comprehension appears to drop. This may be due to the fact that the student did not, in fact, read the material, but just sat quietly until the teacher asked the questions. Only observation on the part of the assessor can catch this type of behavior that would invalidate the results of the measures.

Comprehension questions, whether administered following oral or silent reading, may be answered on the basis of the reader's background of experience and knowledge rather than on the information contained in the passage itself. The teacher needs to look carefully at this possibility in establishing reading levels, especially when comprehension appears to be a great deal higher than word recognition. Sometimes the questions asked provide clues to the desired answer. This may also produce an inflated comprehension score. In establishing overall reading levels, then, it is important to be cautious when it appears that a reader can understand a passage very well when that student has not been able to read the words very well. When comprehension scores are several levels higher than word recognition scores, on either silent or oral reading, the teacher needs to take another look for possible explanations.

How are IRI results used to determine reading levels?

The first level to be established is the *independent reading level*. If a student fails to meet *either word recognition or comprehension criteria*, there is reason to believe that this level of material is not at the student's independent reading level. It would appear that the student needs assistance with either the word recognition or comprehension skills before this level of material could be considered at the independent reading level.

The second level to be established is the *instructional reading level*, a higher reading level than the independent reading level. In order for a student to be considered for instruction at any particular reading level, neither word recognition nor comprehension percentages should fall below the level's criteria. It would, however, be possible for a student to have an independent level ability in either word recognition or comprehension but still need instruction in the other of these areas. When this happens, the level at which the student needs instruction in either reading skill area becomes the instructional level—until such time as the weak area can be strengthened. It is possible for a student to have a range of instructional levels. This often happens when the student is independent in one area and instructional in the other area. In this case, a decision concerning in which of these reading levels actually to instruct the student should be made.

Look at Figure 12-11 to determine Joni's instructional level. Although there is an instructional range for Joni of primer through first-reader level, instruction probably should begin at the first-reader level. This decision was based on the fact that Joni's scores were almost equal in both levels, and starting her instruction at the first reader level is justified by the strength of her scores.

The third level to be established is the *frustration level*. It is of utmost importance that students are not taught at the frustration level. Avoidance of this is one of the prime reasons for assessing students' reading levels and skills. If a student is frustrated by either word recognition or comprehension at a given level, that level is the frustration level. Joni's frustration level in Figure 12-11 would be at the second-grade level. The score in silent comprehension at this level was the deciding factor.

A final word of caution concerning the establishment of the overall reading levels is that whenever there is some doubt about whether or not a student is independent or instructional at a given level, it is *always better to err toward the lower level than to err toward the higher one*.

Look at Greg's listening scores below to see that his potential for reading is fourth-grade level. Even though he scored higher than 75 percent at this level, his score at fifth-grade level fell below the 75 percent criterion used to determine potential.

Level	Listening Score
4	80%
5	50%
6	40%

Analyzing Word Recognition Skills

What can an
analysis of an IRI
indicate about
word recognition
skills?

The passage in Figure 12-9 contains fifty-one words. On the first line there are no errors to be counted, only errors that are judgmental in nature. On the second line there are four errors that count: *makes* for *make*, insertion of *a*, misreading of *drifts* as *drift*, and omission of *very*. On the third line there are four errors. One of these is the repeated omission of the word *very*. Since this same error has occurred in the second line, it will not be counted again; however, the unknown word and the misreading of *nobody* will count. The fourth line has only one error that would count—the misreading of *outside*. The last line contains two unknown words that count. This makes a total of nine errors in a fifty-one word passage. Although there are also several judgmental types of errors, no consideration needs to be given to these errors in this passage since the reader was obviously well below instructional level with word recognition accuracy of about 80 percent. Notice that most of the errors do make sense. This indicates that the reader effectively uses context clues but has too much difficulty with word recognition in general. This reader would need to be taught at a lower level for a period of time until more comfort is attained with recognizing words.

In the passage contained in Figure 12-9, there were several compound words—five to be exact: *today, nobody, outside, maybe,* and *snowman*. Of these five compound words, the reader missed two. Based on this small sample, there is reason to believe that this reader has some difficulty with compound words. There are also two words that the reader apparently does not know, and one word omitted both times that it occurred. Try to verbalize an analysis of the other errors contained in Figure 12-9. Notice that one ending was omitted and that there were numerous hesitations as well as an insertion, a substitution, and a repetition.

It is also important to look at a reader's strengths. Based on this passage, the teacher could be relatively certain that the student knows initial consonants since there were no errors in this area. Consonant blends seem to be fine; there are no digraphs. Medial vowels in single-syllable words were correct, but words containing vowel digraphs gave this reader difficulty.

Look at Figure 12-12 where the first column presents the words a reader missed in another selection. The second column contains the word that the reader said, and the third column presents an analysis of the type of word recognition error made. This figure shows a possible analysis of errors. Careful examination of this figure reveals several recurring errors. There are three errors related to r-controlled vowels and three errors related to blends. Sometimes blends and digraphs have been confused. A diagnostic teacher would be able to see some areas of phonics instruction that might be helpful to this reader. When analyzing the word errors, look for a *pattern of errors*. One mistake does not necessarily mean there is a problem. Do not be overanalytical.

FIGURE 12-12
Word Error Analysis

Word Was	Reader Said	Error
hop	hope	CVC; CVe
was	saw	basic sight vocabulary (was and saw)
fish	first	i-ir; sh-st medial vowel; digraph-blend; r-controlled vowel
shave	stove	medial vowel; VCe digraph-blend
stop	shop	st-sh
cute	cut	CVe; VCV
horse	house	or-ou r-controlled vowel diphthong
pay	play	blend
cart	cat	r-controlled vowel

Analyzing Comprehension Ability

How can an IRI be analyzed to determine comprehension ability?

The following steps are used to complete the comprehension error analysis:

1. *Count the number of each type of question asked for each story read.*
2. *Count the number of each type of question missed for each story.*
3. *Calculate the percentage of questions missed for each story to determine percentage of error.*
4. *Compare the percentages of error and determine major comprehension needs.* At the instructional level, 75 percent comprehension is expected; that means that a 25 percent error is acceptable. A greater percentage of error at or below the instructional level can be considered a weakness in comprehension. In Figure 12-13 Chuck's weaknesses are circled and fall in the areas of main idea, detail, and cause and effect. His strengths are in vocabulary and inference.

Using the IRI in Program Planning

The functional reading levels derived from the administration of an IRI can be used for forming instructional groups in the classroom. The analysis of word recognition and comprehension weaknesses can be used for forming skill groups. The procedures for these grouping tactics are discussed in Chapter 13.

FIGURE 12-13
Comprehension Error Analysis

Name _____ Chuck _____ Instructional Level ____3____

Frustration Level ____4____

		Levels		
Skills	**1**	**2**	**3***	**4**
Main idea	1/1 = 100%	1/1 = 100%	1/1 = 100%	1/1 = 100%
Vocabulary	0/2 = 0%	0/1 = 0%	0/1 = 0%	1/1 = 100%
Detail	1/4 = 25%	1/3 = 33⅓%	2/3 = 67%	2/2 = 100%
Inference	0/0 = –	0/1 = 0%	0/2 = 0%	2/4 = 50%
Cause/effect	0/1 = 0%	1/1 = 100%	1/2 = 50%	1/1 = 100%

Major Weaknesses: Main idea   Strengths: Vocabulary
                   Detail   Inference
                   Cause/effect

*Instructional Level

SPECIFIC SKILLS TESTING

What is the place of specific skill testing in assessment?

Further information concerning specific skill strengths and weaknesses may be desirable when a student's performance on an IRI or GRI has been particularly low, resulting in very little material for analysis. When this is true, the teacher may want to use any one of a number of published tests designed to test specific skill areas. Many basal series also include such tests as part of the supplementary material for the series. Many of these tests are criterion-referenced tests, meaning that the student must earn the designated level of accuracy on the test for a specific skill before moving on to the next skill.

Word Recognition Skill Tests

When it seems advisable to administer specific tests to a student, it may be appropriate to begin with a test of the student's knowledge of basic sight vocabulary. One such specific test is the Kucera-Francis list (Johnson, 1971). By administering such a test, the assessor will be able to determine the student's progress toward mastery of these words and be aware of which of these words still need to be taught, retaught, or reinforced in future lessons.

Other sources for word recognition skills tests are those that accompany the basal reader series being used in the classroom. These tests are usually designated to be administered at the end of a unit or book in the basal series and include only those skills taught in that segment of work.

Other specific reading skill tests in the area of word recognition might be teacher-made. Such tests would concentrate on areas of skill development that appeared to be weak based on the error analysis of the IRI.

Comprehension Skill Tests

It is not easy to devise specific comprehension skill tests since comprehension *must* be checked in direct relationship to material read. The best specific measure of the student's ability to comprehend is directly related to the answers the student is able to give in response to questions about what has been read.

Additional specific information for particular comprehension skills may be informally determined based on actual reading lessons. During the guided-reading portion of the DRL, the teacher might concentrate on a particular type of comprehension question, being very careful to note which students seem to be having difficulty with answering that type of question. On another day, another DRL might concentrate on still another type of comprehension, and so on, until each specific type of error could be analyzed based on these lessons.

Teacher-made tests could be devised for the specific meaning vocabulary. An example of such a test would be one that consists of a list of antonyms in two columns; the students would be required to match those words that had opposite meanings. Similarly, a test for synonyms or multiple meanings of words might be devised. Another specific comprehension skill test that might be teacher-devised could be related to the figurative language skills. Again, students might be asked to match the figurative expression to its meaning. In still another area, students might be asked to sort out facts from opinions on a given list of statements, or mark a set of statements as real or fantasy.

Study Skill Tests

A student in middle- and upper-grade levels who is making normal progress in the word recognition and comprehension skill areas would be expected to begin to develop strength in the area of study skills. At this point of development, specific study skills tests would be useful. Again, there are such tests available from publishers (Warncke & Shipman, 1984), and many basal reader series include such tests as supplementary materials to the series.

Informal, teacher-devised measures of study skill strengths may be valuable. Teachers can devise worksheet-type activities to assess such areas as alphabetical order, locating information, knowledge of book parts, outlining, interpreting graphic and pictorial materials, and so forth.

It is important to remember when assessing specific reading skills that the reading materials should not be taxing for the student in terms of word recognition or comprehension, since this might adversely influence the ability to complete the task. We do not recommend total and comprehensive specific skill testing; rather, we suggest selective testing of apparently weak areas that are necessary at a particular level of instruction.

PUTTING IT ALL TOGETHER

Once all testing instruments have been administered, the last task is that of summarizing total results for each student and/or the entire class. This process is discussed in detail in Chapter 13.

PRACTICE EXERCISE

Directions

This series of exercises is designed to help you practice and check your knowledge of informal classroom assessment. Complete each exercise, then check your answers with those in the Answer Key at the end of the text.

Part I

Mark each of the following statements true (T) or false (F). Explain each false (F) response.

_____ 1. The independent reading level is the highest reading level.

Comment _____

_____ 2. In order for a student to be at the instructional level, his word recognition ability should be at least 95 percent.

Comment _____

_____ 3. A student is considered frustrated if either word recognition or comprehension is difficult for him.

Comment _____

_____ 4. Students should be taught at the independent level.

Comment _____

_____ 5. It is better to teach with material that is too easy than with material that is too hard.

Comment _____

_____ 6. It is appropriate to teach on a student's frustration level.

Comment _____

_____ 7. A student has the potential to read at his listening level.

Comment _____

_____ 8. A student should be 99 percent accurate in word recognition and 90 percent accurate in comprehension to be considered independent at that level.

Comment _____

_____ 9. A score of 75 percent accuracy in comprehension is all right at the reader's instructional level.

Comment _____

_____ 10. A student may only have one instructional level.

Comment _____

_____ 11. A GRI measures only silent comprehension.

Comment _____

_____ 12. Listening ability or potential can only be measured by an IRI.

Comment _____

_____ 13. The best instruments for measuring students' specific reading skills are standardized tests.

Comment _____

_____ 14. Interest inventories should only be given to students who are at least a first-grade instructional level in reading.

Comment _____

_____ 15. A record-keeping system is a vital component of an assessment program.

Comment _____

Part II
Choose the best answer for each item.

1. Reading assessment provides the teacher with the means of
   a. establishing a rationale for giving a report card grade in reading
   b. adjusting teaching to students' needs
   c. comparing students to a national norm
   d. determining the student's intellectual ability
   e. all of the above

2. A student's potential for reading is a measurement of the student's _____ ability.
   a. listening
   b. intellectual
   c. reading
   d. word recognition
   e. a and c

3. Reading mannerisms may indicate
   a. frustration
   b. faulty reading habits
   c. visual problems
   d. all of the above
   e. b and c

4. The word list in an IRI is used *primarily* to
   a. get the student accustomed to reading aloud
   b. determine the student's sight vocabulary proficiency
   c. determine on which level to begin the oral reading paragraphs
   d. determine where to begin the silent reading of paragraphs
   e. determine where to begin the assessment of potential

5. A GRI can provide information about
   a. functional levels
   b. comprehension ability
   c. reading mannerisms
   d. word recognition ability
   e. a, b, and c

Use Charts A and B of IRI results to complete items 6 to 10.

Chart A

Level	Word Recognition	Comprehension Skills	Comprehension Skills Silent
PP	Independent	Independent	Independent
P	Independent	Instructional	Instructional
1	Instructional	Instructional	Instructional
2	Instructional	Frustration	Independent
3	Frustration	Frustration	Frustration

Chart B

Level	Word Recognition	Comprehension Skills	Comprehension Skills Silent
1	Instructional	Instructional	—
2	Independent	Instructional	Instructional
3	Instructional	Instructional	Independent
4	Frustration	Instructional	Frustration
5	Frustration	Instructional	Frustration

6. Chart B indicates that
   a. too much testing was done
   b. not enough testing was done
   c. the student's potential is third grade
   d. a and c
   e. none of the above

7. The instructional level for the reader for Chart A is
   a. PP
   b. P
   c. first grade
   d. second grade
   e. third grade

8. The independent level for the reader for Chart B is
   a. not determined
   b. first grade
   c. second grade
   d. fourth grade

9. The frustration level for the reader in Chart A is
   a. not determined
   b. second grade
   c. third grade

10. The instructional level for the reader in Chart B is
    a. not determined
    b. first grade
    c. second grade
    d. third grade
    e. fourth grade

Use Chart C of GRI results to complete items 11–13.

Chart C

Level of Story	Reading Level	Percentage
PP	Independent	100
P	Independent	100
1	Instructional	80
2	Independent	90
3	Independent	90
4	Instructional	80
5	Instructional	80
6	Instructional	75
7	Frustration	70
8	Frustration	40

11. The frustration level is
    a. seventh grade
    b. eighth grade
    c. not determined

12. The independent level is
    a. P
    b. first grade
    c. second grade
    d. third grade

13. The instructional level is
    a. not determined
    b. first grade
    c. fifth grade
    d. sixth grade
    e. fourth grade

Part III

Count the word recognition errors on each line of the marked passage below. Total the errors and determine the percentage of accuracy. Label the percentage as related to the criteria for the word recognition portion of reading levels.

Errors per Line

Termites are small insects. They look a   _____(1)

little like large ants. They live in rotten wood.   _____(2)

They live by eating the wood. They cause much   _____(3)

damage because they destroy the wood they live   _____(4)

in. Sometimes they get into the new wood of   _____(5)

houses. If they are not stopped, they can   _____(6)

cause the house to fall down.   _____(7)

Total number of errors _____
Total number of words _____
Percentage of accuracy _____
Word recognition reading level _____

Part IV

Ask someone to read the following selection to you, making all kinds of word recognition mistakes. It would probably be a good idea to get someone in your class to read it for you, since that person would know what types of errors to make. While the person reads to you, mark the errors made, ask the following comprehension questions, then analyze the word recognition and comprehension errors. Go on to determine that person's reading level for this passage and his specific skill strengths and needs.

Peanut butter cookies can be made by putting one cup of _____

peanut butter, one cup of sugar, and one egg together. _____

These three ingredients should be carefully mixed. _____

Then the baker should form small balls of the dough and _____

pat them down with the tines of a fork before baking _____

them. They should be baked for about ten minutes in a _____

350-degree oven. They are quite good. _____

Comprehension Questions

1. What might be a good title for this selection? (main idea)
2. What three things should be put together to make the cookies? (detail)
3. What should the baker do after the cookies are formed into balls, but before baking the cookies? (sequence)
4. How long should they bake? (detail)
5. How is this cookie recipe different from most recipes? (critical reading)
6. About how many cookies would this recipe make? (inference) What makes you answer as you do?
7. What are the tines of a fork? (vocabulary)
8. Would you enjoy these cookies? Why? (critical)

Total number of words _____

Total number of errors _____

Percentage of accuracy _____

Word recognition reading level _____

Analysis of Word Recognition Errors

(complete the chart below)

	Word Was	*Reader Said*	*Errors*
1.	_____	_____	_____
2.	_____	_____	_____
3.	_____	_____	_____
4.	_____	_____	_____
5.	_____	_____	_____
6.	_____	_____	_____

Patterns of word recognition errors:

Analysis of Comprehension Errors

(complete the chart below)

Type of Questions	Proportion of Errors	Error Percentage
Main idea	_____/1	_____
Detail	_____/2	_____
Sequence	_____/1	_____
Critical	_____/2	_____
Inference	_____/1	_____
Vocabulary	_____/1	_____

Comprehension problems:

Total number of questions _____

Total number of errors _____

Percentage of accuracy _____

Comprehension reading level _____

Overall reading level _____

13

Classroom Organization and Management

What will you
learn in this
chapter?

The real test of being able to teach reading comes in knowing how to organize the class for instruction and how to manage the program that is designed to meet students' needs. The concern of this chapter is to focus on how to use the knowledge learned thus far in this text to plan and operate the classroom reading program.

As you read this chapter you will learn guidelines and techniques for organizing the class for reading instruction and management techniques for a flexible and efficient reading program.

ORGANIZING A CLASSROOM READING PROGRAM

How should a
classroom be or-
ganized for read-
ing instruction?

Organization of the reading program is the manner in which the teacher determines the best way to teach students to read. It involves interpreting information the teacher has concerning the students' reading abilities and needs, analyzing the reading similarities and differences of the class, selecting the appropriate grouping patterns that will enhance instruction, and implementing a systematic plan for reading instruction.

Initial Organization

An organized plan for reading instruction allows the teacher to systematically improve the reading performance of all students in a class. Organization is not rigid and should change throughout the school year. The following basic steps for developing a plan should help with the initial organization of the classroom.

1. *Gather and interpret diagnostic information concerning your students.*
2. *Plan the basic instructional groups.* These are the groups for instruction that follow the reading program or the scope and sequence.
3. *Plan the type of additional grouping patterns that would be needed along with the basic instructional groups.* These patterns should be based on the students' skill needs and interests as well as the teacher's purpose.
4. *Select the materials to be used with each group.* For the basic instructional group this involves selecting the basal series and/or other material assigned to each group.

Regardless of the initial organizational plan chosen, it should be flexible and change with the needs of the students. How to make these changes will be discussed later. We firmly believe that any effective organization is based on individualized instruction.

Individualized Instruction

The effective reading program employs individualized instruction in that it systematically provides students with reading instruction based on their needs. From our point of view, individualization does *not* mean one-to-one instruction for the entire class; however, individualization of reading instruction may involve, from time to time, teaching an individual student. Individualization of reading instruction means that the instructional program for each student is planned around that student's strengths and needs as determined by assessment. It means that the total class is studied by the teacher and then a plan is developed for reading instruction. This may entail grouping as well as some individual work. In any effective reading program, it is very likely that all students will be grouped at some time for instruction. *Flexible* grouping means that groupings will change as needs change. Some students will work in groups while others work individually. Therefore, both group and individual instruction are employed in the concept of individualized instruction (Rosenshine & Stevens, 1984).

GROUPING PATTERNS

What is the basis for forming basic instructional groups, and what steps are involved?

The effective teacher of reading is familiar with various types of grouping for instruction and is able to make competent decisions about which grouping practices are appropriate for a particular time in a specific classroom.

Basic Instructional Groups

The first organizational challenge of the classroom teacher is to develop instructional groups that systematically lead the student along a continuum toward mature reading. The *basic instructional groups* are the ones in which the bulk of reading instruction occurs and in which the students are guided in using all the skills and processes they have been taught.

The basic instructional groups are organized on the basis of information about the students' functional reading levels. The students assigned to a specific basic instructional group would be able to read the same level material with no students being frustrated because the material is too difficult and no student being unchallenged because the material is too easy. The students within the basic instructional group may differ in specific skills or process needs but should be able to handle the material with appropriate instruction from the teacher.

How may a teacher go about organizing basic instructional groups in a classroom? First, record the information about each student's functional levels that was gathered during diagnosis. Figure 13-1 contains this information for a hypothetical third-grade class. A teacher might find it easier to record the information given in Figure 13-1 on

FIGURE 13-1
Third-Grade Class List

Student	Independent Reading Level	Instructional Reading Level	Frustration Reading Level
1. Mike	PP	1-2	3
2. Sue	1	2	3
3. Ann	1	2-3	4
4. Tom	3	4-5	6
5. Ed	2	3	4-5
6. Sara	P	1-2	3
7. Winnie	1-2	2-3	6
8. Larry	3	4-5	6
9. Hank	3	4	6
10. Joan	1	2	3-4
11. Joe	2	3	4
12. Rick	3	4	6
13. Edna	PP	1	2
14. Kay	PP	P	1
15. Bill	3	4-5	6
16. Mark	4	5-6	7
17. Mary	2	3	4
18. Peggy	1	2-3	4
19. Ruth	2	3	4
20. Don	2	3	4
21. George	1	2-3	4
22. Dick	2	3	4
23. Jim	2	3-4	5
24. Jack	2	3-4	5

FIGURE 13-2
Student Record Card

Name _____ Age _____ Date_____

Reading Levels

Independent _____ Instructional _____ Frustration _____

Potential _____

Put a (+) on those areas mastered.

Prereading

Letter Name _____	Initial	Prefixes _____	Main Idea _____
Visual	Consonants _____	Suffixes _____	Sequence _____
Discrimination _____	Final		
Auditory	Consonants _____	Endings _____	Inferencing _____
Discrimination _____	Blends _____	Compounds _____	Dictionary _____
Left-Right _____	Digraphs _____	Syllabication _____	Table of
Listening _____	Long Vowels _____		Contents _____
Spelling		*Comprehension-*	Index _____
Vocabulary _____	Short Vowels _____	*Study Skills*	
Oral Sentence	r-controlled	Vocabulary _____	Maps _____
Structure _____	Vowels _____		
	Vowel	Context _____	Graphs _____
Word Recognition	Generalizations _____	Details _____	
Sight			
Vocabulary _____	Diphthongs _____		

(Comments on Back)

index cards or on a card similar to the one shown in Figure 13-2. Cards are more convenient for formulating the groups since they can be shuffled as groups are formed. Next, follow these steps designed to form basic instructional groups.

1. *List the names of all the students who have the exact same recorded instructional reading level.* Using cards, simply stack the cards in groups. Continue the listing or stacking until every name or card has been placed. Figure 13-3 indicates appropriate grouping for the hypothetical third-grade class.

Most teachers think that it is not possible to manage ten reading groups. Now notice the overlap at various instructional levels such as 1-2, 2-3, 3-4, 4-5, and 5-6. Some students have an instructional range that includes more than one grade level.

2. *Regroup the students by studying the groups that have overlap (1-2, 2-3, etc.) until you have arrived at a manageable number of groups.* Several guidelines may be used to do this.

FIGURE 13-3
Students' Instructional Levels

P	1	1-2	2	2-3	3	3-4	4	4-5	5-6
Kay	Edna	Mike	Sue	Ann	Ed	Jim	Hank	Tom	Mark
		Sara	Joan	Winnie	Joe	Jack	Rick	Bill	
				Peggy	Mary			Larry	
				George	Ruth				
					Don				
					Dick				

a. It is better to place a student at a level that is too easy rather than to begin at a level that is too difficult.

b. Look at independent and frustration levels. Notice Winnie's scores in Figure 13-1. They should help in forming the decision that she could best be placed in a third-grade level rather than a second-grade level. Her sixth-grade frustration and first-second grade independent levels would lead you to that decision. George's independent and frustration scores indicate that a second-grade instructional level would be the best choice for him. Complete groupings for this class and compare the results with those in Figure 13-4.

There are many ways to organize this class for basic instructional groups. The major point which was kept in mind while working out the plan given in Figure 13-4 is that students need to be started in instructional materials where they can have success without being bored or insulted.

3. *Try out the basic instructional groups for a week to see if they are appropriately organized.* This step will help to confirm or reject decisions. Using the reading materials selected for them, teach a Directed Reading Lesson and give some independent work. At the end of the week of tryouts, make the needed changes.

During the trial period, look for these things:

a. Are the students able to work independently?

FIGURE 13-4
Suggested Basic Instructional Groups

1	2	3	4	Individualized
Edna (1)	Sue (2)	Ed (3)	Hank (4)	Mark (5-6)
Mike (1-2)	Joan (2)	Joe (3)	Larry (4-5)	Kay (P)
Sara (1-2)	Ann (2-3)	Mary (3)	Rick (4)	
	Peggy (2-3)	Ruth (3)	Tom (4-5)	
	George (2-3)	Don (3)	Bill (4-5)	
		Dick (3)		
		Jim (3-4)		
		Jack (3-4)		
		Winnie (2-3)		

b. Is the vocabulary load of the material too great?

c. Are students able to retain new vocabulary that has been taught?

d. Is the range of performance within the group too great?

After the tryout period is over and adjustments are made, proceed with the basic instructional groups. The *major* organizational component of an effective reading program is complete.

Specific Skill Groups

How does a teacher form other kinds of groups and why?

Another type of group to be considered is the one in which the instruction focuses on the specific skill needs of the students that are not in the scope and sequence for their basic instructional group, that is, skills that students should have mastered but have not. These specific skill groups should be organized within the basic instructional groups. If teachers set up skill groups without paying attention to the instructional reading levels of the students, it leads to two major problems. Students in the skill groups have such a wide range of reading levels that it is next to impossible to teach anything, and the wide range of reading levels within the group makes the application of skills difficult. Three steps should be followed in organizing skill groups:

1. Within each basic instructional group determine the word recognition skills and comprehension skills and processes each student needs to have for initial instruction.
2. Group together within the basic instructional group those students who have the same needs.
3. Consider combining students from several different instructional levels who have the same needs *only* when they do not fit in their basic instructional group.

Interest Groups

Grouping students for basic instructional needs and specific skill needs is important; however, research indicates that oftentimes the low-achieving student does not profit from these groupings as much as the higher achieving student (Anderson et al., 1985). The formation of interest groups can be used to foster improved instruction for low-achieving students.

Many times one student or a group of students will be interested in a particular topic or book that someone else or another group is reading; however, because of the basic instructional or specific skill group they are in, they are unable to take advantage of this interest. It is important that opportunities be created for students to work in interest and/or peer groups.

Time should be scheduled regularly for such groups to get together and work on areas of interest. This may involve listening activities, having one student read to others, having students act out a story, or doing a variety of other creative activities. Interest groups should motivate students and give them a more positive feeling about themselves.

Peer Groups

Peer groups can do many of the same types of activities as the interest groups, but here the concern is letting friends who like to be together be together. Peer groups could play games to practice skills as well as do any of the creative, fun types of experiences that relate to reading. It is too easy to neglect this type of grouping. However, it allows students to learn from each other. Some students are competitive in such groupings and truly grow to meet the challenge of friends.

Subject Groups

Subject groups can be used when the teacher wishes to put students together to work on a special subject-area project such as a social studies unit. Students with different reading levels may be grouped to complete parts of a project. For example, some students in a science group may have to read only simple directions to gather materials for a group experiment while others in the group must read to research a topic related to the experiment. These groups often represent the best combination of reading and subject matter.

Whole Group

Currently some schools are returning to large-group reading instruction by combining students of similar instructional levels together. This most often occurs in buildings where more than one section of a particular grade level exists. Students from the various classrooms who read at the same instructional level, perhaps regardless of age or grade level, are regrouped for reading instruction. The philosophy is that this type of "homogeneous" grouping allows like students to work together in a longer instructional period and permits the teacher to be more effective.

Not all reading specialists agree with this trend. Some of the possible problems are that there is less time for direct interaction between the teacher and each student; all of the students who read at the same instructional level may not have the same reading strengths and weaknesses; the opportunity is diminished for students to learn how to work independently as the teacher attends to other groups in the classroom; when the teacher works with a large group, the chance of a student(s) becoming lost or withdrawing from the group activity unnoticed increases.

Implementation of individualized instruction has been the goal of reading teachers for the past few decades. How whole class or large-group instruction impacts on this remains to be seen. At the least, reading educators should maintain an open mind while investigating this current trend or any future trend.

Organizational Pattern Changes

All grouping that is done as a part of the instructional program in reading should be flexible. Students will grow and change in two basic ways in reading: reading levels and specific skill needs. There are likely to be more frequent changes in specific skill groups than there are in basic instructional groups.

Changes in basic instructional groups should be made on the basis of teacher observation and judgment of student work and/or hard evidence from tests such as an IRI or a GRI. Many students complete materials and still need more work at the same level.

Skill group changes become evident as the teacher works with the groups. Those in a group who master skills move on while those who need more instruction may separate from the group and join another group. The best evidence of skill mastery is the application of the skill as the student reads. Students may do workbook pages correctly or even score satisfactorily on a skills test and not be able to apply the skill(s) when reading. Applying skills when reading is the true measure of skill mastery and should override contradictory test or workbook scores.

The application of the concepts of organization to the classroom where *beginning* reading instruction is taking place requires a special note. Basic instructional groups are organized at first around pupil readiness for learning to read. The groups may even resemble the specific skill groups more than basic instructional groups because they will be focusing on the specific prereading skills and abilities that need to be developed. The same principles of organization should be applied to the classroom for beginning readers as would be used with any other class. These principles must just be viewed slightly differently as the program begins.

MANAGEMENT OF THE CLASSROOM READING PROGRAM

What are the areas of management techniques, and how are they implemented?

Management of the classroom reading program refers to the procedures used in keeping the program running smoothly. This includes the techniques a teacher employs for keeping records of students' reading needs and progress, the scheduling of the instructional activities, and the maintenance of a favorable learning environment.

Management includes all the details that make a difference in whether or not a reading program functions efficiently. The lack of a good management system is one of the things that separates the effective classroom reading teacher from the mediocre or unsuccessful one. *A good management system depends on preplanning and continuous planning.* Students who work in a well-managed classroom are more apt to be able to attend to instruction and their tasks (Johnson & Bany, 1970).

Record Keeping

An effective reading program should have some record-keeping system for plotting student growth. This system should be one which is school-wide or system-wide. These records should be passed along from year to year and should provide each teacher with a clear profile of what has taken place in the students' reading development.

Many types of reading records may be used. The sample presented in Figure 13-2 is an example of an informal card that provides enough space for a teacher to keep track of what is going on in a student's reading during a particular school year.

Figure 13-5 presents a more complete type of record. Ideally, records should be simple but useful in providing teachers with the type and quality of information needed to operate effectively in teaching reading. It is important that records be kept systematically. Each school may develop its own records or select and adapt records that have been published or developed by other schools. (Permission must be obtained from copyright holder or the school to use or adapt record forms already printed.) Each category cited below should be included in the records.

Reading Levels.   This area of the record should give information about the student's independent, instructional, and frustration reading levels. Potential should also be noted. Figure 13-5 presents a sample record sheet that was developed by an individual school. This type of record could be adapted to fit any school's reading program.

Specific Skill Growth.   There has been a tendency to make specific skill growth overly detailed. Some schools may want more detail than others, but caution should be exercised in not making the record so detailed that it becomes a cumbersome, useless burden to the teacher. The skill record should reflect those skills taught to the student and those mastered and retained by the student. The record presented in Figure 13-5 provides for such information.

FIGURE 13-5
Sample Reading Record

Reading Skills Checklist

Name _____ Age _____

Reading Levels	Date	( )	( )	( )	( )	( )	( )
Independent		____	____	____	____	____	____
Instructional		____	____	____	____	____	____
Frustration		____	____	____	____	____	____
Potential		____	____	____	____	____	____

Student Test Data
Specific Skills: + mastered; – not mastered; ⊕ retained; blank = not taught

Prereading	1	2	3	4	5	6	**Comments**
Letter Names							
Visual Discrimination							
Auditory Discrimination							

FIGURE 13-5
Sample Reading Record (continued)

Prereading	1	2	3	4	5	6	Comments
Left-Right							
Listening							
Speaking Vocabulary							
Oral Sentence Structure							

Word Recognition	1	2	3	4	5	6	Comments
Sight Vocabulary (Level)							
Initial Consonant							
Final Consonant							
Silent Consonant							
Blends							
Digraphs							
Long Vowels							
Short Vowels							
r-controlled Vowels							
Two Vowel Rules							
Medial Vowel Rule							
VC Rule							
Open Syllable Rule							
Diphthongs							
Prefixes							
Suffixes							
Inflectional Endings							
Compounds							
Contractions							

FIGURE 13-5
Sample Reading Record *(continued)*

Word Recognition	1	2	3	4	5	6	Comments
VCC Rule							
VCV Rule							
le Rule							
Affix Rule							

Comprehension-Study Skills	1	2	3	4	5	6	Comments
Vocabulary							
Context Clues							
Details							
Main Idea							
Sequence							
Inferencing							
Critical/Evaluation							
Dictionary							
Table of Contents							
Index							
Maps							
Graphs							

Materials Used

Grade 1	
Grade 2	
Grade 3	

FIGURE 13-5
Sample Reading Record (continued)

Materials Used

Grade 4		
Grade 5		
Grade 6		

Teacher Comments

Grade 1		
Grade 2		
Grade 3		
Grade 4		
Grade 5		
Grade 6		

Materials Used.   Materials that have been used for *direct instructional* purposes should be noted. The record does not need to include every piece of material or exercise used by a student but should indicate the major sources used during a year. The sample record presented in Figure 13-5 shows one way of recording materials.

Teacher Comments.   A final inclusion in the reading record is a provision for noting comments by the teacher. Figure 13-5 provides space for any teacher to add comments concerning the student's reading progress. Only appropriate comments that clarify other items on the record form need to be included. Therefore, teachers should only make comments that will aid future teachers as they plan a student's reading program (Cooper & Worden, 1983).

Published Reading Records

Most basal reader series have some type of record-keeping system available that correlates with the materials of the series. The disadvantage of some of these systems is that they are complicated and time consuming to use.

There are also computer programs available for record keeping. Some basal reader series also have these available for teacher use. These systems have the advantage of a reader-made format into which the teacher simply enters the appropriate data. Modifying the software to meet the desires of the individual teacher is not always readily accomplished. The teacher must decide the merits of the program in relation to the type and amount of records necessary to aid with the smooth operation of a reading program.

Scheduling Reading Activities

What should a teacher know about planning a time schedule?

The amount of time devoted to direct instruction in reading may vary from one hour to several hours a day, depending on the school and grade level. The way this time is used for groups and individuals within the classroom program depends on students' needs. One of the best ways to learn to manage classroom time is to attempt to predict what will happen before each day begins. The more skilled the teacher becomes at predicting, the easier management of time will be.

Developing a Time Schedule

In developing a time schedule and making it work, a number of guidelines should be followed. As the teacher begins to plan time schedules, the following points should be considered:

1. The younger the students, the shorter their attention spans are likely to be; therefore, plan in segments of time that are in line with students' attention spans. At the beginning primary levels, these segments may be as short as ten minutes or less.
2. The teacher should work with groups or individuals throughout the reading period. The students should not all be working independently for long periods.
3. The less able readers need frequent, direct contact with the teacher. These contacts may not be long.
4. Individualized instruction does not mandate that each student or group of students have the same amount of teacher time. Some need daily, direct contact with teacher; others may be able to work independently for longer periods.
5. To provide a smooth-running schedule, routines of behavior and operation should be developed. This includes independent activities available for students when the assigned work is complete.

How are the sample schedules alike and different?

Figures 13-6 and 13-7 present sample schedules for a primary-level teacher and an intermediate-level teacher, respectively. Notice that the segments of time used for planning the schedule are shorter in the primary schedule. This is to account for the students' short attention span. The teachers in each of these classes have a range of reading levels to deal with each day.

FIGURE 13-6
Primary-Level Time Schedule

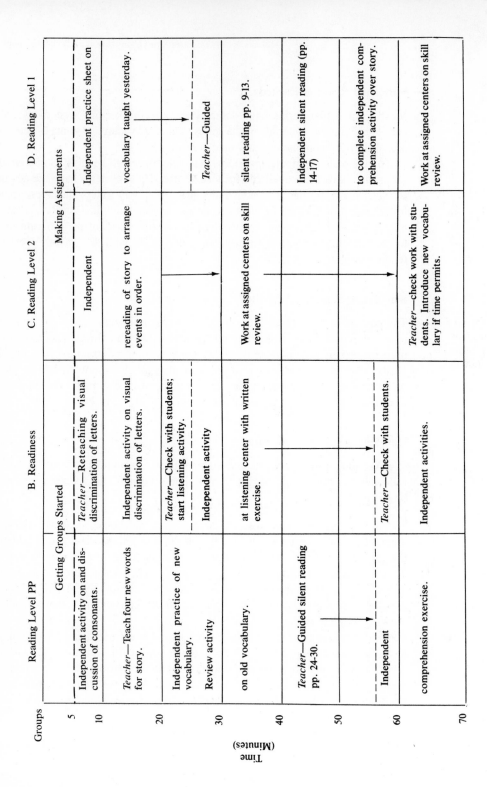

FIGURE 13-7
Intermediate-Level Time Schedule

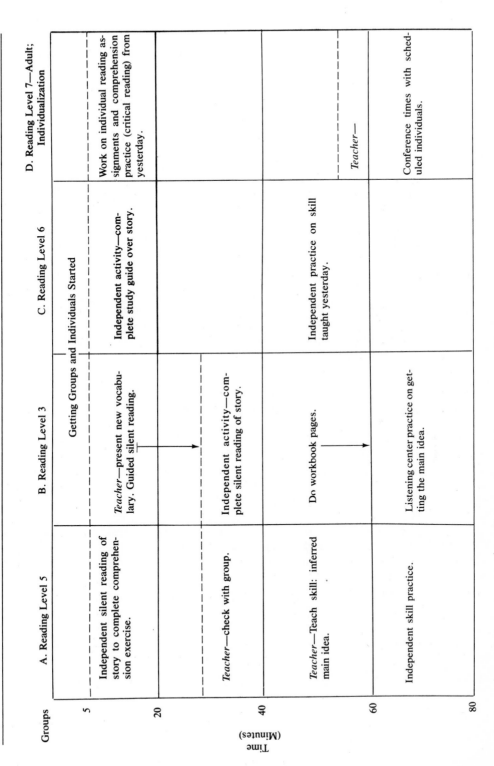

Groups	A. Reading Level 5	B. Reading Level 3	C. Reading Level 6	D. Reading Level 7—Adult; Individualization
		Getting Groups and Individuals Started		
5	Independent silent reading of story to complete comprehension exercise.	*Teacher*—present new vocabulary. Guided silent reading.	Independent activity—complete study guide over story.	Work on individual reading assignments and comprehension practice (critical reading) from yesterday.
20	*Teacher*—check with group.	Independent activity—complete silent reading of story.		
40	*Teacher*—Teach skill: inferred main idea.	Do workbook pages.	Independent practice on skill taught yesterday.	
60	Independent skill practice.	Listening center practice on getting the main idea.		*Teacher*—
80			Conference times with scheduled individuals.	

Time (Minutes)

Look at the schedules in terms of each teacher's activities. In both schedules notice that the teacher is always actively involved with a group or an individual where some type of instructional task is being performed; these tasks range from teaching new vocabulary or skills to conferring with individuals.

Another important point to notice in each of the sample schedules is that each teacher uses a variety of types of activities for both independent work and teacher-directed instructional tasks. Activities assigned as independent work are related either to the teaching taking place on the particular day or are related to previously taught lessons.

The amount of time spent with each group or individual varies in terms of needs and the task to be accomplished. For example, in the intermediate schedule, one group has no direct contact with the teacher on this particular day. Teachers have operated far too long with the misconception that the teacher must spend an equal amount of time with each group each day. Teachers must learn to adjust the time spent with a group or individual to suit the needs and task at hand. It is equally poor practice to simply assign the better readers task after task to get them out of the way. The better readers need direction in using the higher level comprehension skills and being challenged to make more sophisticated use of their reading in general.

Avoid getting into the rut of one pattern of operation where the same group always begins. This will prevent having the flexibility and management skills that are needed to be an effective classroom reading teacher.

MAINTAINING A FAVORABLE LEARNING ENVIRONMENT

What is a favorable learning environment, and what routines should be developed?

The authors believe that a classroom that has a positive atmosphere in which students practice self-discipline is a classroom that has a favorable climate for learning.

To a great extent children learn to do and become what we expect them to be. As long as they know what our expectations are, their actions will reflect them. With this in mind, think about the role of routines and independent activities in the organization and management of the classroom reading program.

The routines that are developed and the independent activities that are used help to provide the time in the schedule when the teacher is free to work with groups or individuals. The entire management of the classroom program hinges on these components.

Students at all levels need to know what they are to do and when they are to do it. The more choices and decisions students have to make on their own, the more basic routines of operation they need. There are three steps to follow in developing routines:

1. Develop general classroom behavior.
2. Let students know what is going to happen and when it will happen.
3. Have sufficient independent activities available.

The first step in developing the routines which will make the reading program run smoothly is taking the time to develop general classroom behavior. This is not laying down the law and spelling out the rules. Rather, it is the time to discuss what constitutes good behavior in an environment where other people must be considered. It is the time when the teacher and students might develop a list of appropriate classroom rules to try. Reasonable consequences of nonconformity should also be discussed. Methods of praise or rewards for accepting responsibility for appropriate behavior are helpful and should be discussed.

The second step in developing routines is letting students know what is going to happen and when it is going to happen. In many instances, students may even participate in the planning of this type of schedule that might be nothing more than a listing on the chalkboard of what will occur at various times during the day. Students then need to be strongly encouraged to budget their time to complete tasks in the assigned time in order to be ready for the next scheduled activity.

The final step in developing classroom routines is having available sufficient independent activities for students to do beyond their assigned work. These activities will give students many opportunities to extend their experiences and will broaden their concepts in addition to providing opportunities to practice skills. If students are to become independent workers and learners, they must be put into situations where they are expected to work independently. These activities fall into two categories: those that fit directly into the instructional process and those which are self-selected by students.

Instructional process activities are assigned to students as a direct part of the instructional process and must fit the objective for the skill or area being developed. The necessary teaching must have taken place to ensure that the students are ready for the independent activity assigned.

Self-selected activities are ones that students would do when they have completed their assigned instructional process activities. They should have clear directions that students can easily understand.

PUTTING IT ALL TOGETHER

A key to operating an effective reading program is having systematic organizational components. The goal is to have individualized instruction based on the needs of students. Guidelines for organizing and grouping have been discussed. Along with the groups, teachers need to have scheduled conference times to work with those individual students who are not working in a group at that particular time.

Basic to the operation of a well-organized classroom reading program is the teaching cycle. This arbitrarily designated period of time when certain skills will be taught forces the teacher into a pattern that requires continuous reevaluation on a scheduled basis and helps to keep the grouping flexible. The real test of the classroom reading teacher is in being able to put all of this together and make it work. Continuous self-evaluation on the part of the teacher is necessary to develop the skills needed to organize and manage an effective reading program. No one has ever said the job would be easy, but it will be exciting, time consuming, challenging, disturbing, frustrating, and rewarding.

PRACTICE EXERCISE

Directions

This series of exercises is designed to help you practice and check your knowledge of the skills needed to organize and manage your reading program in the classroom. Complete each exercise, then check your answers with those in the Answer Key at the end of the text.

Part I

Match the terms in column A with the correct definitions in column B. Some items in column B will not be used.

Column A

_____ 1. individualization

_____ 2. basic instructional group

_____ 3. organization

_____ 4. interest groups

_____ 5. management

_____ 6. self-selected activities

_____ 7. specific skill group

_____ 8. peer groups

Column B

a. the level where a student can read alone

b. friends working in reading together

c. teacher meeting with a single student to go over work

d. a record of progress

e. activities that might be used by students after all assigned work has been completed

f. groups organized for skill work

g. the procedures for keeping the class running smoothly

h. planning a reading program based on the needs of each student

i. planning for reading instruction

j. groups organized around the functional levels

k. students working together on an area of interest

Part II

Study the following fifth-grade class list and answer the questions that follow.

		Reading Levels		
Students	Interests	Independent	Instructional	Frustration
Mike	Space	6	7-9	10
Sue	Travel	3	4-5	6
Ted	Adventure	3	4	5
Les	Everything	5	6	7

Students	Interests	Reading Levels		
		Independent	**Instructional**	**Frustration**
Patsy	Horses	4	5	6
Karen	Crafts	1	2-3	4
Tom	Rockets	4	5-6	7
Mary	Auto Racing	1	2	3
Larry	Adventure	1	2	3
Bill	Funny Stories	7	8-9	?
Mae	Romance	3	4	5
Kay	Animals	3	4	5
Frank	Space	4	5	6
Niki	Travel	4	5-6	7
Ann	Adventure	3	4	5
Mark	Crafts	1	2-3	4
Leo	Auto Racing	6	7-8	9
Carl	Animals	3	4	5
Dick	Dogs	4	5	6
Ruthie	Anything	4	4-6	7
Dori	Horses	3	4-5	6

1. Which of the three reading levels would you review first in determining grouping for use of a basal reader?
   a. independent
   b. instructional
   c. frustration
   d. all

2. How many basic instructional groups will you have for this class?
   a. four
   b. three
   c. ten
   d. five

3. Whom would you place in a basic instructional group at fourth-grade level?
   a. Carl, Ann, Dori, Niki, Sue
   b. Ann, Ted, Kay, Sue, Mae
   c. Ted, Mae, Kay, Ann, Carl
   d. Sue, Ted, Dori, Ann, Mae

4. At which level would you place Karen and Mark?
   a. second grade
   b. third grade
   c. fourth grade
   d. first grade

5. Which students would be the most likely candidates for an individualized basic instructional group?
   a. Mike
   b. Les, Leo
   c. Mike, Leo, Bill
   d. None

6. Whom would you put in an interest group working on animals?
   a. Ted, Larry, Ann, Ruthie
   b. Patsy, Kay, Carl, Dick, Dori
   c. Dori, Ruthie, Carl, Niki, Bill
   d. Mary, Tom, Les, Ann, Mark

Part III
Study the time schedule on page 257 and answer the following questions.

1. What is missing from the beginning of this schedule?

2. In the second time slot, what has this teacher done that is in violation of a major management principle?

3. What principle(s) has this teacher failed to follow in planning the schedule for Groups C and D?

4. Instructionally, what is wrong with the schedule for Group B?

5. Instructionally, what is wrong with the schedule for Group A?

Third-Grade Time Schedule For Mr. Jones

Groups / Time (Minutes)	A. Reading Level 3	B. Reading Level 4	C. Reading Level 1	D. Reading Level 2
20	Independent silent reading.	Teacher—Present new vocabulary for story to be read.	Independent work.	Independent skill work and silent reading.
40		Independent silent reading.		
60	Teacher—discussion of story.		Independent work at learning centers.	
80	Independent practice of new skill.	Teacher—practice new vocabulary.		

Part IV
Each of the following groups of items relates to organization and management of the classroom reading program. Study each group; circle each item that does not belong and tell why. The first one is done for you.

1. Reading levels, materials used, specific skills, (days absent)

   Others are information to be kept on reading record.

2. Scheduling, basic instructional groups, classroom routines, independent activities.

3. Interests, reading levels, skill needs, conferences

4. Capable readers, time slots, more frequent, less able readers

5. Reading card, teacher made, published, self-contained

Answer Keys

CHAPTER 1

Part I
1. f
2. b
3. a
4. g
5. e
6. d
7. c

Part II
1. b
2. c
3. b
4. d
5. a
6. b
7. c
8. b
9. d
10. b
11. c
12. a

Part III
Answers will vary; check with your instructor.

Part IV

Answer will vary; check with your instructor.

Part V

Answers may vary.
1. bilingual—build oral language, use language experience method
2. cultural, dialectical, or language different—fill in gaps in knowledge, have frequent oral reading
3. handicapped—individualize, move slowly
4. gifted—challenge, individualize

CHAPTER 2

Part I
1. a. oral language development
   b. experiential background
   c. auditory discrimination ability
   d. visual discrimination ability
   e. directionality
2. Readiness is ongoing; prereading before formal reading instruction. Some factors are same in each.
3. sleep and food, for example
4. real and vicarious

Part II
1. directionality
2. visual discrimination
3. auditory discrimination
4. experiential background/language development
5. oral language development

Part III
1. T
2. T
3. T
4. F
5. F

Part IV
1. e
2. c
3. a
4. d
5. d

CHAPTER 3

Part I

1. b	6. d
2. a	7. b
3. c	8. a
4. c	9. c
5. b	10. c

Part II

1. Sentences 1, 2, and 3—the reader must note the details given to ultimately understand who is being followed.
2. Sentence 5—the reader notes that the person walks and then steps.
3. Sentence 4—as ugly as a Halloween monster; also sentence 8.
4. Paragraph 1—the reader must determine that this person is following an ugly man. This is inferred.
5. Sentences 1, 2, and 3—the reader must infer that this is a man.
6. Sentences 9 and 10—the reader must judge that the author is trying to sway the reader.
7. Sentences 7 and 8—sentence 8 is fact. Sentence 9 is opinion.
8. Sentences 5 and 6—the word *dense* is clearly defined from context.
9. Throughout the paragraphs the reader would have to monitor to understand.
10. Sentence 1—recognizing that the author is telling the story or using first person. Sentences 4 and 8—the author is using similes.

Part III

1. f	9. g
2. j	10. e
3. l	11. n
4. c	12. o
5. i	13. b
6. m	14. k
7. a	15. d
8. h	

Part IV

1. barriers to critical reading
2. types of literature; part of literary appreciation
3. a strategy for teaching monitoring
4. propaganda techniques
5. types of context clues

CHAPTER 4

Part I

1. d	11. c
2. a	12. b
3. c	13. b
4. a	14. c
5. d	15. b
6. d	16. c
7. c	17. d
8. b	18. b
9. b	19. d
10. a	20. b

Part II

1. d—final *e* or CVCe generalization
2. b—soft *g* generalization or
   e—CVC generalization
3. c—CVC generalization
4. e—CVVC generalization
5. e—if only first syllable of music is considered; c if second syllable is—open syllable generalization
6. d—controlled vowel sound

Part III

1. d	8. n
2. h	9. p
3. c	10. o
4. f	11. l
5. j	12. b
6. k	13. a
7. m	14. i or l

Part IV

1. ē/kon, ĕk/on
2. rōash/ing
3. whŏch/mĕnt
4. slŭp/pĕl/gŭg, slŭpp/ĕl/gŭg
5. prē/sīl/năp/ĭsh/mĕnt, prē/sīl/nā/pĭsh/mĕnt
6. drăck/le
7. măs/tle, măst/le
8. krŏm/sŭl
9. blēt/ing

Part V

1. b

2. a

3. a

4. c

5. d

6. b

7. c

8. d

9. a

10. a

CHAPTER 5

Part I

1. completed in practice exercise
2. alphabetical order—all others have to do with outlining
3. almanac—not related to maps
4. bar graph—not related to dictionaries
5. thesaurus—not related to locating materials in a library

Part II

1. h, n

2. e

3. g

4. k

5. j

6. b, o, p

7. m, n

8. c

9. a

10. l

11. i

12. f

13. d

14. b, o, p

15. h

Part III

1. b

2. d

3. a

4. d

5. c

6. a

7. b

8. d

9. d

10. a

CHAPTER 6

Part I

1. c

2. b

3. b

4. c

5. d

6. a

7. c

8. a

9. a

10. d

Part II

1. a	6. a
2. c	7. b
3. a	8. a
4. c	9. b
5. b	10. c

Part III

1. T	6. T
2. T	7. T
3. F	8. F
4. F	9. T
5. T	10. T

Part IV

1. a
2. d
3. d
4. e
5. e

CHAPTER 7

Part I

1. VCCV and/or short vowel
   teach
2. meaning vocabulary, antonyms
   practice
3. phonics—maybe VCe and/or the blend *gr*
   T, P, or A (be prepared to defend your choice)
4. meaning vocabulary, homophones
   practice
5. consonant digraphs
   teach (decoding—symbol/sound)
6. meaning vocabulary—synonyms
   practice
7. vocabulary
   apply
8. vocabulary
   teach
9. study skills—organizing information
   apply (science teacher probably didn't teach outlining)

10. study skills—locating information
    apply (student went to library without teacher direction)
11. phonics—consonant blends
    teach—substitution
12. context clues
    practice
13. literal comprehension of detail
    teach
14. vowel digraph (*ea*) generalization
    apply (guided silent reading)

Part II
1. d
2. a
3. b,c
4. b
5. c,d,e

6. b
7. a,b,c,d
8. e
9. a,d
10. d

Part III
1. Completed in practice exercise.
2. Direct instruction; correct.
3. Comprehension; error; Steps should be modeling, concept, listening, reading.
4. Study skills; error; modeling should follow skills.
5. Direct instruction; error; apply should be listed last.

CHAPTER 8

Part I
1. a, h
2. b, d
3. b, g
4. a, h, c

5. a, f, h
6. a
7. b, e, i
8. j

Part II
1. dictionary; c, a, d, b
2. adjusting to context clues; d, b, a, c, e
3. whole word; b, d, c, a, e
4. compare and contrast; b, a, c
5. word analysis; a, c, d, b
6. vocabulary prediction; b, d, a, c
7. picture clues; a, b

Part III

1. d—others are preteaching strategies
2. c—others are techniques for building background
3. a—others are expansion and enrichment strategies
4. d—others are part of the instructional model

Part IV

1. b—locating entry words and selecting correct meaning require knowledge of alphabetical order
2. d—all vocabulary strategies attend to word meaning
3. a—overemphasis on picture clues leads to readers who lack analysis skills required for independence

CHAPTER 9

Part I

1. d	6. d
2. a	7. b
3. c	8. c
4. d	9. b
5. a	10. b

Part II

1. Answers will vary; should require reader to focus on entire selection.
2. What color is the snowshoe rabbit's fur in winter? (white)
3. Answers will vary; check with your instructor.
4. Answers will vary.
5. Answers will vary.

Part III

Answers will vary; check with your instructor.

CHAPTER 10

Part I

1. T	6. F
2. F	7. F
3. T	8. F
4. T	9. T
5. F	10. T

Part II
Answers will vary and should be discussed with classmates and instructor.

CHAPTER 11

Part I

1. c	6. e
2. a	7. d
3. c, d	8. d
4. a	9. c
5. b	10. d

Part II

1. a	4. d
2. d	5. d
3. c	6. c

Part III
1. F—the range for most basal readers is from prereading through junior high school
2. T
3. F—students choose materials in the individualized approach
4. F—teachers' manuals are vital components of the basal reader approach
5. T
6. F—an eclectic approach can be effective for teaching reading
7. F—the teacher is the key
8. F—the DRL is based on the basal reader approach
9. T

CHAPTER 12

Part I
1. F—the highest level is frustration
2. T
3. T
4. F—students should be taught at the instructional level
5. T
6. F—students should be taught at the instructional level
7. T
8. T
9. T
10. F—students may have an instructional range

11. F—it can also measure potential
12. F—potential can also be measured by a GRI
13. F—teacher-made and other informal tests can be used
14. F—there are interest inventories for nonreaders
15. T

Part II

1. b
2. a
3. d
4. c
5. e
6. b
7. c

8. a
9. b
10. d
11. a
12. d
13. d

Part III

Line 1—2
Line 2—4
Line 3—2
Line 4—3
Line 5—2
Line 6—2
Line 7—1

Total number of errors: <u>16</u>

Total number of words: <u>56</u>

Percentage of accuracy: <u>72</u>

Word recognition reading level: <u>Frustration</u>

Part IV

Answers will vary; check by reviewing in text and/or in class discussion.

CHAPTER 13

Part I

1. h
2. j
3. i
4. k

5. g
6. e
7. f
8. b

Part II

1. b
2. a
3. c

4. a
5. c
6. b

Part III

1. no time is indicated to get groups started
2. all groups are working independently at the same time
3. less able readers need direct teacher contact frequently and for shorter periods of time
4. vocabulary practice came after independent silent reading; it should have come before silent reading
5. there is no teaching of a new skill to be practiced unless it was taught on another day

Part IV

(accept any reasonable answer)
1. Completed in practice exercise.
2. Basic instructional groups; others have to do with management.
3. Conferences; others form basis for organizing.
4. Capable readers; others pertain to scheduling with less able readers.
5. Self-contained; others have to do with progress records.

A
Affix Listing

Prefixes	Meaning	Examples
ad	to, toward, in; addition to	adjacent, adjoin
com (con)	with, together	compel, conclude
de	down, away, off; reversing, undoing, or taking away	deport, denature
dis	not; destroying of, lack of; to take away, remove; to make not, undo, reverse	disable, discourage, discard, disappear, disassemble
ex	out; beyond; thoroughly; formerly but not now	expire, expand, exquisite, ex-wife
in (il, im, un, ir)	in, within, toward; not	incline, incrust, indistinct
inter	between, among; mutual or mutually	interlock, interact
mis	amiss, wrong, bad	mistrial, mistook

Prefixes	Meaning	Examples
mono	one, single	monogamy
non	not	noncomplying, nonactive
pre	before	prenatal, predict
pro	forward, onward; in the place of; before	promote, protest
re	back; again	rewrite, remake
sub	under; bordering upon; by or forming a further division	submit, sublease
trans	over, across; into a changed form or condition; on or to the other side of	transmit, transplant, transfer
un	to do; remove from completely; not	untwist, unpile, unoccupy

Suffixes	Meaning	Examples
-able	capable of being	debatable, cookable
-age	act or process of; result of; fee charged for the use of; the home of	footage, orphanage, mileage
-ation	act of doing or the state of being; the thing that	consternation, consultation
-ative	tending to or given to; of the nature of or relating to	manipulative, talkative
-ed	possessed of, provided or furnished with; having the characteristic of	educated, informed
-ent	having the quality, manner, or condition of a person or thing; person or thing that	independent, president
-er	one who has to do with; one of size, capacity, value or date; resident of; person or thing that performs an action; used to form the comparative degree	walker, easterner, worker, happier
-est	used to form superlative degree	warmest, liveliest

Suffixes	Meaning	Examples
-ful	full of, bounding in; tending to, able to; quantity that would fill	careful, scornful, spoonful
-ing	used to form present participle; act or act of; things produced by one who; things used in making	doing, walking, leavings
-ism	act of doing; condition of being; belief or practice of; a characteristic or peculiarity of expression; an abnormal condition resulting from an excess of something	idealism, communism, truism
-less	without; beyond the range of; unable or without the power to	careless, powerless, sightless
-ly	like in appearance or manner, befitting; every; manner or way that is	kingly, daily, quickly
-ment	something that results from or is subject to; a thing that does or causes; act, process, or art of; condition of being	amendment, judgment, supplement
-ness	quality or condition of being	showiness
-sion	action of	compulsion
-tion	action of; an instance of, result of; condition of being	coordination, reception

B
Sample Ideas for Practice Activities

Included here are a few basic ideas for practice activities. They are intended only to assist you to begin to think about kinds of activities that might give the learner drill or reinforcement of a skill. There are numerous books of such ideas published.

There are any number of variations of many basic activities. Similar activities may also have a wide variety of titles and uses. Sometimes the game has a catchy title that will serve many lessons. With this in mind, many teachers find it desirable to make the basic game boards or cards without the actual activity written on them. The basic materials can then be laminated or covered with clear contact paper or acetate. After the material has been covered, the teacher can write the needed activity on it with water-based pens, grease pencils, or crayons, which can later be erased with a tissue, leaving the basic material ready to be reused with a new activity.

As games are incorporated for practice, sometimes it is advisable for the teacher to play the game or complete the activity with the students. Later, it is frequently desirable for students to take turns in the role of the teacher. It is quite possible for the rules to be established that the winner will be the next "teacher." Sometimes activities may be made self-correcting, so they may be used independently.

One basic activity that can have many variations is the game of bingo. Once the basic grid cards have been made and covered with plastic, the skill to be practiced may be varied as needed. The title can also be changed to fit the topic of the skill being practiced.

In a letter-matching activity, the teacher might hold up a capital letter and instruct the learner to cover the matching lowercase letter; the teacher names a letter, and the learner covers the letter named; the teacher says a word, and the learner covers the letter it begins with; the teacher says a word, and the learner covers the letter it ends with; and so forth.

Antonyms, synonyms, and homonyms can be practiced. Words of one type would be written on the grid and the paired word could be called out for students to cover the appropriate word from the grid. Usually only one type of word would be practiced during any given game.

Auditory discrimination of vowel sounds could be practiced by having students cover on the grid the vowel letter that is heard in the word read by the teacher.

Words and their meanings can be matched on a grid. The words would be printed on the grid and the meanings read aloud for the words to be covered.

Word-matching activities are also sometimes used to ensure recognition of new vocabulary. This kind of activity might include having one student read new words aloud while others cover the word called out. The winner becomes the word caller for the next game.

Names of the parts of a book could be placed on the grid. When a book part is shown, its name is covered; or when its use is described, its name could be covered.

Another basic material for a variety of activities is the round cardboard that comes under pizzas. Round cardboard activities can be useful in many ways. When using these cardboard circles, it is frequently necessary to add color to them in some way since they are usually drab in appearance. One of the more common uses is to attach two circles of different sizes with a brad clip in the middle, so each circle can be turned. Of course, more than two circles could be included if appropriate for the activity. After the rounds are attached, there are many possibilities for matching activities.

Initial Consonant Substitutions

The inner circle could contain one or more phonograms minus the initial letter or letters (blends or digraphs), the outer circle would contain either several initial consonants, several blends, or several digraphs to be matched to the inner circle phonogram for pronunciation. If a lesson dealt with teaching *one* initial sound, then *only* one sound would be around the outer ring to be practiced with each phonogram. When several are on the outer ring, all but one should already be known, or the entire activity is designed for practice of a review lesson.

Final Consonant Substitutions

The same process could be followed as described in initial consonant substitution. In either activity, it would be important to have the *words pronounced*. At higher levels, there might be three circles with initial and final sounds being substituted.

A single round of cardboard can be made colorful and eye appealing. It can be covered and written on so clothespins could be clipped to it in a variety of matching activities.

True or false statements can be written. The learner would use clothespins to identify the statements that are true or false on the board. The reverse kind of activity could also be used where the clothespins say True or False, and the statements are on the round cardboard. This could be used with reality versus fantasy statements in the same manner.

Contractions and their original two words can also be clipped to the round cardboard. Either the clothespins or the board might contain the contracted form of the word.

Affixes might be clipped to the round cardboard to make new words. If prefixes are being studied, and they are to be clipped on, then the base word would be written with the beginning of the word at the outer edge of the circle. If suffixes were being studied, the base word would need to be written beginning toward the center of the cardboard so that the ending of the word would be at the outer edge.

An electric board or answer board also provides many opportunities for a variety of activities with the same basic material. Basically, it includes one column for questions and another for answers. These two columns are wired together on the back of the board so that when the electrical circuit is completed with a correct answer, either a bell rings or a light bulb lights up. When electric boards are used for practice frequently, it is necessary to change the wiring on the back so that the correct answer for each question is not always in the same position.

Electric Board

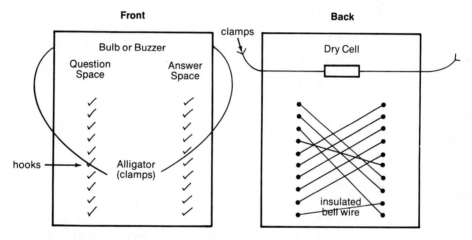

Directions for the Construction of Electric Boards

Materials Needed:

Quantity	Thickness	Width	Length	Kind	Part
1	½ in.	18 in.	24 in.	plywood	panel
1				1½ volt buzzer	sounder
1				D-flashlight battery	energy source
1				battery holder size D	
2				alligator clips	probes
20				L hooks	question and answer card holders

Directions for the Construction of Electric Boards *(continued)*

				Materials Needed:	
Quantity	Thickness	Width	Length	Kind	Part
1 roll			15 ft.	insulated bell wire	circuit
20		1⅝ in.	3½ in.	cardboard	question and answer cards

Construction Hints: Cut out the panel and locate the position for each of the twenty L hooks. Secure hooks into panel until they protrude through the back side approximately one-sixteenth inch. Following the wiring diagram shown in the back view of the drawing, solder bell wire to the points of the L hooks. Mount buzzer in position. Fasten battery holder in place. Wire battery holder and buzzer with insulated bell wire. Cut two pieces of insulated bell wire long enough to reach from the back to the L hooks on the front side of the panel. Fasten one wire to the battery clip (opposite the end connected to the buzzer) and the other wire to the unused buzzer terminal. Solder an alligator clip to each of these two wires. Place a flashlight battery in the battery clip. Check your wiring by clamping one clip on the one hook and the other clip on the hook that completes the circuit on the back side. Prepare twenty cards for the game you have chosen. Ten cards are used for questions, and ten are used for correct answers. Place the questions on the left side and the answers on the right, being sure the answers are placed on the L hook that completes the circuit. Identification questions can be used by pasting pictures on cards and using names on the cards that hang on the answer side.

In addition to an electric board, there are other simpler types of matching activities. Among them would be a piece of cardboard with notches cut out on each side. The cardboard would be covered with plastic, and items to be matched would be written adjacent to each notch. Simple rubber bands could then be used to join the ideas to be matched.

Notched Cardboard and Rubber Bands

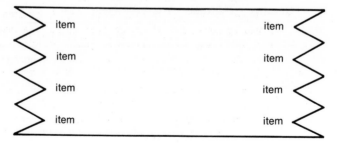

Another similar idea for a matching activity would be to use a piece of cardboard that had been covered, with holes punched along both vertical edges. After items had been written next to each hole, students could match the items by threading shoe-strings between the matching items.

Hole-Punched Cardboard and Shoestrings

One additional matching idea would include the use of manila file folders and library card pockets. The folder might contain items written next to blank lines. The ideas to be matched with the written items would be found in the library card pocket. These items would be taken out and placed on the blank lines next to the written items in the folder.

Manila Folder and Library Card Pockets

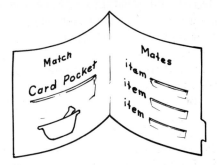

Card games may also be used for skill practice. Laminated cards can be made; words can be written on top of the lamination to make the cards versatile.

The Old Maid idea could be used when students attempt to match compound words or contractions as they draw cards from each other.

Going fishing is another card game idea. Each student is dealt several word cards. The remaining cards form a draw pile. Students ask for a word that rhymes with, has the same beginning sound, has the same vowel sound, or other characteristics of the ones held. If the other player doesn't have such a card in hand, he must go fishing by drawing a card from the extra pile. Pairs of cards are counted at the end of the game.

Crazy Eights is a card game in which students must match each discarded card to the top card in the center stack. Hands are dealt, and one card is turned up in a discard stack. The object of the game is to get rid of all cards dealt. If no match is possible, a new card must be drawn. What has to be matched would depend on the lesson. Possibly the discard should have the same beginning sound or rhyme with the top word. Wild cards can be included to change the pattern of discards. The player who plays the Crazy Eight wild card names what the next pattern will be.

Dominoes can be played with cards when words are written on both ends of the cards. This would be a matching activity. One end might have a prefix and the other a base word. Some cards might have a prefix on both ends or a base word on both ends.

Board games with or without spinners can have many variations. These can be made colorful and are easily stored by using file folders. However, they are more durable when made from cardboard. Any design may be used to make spaces for students to move markers around the board. Some spaces might give a free turn, tell the player to move back one space, tell him to move forward two spaces, or move to any designated spot on the board. Other spaces on the board could be left blank to be filled in on top of the lamination as the game is used for practice of a particular skill. Cards can be drawn to tell students where to move, or a spinner may tell students how many spaces to move and then read directions or words on that space from the board.

Flannel boards with letters and/or objects can be useful both in teaching and practicing a skill. Sentence strips could be arranged in correct sequence or consonant substitution activities can be carried on.

Pocket file folders can be used for categorizing types of activities. One pocket could be for words that have a short *a* sound; the other pocket for those that do not have a short *a* sound. Boxes or cans can also be used for sorting activities: one box for true statements and one for opinion; one for words that begin the same way and the others for those that do not begin with the sound. Cans, boxes, or pocket files should be attractive.

References

Aaron, I. E. (1971). Learning of basal reading skills by mentally and nonmentally handicapped children. *International Reading Association Conference Papers, 15*, 85–93.

Adams, M., & Bertram, B. (1980). *Background knowledge and reading comprehension* (Reading Education Report No. 13). Urbana, IL: Center for the Study of Reading, University of Illinois. (ERIC Document Reproduction Service No. ED 181 431)

Allen, R. V. (1961). *Report of the reading study project* (Monograph No. 1). San Diego: Department of Education, San Diego County.

Allen, R. V. (1976). *Language experiences in communication*. Boston: Houghton Mifflin.

Anderson, R. C., Hiebert, E. H., Scott, J. A., & Wilkinson, I. A. G. (1985). *Becoming a nation of readers: The report of Commission on Reading*. Washington, DC: The National Institute of Education.

Anderson, R. C., & Freebody, P. (1981). Vocabulary knowledge. In J. T. Guthrie (Ed.), *Comprehension and teaching: Research reviews*. Newark, DE: International Reading Association.

Anderson, T. H., & Armbruster, B. B. (1984). Studying. In P. D. Pearson (Ed.), *Handbook of reading research* (pp. 657– 679). New York: Longman.

Aukerman, R. C., & Aukerman, L. R. (1981). *How do I teach reading?* New York: John Wiley & Sons.

Bailey, M. H. (1967). The utility of phonic generalizations in grades one through six. *The Reading Teacher, 20*, 413–418.

Baker, L., & Brown, A. L. (1984a). Cognitive monitoring in reading. In J. Flood (Ed.), *Understanding reading comprehension* (pp. 21–44). Newark, DE: International Reading Association.

Baker, L., & Brown, A. L. (1984b). Metacognitive skills in reading. In P. D. Pearson (Ed.), *Handbook of reading research* (pp. 353–394). New York: Longman.

Baumann, J. F. (1984). The effectiveness of a direct instruction paradigm for teaching main idea comprehension. *Reading Research Quarterly, 20*(1), 93–115.

Beck, I. L. (1984). Developing comprehension: The impact of the directed reading lesson. In R. C. Anderson, J. Osborn, & R. J. Tierney (Eds.), *Learning to read in American schools: Basal readers and content texts.* Hillsdale, NJ: Lawrence Erlbaum Associates.

Beck, I. L., Omanson, R. C., & McKeown, M. G. (1982). An instructional redesign of reading lessons: Effects on comprehension. *Reading Research Quarterly, 17*(4), 462–481.

Bloomfield, L., & Barnhart, C. (1961). *Let's read: A linguistic approach.* Detroit: Wayne State University Press.

Brown, A. L. (1980). Metacognitive development and reading. In R. J. Spiro, B. C. Bruce, & W. F. Brewer (Eds.), *Theoretical issues in reading comprehension* (pp. 453–481). Hillsdale, NJ: Lawrence Erlbaum Associates.

Brown, A. L., & Day, J. D. (1983). Macrorules for summarizing texts: The development of expertise. *Journal of Verbal Learning and Verbal Behavior, 22*(1), 1–14.

Burns, P., & Roe, B. (1985). *Informal reading inventory.* Boston: Houghton Mifflin.

Burns, P., Roe, B., & Ross, E. (1984). *Teaching reading in today's elementary schools.* Boston: Houghton Mifflin.

Chaffee, J. (1985). *Thinking critically.* Boston: Houghton Mifflin.

Clymer, T. (1963). The utility of phonic generalizations in the primary grades. *The Reading Teacher, 16*, 252–258.

Cooper, J. D. (1986). *Improving reading comprehension.* Boston: Houghton Mifflin.

Cooper, J. D., Warncke, E., Ramstad, P., & Shipman, D. (1979). *The what and how of reading instruction.* Columbus, OH: Merrill.

Cooper, J. D., & Worden, T. W. (1983). *The classroom reading program in the elementary school.* New York: Macmillan.

Davis, F. B. (1944). Fundamental factors of comprehension in reading. *Psychometrika, 9*(3), 185–197.

Davis, F. B. (1972). Psychometric research on comprehension in reading. *Reading Research Quarterly, 7*(4), 628–678.

Day, J. D. (1980). *Training summarization skills: A comparison of teaching methods.* Unpublished doctoral dissertation, University of Illinois, Champaign.

Dolch, E. W. (1942). *Basic sight word test.* Champaign, IL: Garrard Press.

Durkin, D. (1978). What classroom observations reveal about reading comprehension instruction. *Reading Research Quarterly, 14*(4), 481–533.

Durkin, D. (1980). Teaching young children to read (3rd ed.). Boston: Allyn and Bacon.

Durrell, D. (1958). Success in first grade reading. *Boston University Journal of Education, 140*, 2–6.

Ekwall, E. E., & Shanker, J. L. (1985). *Teaching reading in the elementary school.* Columbus, OH: Merrill.

Emans, R. (1967). When two vowels go walking and other such things. *The Reading Teacher, 21*, 262–269.

Fay, L. (1965). Reading study skills: Math and science. In A. J. Figurel (Ed.), *Reading and inquiry.* Newark, DE: International Reading Association.

Foerster, L. M. (1976). Teaching reading in our pluralistic society. *The Reading Teacher, 30*, 146–150.

Gates, A. I. (1937). The necessary mental age for beginning reading. *Elementary School Journal, 37*, 497–508.

Goodman, K. S., & Buck, C. (1973). Dialect barriers to reading comprehension revisited. *The Reading Teacher, 27*, 2–6.

Hansen, J. (1981). Inferential comprehension strategy for use with primary grade children. *The Reading Teacher, 34*, 665–669.

Hansen, J., & Pearson, P. D. (1983). An instructional study: Improving the inferential comprehension of good and poor fourth-grade readers. *Journal of Educational Psychology, 75*, 921–929.

Harris, A. J. (1968). Research on some aspects of comprehension, rate, flexibility, and study skills. *Journal of Reading, 12*, 205–210.

Hayes, D. A., & Tierney, R. J. (1982). Developing readers' knowledge through analogy. *Reading Research Quarterly, 17*(2), 256–280.

Hunt, D. E. (1976). Teachers' adaptation: Reading and flexing to students. *Journal of Teacher Education, 27*, 268–275.

Johnson, D. (1971). The Dolch List reexamined. *The Reading Teacher, 24*, 455–456.

Johnson, D. D., & Pearson, P. D. (1984). *Teaching reading vocabulary* (2nd ed.). New York: Holt, Rinehart & Winston.

Johnson, L. V., & Bany, M. A. (1970). *Classroom management.* New York: Macmillan.

Johnston, P. (1981). *Prior knowledge and reading comprehension test bias.* Unpublished doctoral dissertation, University of Illinois, Champaign.

Johnston, P., & Pearson, P. D. (1982). *Prior knowledge, connectivity, and the assessment of reading comprehension* (Technical Report No. 245). Urbana, IL: Center for the Study of Reading, University of Illinois (ERIC Document Reproduction Service No. ED 217 402)

Lesgold, A., Resnick, L. B., & Hammond K. (1985). Learning to read: A longitudinal study of word skill development in two curricula. In T. G. Waller & G. E. MacKinnon (Eds.), *Reading research: Advances in theory and practice* (pp. 107–138). New York: Academic Press.

Loban, W. D. (1963). *The language of elementary school children.* Champaign, IL: National Council of Teachers of English.

Mangieri, J. N., & Kahn, M. S. (1977). Is the Dolch List of 220 basic sight words irrelevant? *The Reading Teacher, 30*, 642–651.

Manzo, A. V. (1968). *Improving reading through reciprocal questioning. Dissertation Abstracts International, 30*, 5344A. (University Microfilms No. 70-10364).

McGreal, T. L., & McGreal, K. M. (1984a, January-February). Practical implications of current teaching research: Part I—The importance of climate to achievement. *Illinois Teacher of Home Economics, 27*(3), 112–116.

McGreal, T. L., & McGreal, K. M. (1984b, March-April). Practical implications of current teaching research: Part II—Planning the use of instructional time. *Illinois Teacher of Home Economics, 27*(4), 162–166.

McKeown, M. G., Beck, I. L., Manson, R. C., & Pople, M. T. (1985). Some effects of the nature and frequency of vocabulary instruction on the knowledge and use of words. *Reading Research Quarterly, 20*(5), 522–535.

Menyuk, P. (1984). Language development and reading. In J. Flood (Ed.), *Understanding comprehension* (pp. 101–121). Newark, DE: International Reading Association.

Meyer, B. J. F. (1975). *The organization of prose and its effects on memory.* Amsterdam: The Hague North-Holland Press.

Meyer, B. J. F., & Freedle, R. O. (1984). Effects of discourse type on recall. *American Educational Research Journal, 21*, 121–143.

Meyer, L. A. (1982). Relative effects of word-analysis and word-supply correction procedures with poor readers during word attack training. *Reading Research Quarterly, 17*(4), 544–555.

Meyer, L., Gersten, R. M., & Gutkin, J. (1983). Direct instruction: A project Follow Through success story in an inner-city school. *Elementary School Journal, 84*, 241–252.

Mier, M. (1984). Comprehension monitoring in the elementary classroom. *The Reading Teacher, 37*(8), 770–774.

Mitchell, K. A. (1980). Patterns of teacher-student responses to oral reading errors as related to teachers' theoretical frameworks. *Research in Teaching English, 14*, 259.

Palincsar, A. S., & Brown, A. L. (1984a). *A means to a meaningful end: Recommendations for the instruction of poor comprehenders.* Champaign, IL: Center for the Study of Reading.

Palincsar, A. S., & Brown, A. L. (1984b). Reciprocal teaching of comprehension-fostering and comprehension monitoring activities. In D. Klahr (Ed.), *Cognition and instruction* (pp. 117–175). Hillsdale, NJ: Lawrence Erlbaum Associates.

Pearson, P. D. (1982). Asking questions about reading (Ginn Occasional Papers, Number 15). Columbus, OH: Ginn.

Pearson, P. D. (1984). *Reading comprehension instruction: Six necessary changes* (Reading Education Report No. 54). Urbana, IL: Center for the Study of Reading, University of Illinois. (ERIC Document Reproduction Service No. ED 251 811)

Pearson, P. D., Hansen, J., & Gordon, C. (1979). *The effect of background knowledge on young children's comprehension of explicit and implicit information.* Urbana, IL: University of Illinois, Center for the Study of Reading.

Perfetti, C. A., & Lesgold, A. M. (1977). Discourse comprehension and sources of individual differences. In M. A. Just & P. A. Carpenter (Eds.), *Cognitive processes in comprehension* (pp. 141–183). Hillsdale, NJ: Lawrence Erlbaum Associates.

Renzulli, J. S., & Smith, L. H. (1980). Revolving door: A truer turn for the gifted. *Learning, 9*, 91–93.

Reynolds, R. E., Taylor, M. A., Steffensen, M. S., Shirey, L. L., & Anderson, R. C. (1982). Cultural schemata and reading comprehension. *Reading Research Quarterly, 17*(3), 353–366.

Rigg, P. (1978). Dialect and/in/for reading. *Language Arts, 55*, 285–590

Robinson, F. P. (1962). *Effective reading.* New York: Harper & Row.

Rosenshine, B. (1980). Skill hierarchies in reading comprehension. In R. J. Spiro, B. C. Bruce, & W. F. Brewer (Eds.), *Theoretical issues in reading comprehension.* Hillsdale, NJ: Lawrence Erlbaum Associates.

Rosenshine, B., & Stevens, R. (1984). Classroom instruction in reading. In P. D. Pearson (Ed.), *Handbook of reading research* (pp. 745–798). New York: Longman.

Ruddell, R. B. (1985). The effect of oral and written patterns of language structure on reading comprehension. In H. Singer & R. Ruddell (Eds.), *Theoretical models and processes of reading* (3rd ed.) (pp. 123–128). Newark, DE: International Reading Association.

Rumelhart, D. E. (1980). Schemata: The building blocks of cognition. In R. J. Spiro, B. C. Bruce, W. F. Brewer (Eds.), *Theoretical issues in reading comprehension* (pp. 33–58). Hillsdale, NJ: Lawrence Erlbaum Associates.

Samuels, S. J., & Kamil, M. (1984). Models of the reading process. In P. D. Pearson (Ed.), *Handbook of reading research* (pp. 185–224). New York: Longman.

Schallert, D. L. (1980). The role of illustrations in reading comprehension. In R. J. Spiro, B. C. Bruce, & N. F. Brewer (Eds.), *Theoretical issues in reading comprehension*. Hillsdale, NJ: Lawrence Erlbaum Associates.

Silvaroli, N. J. (1986). *Classroom reading inventory* (5th ed.) Dubuque: William C. Brown.

Sinatra, R. (1981). Using visuals to help the second-language learner. *The Reading Teacher, 34*, 539–546.

Spache, G. D. (1963). *Toward better reading*. Champaign, IL: Garrard Press.

Spache, G. D. (1976). *Investigating the issues of reading disabilities*. Boston: Allyn & Bacon.

Strang, R. (1968). *Reading diagnosis and remediation*. Newark, DE: International Reading Association.

Trelease, J. (1985). *Read-aloud handbook*. New York: Penguin Books.

Vacca, J., Vacca, R., & Gove, M. (1987). Reading and learning to read. Boston: Little, Brown.

Veatch, J. (1978). *Reading in the elementary school* (2nd ed.). New York: John Wiley & Sons.

Warncke, E. W., & Shipman, D. A. (1984). *Group assessment in reading: Classroom teacher's handbook*. Englewood Cliffs, NJ: Prentice-Hall.

White, R. E. (1981). The effects of organizational themes and adjunct placements on children's prose learning: A developmental perspective. *Dissertation Abstracts International, 42*, 2042A–2043A. (University Microfilms No. 81–25, 038)

Wolfram, W. A. (1979). *Reading and dialect differences*. Arlington, VA: Center for Applied Linguistics.

Woods, M. L., & Moe, A. (1985). *Analytical reading inventory* (3rd ed.). Columbus, OH: Merrill.

Name Index

Subject Index

References to figures appear in bold type.